# First World War

## and Army of Occupation

# War Diary

## France, Belgium and Germany

51 DIVISION
Headquarters, Branches and Services
Royal Army Ordnance Corps
Deputy Assistant Director Ordnance Services
1 May 1915 - 31 January 1919

WO95/2853/1b

The Naval & Military Press Ltd
www.nmarchive.com
**Published in association with The National Archives**

Published by

The Naval & Military Press Ltd

Unit 10 Ridgewood Industrial Park,

Uckfield, East Sussex,

TN22 5QE England

Tel: +44 (0) 1825 749494

www.naval-military-press.com

www.nmarchive.com

*This diary has been reprinted in facsimile from the original. Any imperfections are inevitably reproduced and the quality may fall short of modern type and cartographic standards.*

# Contents

| Document type | Place/Title | Date From | Date To |
|---|---|---|---|
| Heading | WO95/2853 51 Div May' 15-Jan ' 19 D.A.D.O.S. | | |
| Heading | 51st Division Dep. Asst Dir. Ordnance Services May 1915-Jan 1919 | | |
| Heading | D.A.D.O.S. 51st Division Vol I 1-31.5.15 | | |
| War Diary | Boulogne | 01/05/1915 | 02/05/1915 |
| War Diary | Busnes | 03/05/1915 | 13/05/1915 |
| War Diary | Prodelles | 14/05/1915 | 17/05/1915 |
| War Diary | Le Gorgue | 18/05/1915 | 19/05/1915 |
| War Diary | Locon | 20/05/1915 | 31/05/1915 |
| Heading | 51st Division D A D O S 51st Division Vol II 1-30.6.15 | | |
| War Diary | Locon | 01/06/1915 | 26/06/1915 |
| War Diary | Le-Nouveau Monde | 27/06/1915 | 30/06/1915 |
| Heading | 51st Division DADOS 51st Division Vol III | | |
| Heading | War Diary Of D.A.D.O.S. 51st Division (Capt. W. Maltby A.O.D) From 1-7-15 To 31-7-15 | | |
| War Diary | Le Nouveau Monde | 01/07/1915 | 25/07/1915 |
| War Diary | Heilly | 26/07/1915 | 31/07/1915 |
| Heading | 51st Division Box 2708 DADOS 51st Division Vol IV 1-31.8.15 | | |
| Heading | War Diary Of D.A.D.O.S. 51st Division From 1st Aug: 1915 To 31st Aug: 1915 | | |
| War Diary | Heilly | 01/08/1915 | 04/08/1915 |
| War Diary | Senlis | 05/08/1915 | 31/08/1915 |
| Heading | 51st Division DADOS 51st Division Vol V September 15 | | |
| Heading | War Diary Of D.A.D.O.S. 51st Division From 1-9-15 To 30-9-15 | | |
| War Diary | Senlis | 01/09/1915 | 30/09/1915 |
| Heading | DADOS 51st Division Vol VI Oct 15 | | |
| Heading | War Diary Of D.A.D.O.S. 51st Division From 1-10-15 To 31-10-15 | | |
| War Diary | Senlis | 01/10/1915 | 31/10/1915 |
| Heading | D.A.D.O.S. 51st Div. Dec Vol VIII | | |
| Heading | War Diary D.A.D.O.S. 51st Division From 1-12-15 To 31-12-15 | | |
| War Diary | Senlis | 01/12/1915 | 26/12/1915 |
| War Diary | Flesselles | 27/12/1915 | 31/12/1915 |
| Heading | D A D O S 51st Div Jan Vol IX | | |
| Heading | War Diary Of D.A.D.O.S. 51st Division From 1-1-16 To 31-1-16 | | |
| War Diary | Flesselles | 01/01/1916 | 31/01/1916 |
| Heading | War Diary D.A.D.O.S. 51st Division From 1/2/16 To 29/2/16 Vol X | | |
| War Diary | Flesselles | 01/02/1916 | 07/02/1916 |
| War Diary | Daours | 08/02/1916 | 28/02/1916 |
| War Diary | Flesselles | 29/02/1916 | 29/02/1916 |
| Heading | War Diary & D.A.D.O.S. 51st (H) Division From 1/3/16 To 31/3/16 Vol XI | | |
| War Diary | Flesselles | 01/03/1916 | 06/03/1916 |
| War Diary | Beauval | 07/03/1916 | 08/03/1916 |

| | | | |
|---|---|---|---|
| War Diary | Frevent | 09/03/1916 | 12/03/1916 |
| War Diary | Hermaville | 13/03/1916 | 31/03/1916 |
| Heading | DADOS 51 Div Vol XII | | |
| War Diary | Hermaville | 01/04/1916 | 30/04/1916 |
| Heading | War Diary Of D.A.D.O.S. 51st (Highland) Division From 1.5.16 To 30.5.16 | | |
| War Diary | Hermaville | 01/05/1916 | 31/05/1916 |
| Heading | Secret | | |
| Heading | War Diary Of D.A.D.O.S. 51st Division From 1/6/16 To 30/6/16 Vol 14 | | |
| War Diary | Hermaville | 01/06/1916 | 30/06/1916 |
| Heading | Vol 15 War Diary Of DADOS 51st H Division From 1st July 16 To 31st July 16 | | |
| War Diary | Hermaville | 01/07/1916 | 14/07/1916 |
| War Diary | Villers Chatel | 15/07/1916 | 15/07/1916 |
| War Diary | Doullens | 16/07/1916 | 17/07/1916 |
| War Diary | Ribeaucourt | 18/07/1916 | 21/07/1916 |
| War Diary | Heilly & Meaulte | 22/07/1916 | 31/07/1916 |
| Heading | Vol 16 War Diary Of DADOS 51st H Division From 1st August To 31st Aug 1916 | | |
| War Diary | Heilly & Meaulte | 01/08/1916 | 09/08/1916 |
| War Diary | Pont Remy | 10/08/1916 | 11/08/1916 |
| War Diary | Reniscure | 12/08/1916 | 15/08/1916 |
| War Diary | L'Halle 'D' Beau | 16/08/1916 | 28/08/1916 |
| War Diary | Steenwerck | 29/08/1916 | 31/08/1916 |
| Heading | Vol 17 51st (H) Division D.A.D.O.S. War Diary September 1916 | | |
| War Diary | Steenwerck | 01/09/1916 | 30/09/1916 |
| Heading | Vol 18 51st (H) Division D.A.D.O.S. War Diary October 1916 | | |
| War Diary | Bus-Les-Artois | 01/10/1916 | 17/10/1916 |
| War Diary | Lealvillers | 18/10/1916 | 31/10/1916 |
| Heading | 51st (H) Division D.A.D.O.S. War Diary November 1916 Vol 19 | | |
| War Diary | Lealvillers | 01/11/1916 | 27/11/1916 |
| War Diary | Bouzincourt | 28/11/1916 | 30/11/1916 |
| Heading | Vol 20 51st (Highland) Division D.A.D.O.S. War Diary December 1916 | | |
| War Diary | Bouzincourt | 01/12/1916 | 31/12/1916 |
| Heading | Vol 21 51st (Highland) Division D.A.D.O.S. War Diary January 1917 | | |
| War Diary | Bouzincourt | 01/01/1917 | 12/01/1917 |
| War Diary | Marieux | 13/01/1917 | 13/01/1917 |
| War Diary | Bernaville | 14/01/1917 | 14/01/1917 |
| War Diary | Buigny St Maclou | 15/01/1917 | 21/01/1917 |
| War Diary | Buigny | 22/01/1917 | 31/01/1917 |
| Miscellaneous | Headquarters "Q" 51st (H) Division | 02/03/1917 | 02/03/1917 |
| Heading | Vol 22 51st (Highland) D.A.D.O.S. War Diary February 1917 | | |
| War Diary | Buigny | 01/02/1917 | 04/02/1917 |
| War Diary | Brailly | 05/02/1917 | 05/02/1917 |
| War Diary | Frohen-Le-Grand | 06/02/1917 | 06/02/1917 |
| War Diary | Roellecourt | 07/02/1917 | 07/02/1917 |
| War Diary | Mingoval | 08/02/1917 | 28/02/1917 |
| Heading | Vol 23 51st (Highland) Division D.A.D.O.S. War Diary March 1917 | | |

| | | | |
|---|---|---|---|
| War Diary | Mingoval | 01/03/1917 | 31/03/1917 |
| Heading | 51st (Highland) Division D.A.D.O.S. War Diary April 1917 | | |
| War Diary | Mingoval | 01/04/1917 | 16/04/1917 |
| War Diary | ACQ | 17/04/1917 | 30/04/1917 |
| Heading | 51st (Highland) Division D.A.D.O.S. War Diary May 1917 | | |
| War Diary | ACQ | 01/05/1917 | 16/05/1917 |
| War Diary | Sheet 51 B Point G 13 D | 16/05/1917 | 31/05/1917 |
| Heading | Vol 26 51st (Highland) Division D.A.D.O.S. War Diary June 1917 | | |
| War Diary | Roellecourt | 01/06/1917 | 03/06/1917 |
| War Diary | Pernes | 04/06/1917 | 04/06/1917 |
| War Diary | Boney | 05/06/1917 | 06/06/1917 |
| War Diary | Eperlecques | 07/06/1917 | 22/06/1917 |
| War Diary | Lederzeele | 23/06/1917 | 30/06/1917 |
| Heading | Vol 27 51st (Highland) Division D.A.D.O.S. War Diary July 1917 | | |
| War Diary | Lederzeele | 01/07/1917 | 13/07/1917 |
| War Diary | Sheet 29 F 27b.8.8 | 14/07/1917 | 31/07/1917 |
| Heading | Vol 28 51st (Highland) Division D.A.D.O.S. War Diary August 1917 | | |
| War Diary | F 27 B.8.8. Sheet 27 | 01/08/1917 | 31/08/1917 |
| Heading | Vol 29 51st (Highland) Division D.A.D.O.S. War Diary September 1917 | | |
| War Diary | Sheet 27 F 27b.8.8. | 01/09/1917 | 28/09/1917 |
| War Diary | Achiet Le Petit | 29/09/1917 | 30/09/1917 |
| Heading | Vol 30 51st (Highland) Division D.A.D.O.S. War Diary October 1917 | | |
| War Diary | Achiet Le Petit | 01/10/1917 | 05/10/1917 |
| War Diary | Sheet 51 B. 52 D.8.4 | 06/10/1917 | 31/10/1917 |
| Heading | Vol 31 War Diary Of D.A.D.O.S. 51st (Highland) Division From 1st To 30th November 1917 | | |
| War Diary | Boisleux Hermaville | 01/01/1917 | 16/01/1917 |
| War Diary | Lechelle | 17/11/1917 | 24/11/1917 |
| War Diary | Baisieux | 26/11/1917 | 30/11/1917 |
| Miscellaneous | The Officer i/c | 18/01/1918 | 18/01/1918 |
| Heading | Vol 32 War Diary 57th H.D. December 1917 | | |
| War Diary | Baijieun | 01/12/1917 | 01/12/1917 |
| War Diary | Bapaume | 02/12/1917 | 02/12/1917 |
| War Diary | Fermicourt | 03/12/1917 | 31/12/1917 |
| Heading | Vol 33 D.A.D.O.S. 51 (H) Division January 1918 | | |
| War Diary | Fremicourt | 01/01/1918 | 20/01/1918 |
| War Diary | Achiet-Le-Petit | 21/01/1918 | 31/01/1918 |
| Heading | Vol 34 War Diary For D.a.D.O.S. 51st (H) Division From 1st To 28th February 1918 | | |
| War Diary | Achiet Le Petit | 01/02/1918 | 12/02/1918 |
| War Diary | Fremicourt | 13/02/1918 | 28/02/1918 |
| Heading | Vol 35 War Diary March 1918 D A D O S 57 Hd | | |
| War Diary | Fremicourt | 01/03/1918 | 21/03/1918 |
| War Diary | Grevillers | 21/03/1918 | 21/03/1918 |
| War Diary | Achiet-Le-Petit | 22/03/1918 | 23/03/1918 |
| War Diary | Bertrancourt | 24/03/1918 | 24/03/1918 |
| War Diary | Marieux | 25/03/1918 | 25/03/1918 |
| War Diary | Occoches | 26/03/1918 | 26/03/1918 |
| War Diary | Neuvillette | 27/03/1918 | 28/03/1918 |

| | | | |
|---|---|---|---|
| War Diary | Fouquieres | 29/03/1918 | 31/03/1918 |
| Heading | Vol 36 War Diary April 1918 D A D O S HD | | |
| War Diary | Fouquieres | 01/04/1918 | 04/04/1918 |
| War Diary | Labouvriere | 05/04/1918 | 07/04/1918 |
| War Diary | Robecq | 08/04/1918 | 11/04/1918 |
| War Diary | Busnes | 12/04/1918 | 15/04/1918 |
| War Diary | Lambres | 16/04/1918 | 19/04/1918 |
| War Diary | Norrent Fontes | 20/04/1918 | 30/04/1918 |
| Heading | Vol 37 War Diary For May 1918 | | |
| War Diary | Norrent Fontes | 01/05/1918 | 06/05/1918 |
| War Diary | Maroeuil | 07/05/1918 | 31/05/1918 |
| Heading | Vol 38 War Diary June 1918 D.A.D.O.S. HD | | |
| War Diary | Maroeuil | 01/06/1918 | 30/06/1918 |
| Heading | Vol 39 War Diary July 1918 D.A.D.O.S. HD | | |
| War Diary | Maroeuil | 01/07/1918 | 11/07/1918 |
| War Diary | Rouellecourt | 12/07/1918 | 13/07/1918 |
| War Diary | Tinquette | 14/07/1918 | 15/07/1918 |
| War Diary | Aubigny | 15/07/1918 | 17/07/1918 |
| War Diary | Ognes | 18/07/1918 | 18/07/1918 |
| War Diary | Pierry-Moussy | 19/07/1918 | 31/07/1918 |
| Heading | Vol 40 War Diary Aug 1918 | | |
| War Diary | Moussy | 01/08/1918 | 04/08/1918 |
| War Diary | Mingoval | 05/08/1918 | 15/08/1918 |
| War Diary | Maroeuil | 16/08/1918 | 18/08/1918 |
| War Diary | Agnes-Les-Duisans | 18/08/1918 | 22/08/1918 |
| War Diary | Maroeuil | 23/08/1918 | 26/08/1918 |
| War Diary | Victory Camp Ecurie | 27/08/1918 | 31/08/1918 |
| Heading | War Diary Septr. 1918 D.A.D.O.S. 51st (H) Div Vol 41 | | |
| War Diary | Victory Camp Ecurie | 01/09/1918 | 13/09/1918 |
| War Diary | Maroeuil | 14/09/1918 | 24/09/1918 |
| War Diary | Vic. Camp Ecurie | 25/09/1918 | 30/09/1918 |
| Heading | Vol 42 War Diary October 1918 D.A.D.O.S. 51st (H) Div | | |
| War Diary | Victory Camp Ecurie | 01/10/1918 | 02/10/1918 |
| War Diary | Chateau D'Acq | 03/10/1918 | 06/10/1918 |
| War Diary | Queant | 07/10/1918 | 10/10/1918 |
| War Diary | Chateau Bourlon | 10/10/1918 | 11/10/1918 |
| War Diary | Escadoeuvres | 11/10/1918 | 13/10/1918 |
| War Diary | Naves | 13/10/1918 | 20/10/1918 |
| War Diary | Avesnes Le Sec | 21/10/1918 | 21/10/1918 |
| War Diary | Lieu-St-Amand | 22/10/1918 | 30/10/1918 |
| War Diary | Iwuy | 31/10/1918 | 31/10/1918 |
| Heading | Vol 43 War Diary For Nov. 1918 | | |
| War Diary | Iwuy | 01/11/1918 | 30/11/1918 |
| Heading | Vol 44 D.A.D.O.S. 51st (H) Div | | |
| War Diary | Iwuy | 01/12/1918 | 31/12/1918 |
| Heading | Vol 45 D A D O S 51st (H) Division January 1919 | | |
| War Diary | Iwuy | 01/01/1919 | 05/01/1919 |
| War Diary | La Louviere | 06/01/1919 | 31/01/1919 |

1

WO 95/2853

51 DIV.

May '15 – Jan '19

D.A.D.O.S.

# 51ST DIVISION

DEP.ASST DIR. ~~VETY~~ ORDNANCE SERVICES

MAY 1915-JAN 1919

121/5513

D.A.D.O.S. 51st Division

Vol I. 1 – 31. 5. 15

Army Form C. 2118.

# WAR DIARY
or
# ~~INTELLIGENCE SUMMARY.~~

(*Erase heading not required.*)

Instructions regarding War Diaries and Intelligence Summaries are contained in F. S. Regs., Part II. and the Staff Manual respectively. Title pages will be prepared in manuscript.

| Place | Date | Hour | Summary of Events and Information | Remarks and references to Appendices |
|---|---|---|---|---|
| | May | | | |
| Boulogne | 1st | 10 pm | Landed at Boulogne with Hd Qrs H Divn | Wh |
| Do | 2nd | 10.30am | Left Boulogne for Lillers by motor car, arrived Lillers at 1.30 pm | Wh |
| | | | Ordnance personnel arrived at Busnes (Hd Qrs 1/H Divn) at 10 pm | |
| Busnes | 3rd | | Visited Hd Qrs Meerut Division for instruction & returned same day | Wh |
| " | 4th | | Visited Hd Qrs 1st Army (DDOS) & returned same day | Wh |
| " | 5th | | Wired to Base for oil & other cleaning material. Established 1 W.O. AOC & two privates AOC at each Bde Group of Highland Division and instructed personnel AOC in duties. | Wh |
| " | 6th | | Purchased White Screens for indicating positions of units to aircraft. | Wh |
| " | 7th | | Visited Bethune & purchased 12 shotguns & ammunition for use in front line trenches for destruction of pigeons | Wh |
| " | 8th | | Wired urgently to base for 6 bicycles for pigeon service. | Wh |
| | | | Made initial distribution of cleaning material to troops. | Wh |
| " | 9th | | Distributed respirators & hypo-sulphate to Infantry units | Wh |
| " | 10th | | Purchased 20 Tubs washing for use of troops | Wh |
| | 11th | | Published back General Routine Orders in Area RO re additional issues of equipment | |
| | | | Continued | |

Army Form C. 2118.

# WAR DIARY
*or*
# INTELLIGENCE SUMMARY.
*(Erase heading not required.)*

Instructions regarding War Diaries and Intelligence Summaries are contained in F. S. Regs., Part II. and the Staff Manual respectively. Title pages will be prepared in manuscript.

| Place | Date | Hour | Summary of Events and Information | Remarks and references to Appendices |
|---|---|---|---|---|
| Busnes | 11th | | approved for various units. Called for indents to complete equipment. | Wh |
| " | 12th | | Nothing of importance occurred. Ordinary Routine Work. | Wh |
| " | 13th | | — Do — | Wh |
| Frodelles | 14th | | Division moved from Busnes to Frodelles. Distributed to troops part issue of Respirators. Infantry only. | Wh |
| " | 15th | | Visited Railhead to pick up stores. Distributed to troops same day. Further distribution of respirators & smoke helmets to Infantry units. | Wh |
| " | 16th | | Visited Railhead to pick up stores & distributed – Railhead changed to Merville on the 16th inst. | Wh |
| " | 17th | | Do. Purchased 200 red flags for use of Infantry | Wh |
| La Gorgue | 18 | | Visited Railhead to pick up stores & distributed to units. Highland Division moved to new billeting area, with Hd Qrs of Division a La Gorgue. | Wh |
| " | 19 | | Visited railhead to pick up stores & distributed them to troops. Arranged ~~with~~ for Ordnance Lorries, to come up to refilling points same time as supply Lorries, which they will accompany in future; this means that ordnance stores will not leave railhead until morning after arrival at railhead. | Wh |
| | | | Continued | |

Instructions regarding War Diaries and Intelligence Summaries are contained in F. S. Regs., Part II. and the Staff Manual respectively. Title pages will be prepared in manuscript.

# WAR DIARY
*or*
# INTELLIGENCE SUMMARY.
(*Erase heading not required.*)

Army Form C. 2118.

| Place | Date | Hour | Summary of Events and Information | Remarks and references to Appendices |
|---|---|---|---|---|
| Locon | 20th | | Visited railhead & distributed stores for troops. Division moved from La Gorgue to Locon | Wh |
| " | 21st | | Visited railhead & distributed stores for troops. 6000 Bonnets Balmoral and Khaki covers received. Wired for sufficient respirators to complete troops as authorized | Wh |
| " | 22nd | | Visited Railhead & distributed stores to troops | Wh |
| " | 23rd | | Do Received 16 Travelling Kitchens for 152nd Inf: Bde | Wh |
| " | 24th | | Visited Railhead & distributed stores to troops Received 19 Travelling Kitchens for 153rd Inf Bde & 3 for 154th Inf: Bde | Wh |
| " | 25th | | Visited Railhead & distributed stores to Troops. Arranged for a barn to be used as an Ordnance refilling depot in a Central Position. From this point stores will be removed by units in baggage wagons | Wh |
| " | 26th | | Visited Railhead & distributed remainder of Travelling Kitchens required for the Infantry units of the Division | Wh |
| " | 27 | | Visited railhead & removed Ordnance Stores required by units | Wh |

1577 Wt. W10791/1773 500,000 1/15 D. D. & L. A.D.S.S./Forms/C. 2118.

Army Form C. 2118.

# WAR DIARY
*or*
# INTELLIGENCE SUMMARY.

*(Erase heading not required.)*

Instructions regarding War Diaries and Intelligence Summaries are contained in F. S. Regs., Part II. and the Staff Manual respectively. Title pages will be prepared in manuscript.

| Place | Date | Hour | Summary of Events and Information | Remarks and references to Appendices |
|---|---|---|---|---|
| Locon | 28th | | Wired to Base for 7500 respirators to hold as a Reserve for Division. Aut. Ordnance Communication wire O.P 5097 of 26.5.15. Also wired to Base for Smoke helmets at the rate of one per man Cavalry RA RE Cyclist Co. Infantry & RAMC. Received instruction to complete Infantry units with 6 Helios per unit. Visited Railhead & despatched stores to Ordnance Refilling point for distribution to troops | Wh. |
| Locon | 29th | | Visited Railhead & despatched stores to Ordnance Refilling Point for distribution to Troops. Wired to Base for 7500 Smoke helmets to be maintained as a Reserve | Wh. |
| Locon | 30th | | Visited Railhead & despatched stores to Ordnance Refilling Point for distribution to Troops. Received 7600 respirators as a reserve for the Division | Wh. |
| Locon | 31st | | Visited Railhead & despatched stores to Ordnance Refilling point for distribution to Troops. Received instructions that Helios for I F units had not yet been approved. which cancelled instructions referred to as received on the 28th inst. | Wh. |

1577 Wt. W10791/1773 500,000 1/15 D. D. & L. A.D.S.S./Forms/C. 2118.

51st Division

121/5971

DADOS. 51st Division

Vol II 1—30.6.15.

Army Form C. 2118.

Instructions regarding War Diaries and Intelligence Summaries are contained in F. S. Regs., Part II. and the Staff Manual respectively. Title pages will be prepared in manuscript.

# WAR DIARY
*or*
# INTELLIGENCE SUMMARY.

*(Erase heading not required.)*

| Place | Date | Hour | Summary of Events and Information | Remarks and references to Appendices |
|---|---|---|---|---|
| Lacon | 1st | | Visited Railhead - changed to Lillers - & drew stores for troops. Received instructions regarding method of repairing smoke helmets. The mica to be replaced by Acetoid transparent eyepieces. | 0/37 2-6-15 Wh. |
| Lacon | 2nd | | Visited Railhead & drew stores for troops. Shewed ADMS piece of acetoid & arranged for method of repair of smoke helmets. | Wh. |
| Lacon | 3rd | | Visited Railhead & drew stores for troops. Distributed 120 local pattern bandoliers for the carrying of bombs between HQ 3 Inf. Bdes. Also distributed 500 local pattern fly killers to the various units in proportion | Wh |
| Lacon | 4th | | Visited railhead & drew stores for troops. Following were received & distributed as shown:- 152nd Inf Bde 3 Hyposcopes & 2 Lens rifles. also 62 Grenade boxes | |
| | | | 153 " Inf Bde 4 " " " " | Wh |
| " | " | | 154th Inf Bde 62 Local pattern Grenade boxes | Wh |
| " | 5 | | Visited Railhead & drew stores for troops | Wh |
| " | 6" | | Do Do Purchase a barrel cart for use of ADMS for the purpose of emptying filth from pools &c | Wh |
| " | 7 | | Visited Railhead & drew stores for troops. Saw DDOS 1st Army at railhead & received notification regarding return of ordnance stores to the base i.e. old & new stores to separated at Railhead by AOC representative before returning to base | Wh |

1577 Wt. W10791/1773 500,000 1/15 D. D. & L. A.D.S.S./Forms/C. 2118.

Instructions regarding War Diaries and Intelligence Summaries are contained in F. S. Regs., Part II. and the Staff Manual respectively. Title pages will be prepared in manuscript.

# WAR DIARY
*or*
# INTELLIGENCE SUMMARY.
*(Erase heading not required.)*

Army Form C. 2118.

| Place | Date | Hour | Summary of Events and Information | Remarks and references to Appendices |
|---|---|---|---|---|
| | | | | HQ 1st Army O.S. 53/3 7-6.15 |
| Lacon | 8th June | | Visited Railhead & distributed stores to Troops. Purchased & distributed to H.Q. 3 Inf: Bdes 100 local pattern hand grenade boxes. Received notification that 4 bomb throwers is being issued to Division | Wh. |
| Lacon | 9th | | Visited Railhead & distributed stores to Troops. Purchased 32 flags red for marking position of troops. 10 Rifles M.L.E. fitted with optical sights received & distributed to | Wh |
| Lacon | 10th | | Visited Railhead & distributed stores to troops. Purchased 30 Washing Tubs for use of troops for bathing purposes | Wh |
| Lacon | 11th | | Visited railhead & distributed stores to troops. 18000 respirators arrived to complete units to 2 respirators per man, as Smoke helmets are not yet available | Wh |
| Lacon | 12th | | Visited Railhead & distributed stores to Troops. 1750 Smoke helmets received & distributed to Inf: units | Wh |
| Lacon | 13th | | Visited Railhead & distributed stores to Troops 1150 Smoke helmets received & distributed to Inf units | Wh |
| " | 14th | | Visited Railhead & distributed stores to Troops. 1000 Smoke helmets received & distributed to Infantry Units | Wh |

1577 Wt. W10791/1773 500,000 1/15 D. D. & L. A.D.S.S./Forms/C. 2118.

Instructions regarding War Diaries and Intelligence Summaries are contained in F. S. Regs., Part II. and the Staff Manual respectively. Title pages will be prepared in manuscript.

# WAR DIARY
*or*
# INTELLIGENCE SUMMARY.
*(Erase heading not required.)*

Army Form C. 2118.

| Place | Date | Hour | Summary of Events and Information | Remarks and references to Appendices |
|---|---|---|---|---|
| Locon | 15/6/15 | | Visited Railhead & distributed stores to Troops. 1 Thresh Disinfector arrived for ADMS of Division | Wh |
| Locon | 16/6/15 | | Visited Railhead & distributed stores to Troops. Purchased 20 yellow screens each with two 6 ft poles, urgently required. 1200 Smoke helmets arrived. | Wh |
| Locon | 17/6/15 | | Visited Railhead & distributed stores to Troops. 1800 Smoke helmets arrived | Wh |
| Locon | 18/6/15 | | Visited railhead & distributed stores to Troops. Wired to Base for 2 Maxim Guns complete with spare part boxes & Tripod mountings for 1/6 Scottish Rifles to replace others lost by shell fire. Repeated to QMG. GHQ & Ordnance 1st Army. Also wired to base for 1 BLC 15 pr gun for 1/3 City of Aberdeen Battery and 1 BLC 15 pr gun for 1/1 Fifeshire Battery. Both guns condemned by IOM. Repeated to Ordnance Communications and Ordnance First Army. Received 1350 Smoke helmets | Wh |
| Locon | 19/6/15 | | Visited Railhead & distributed stores to Troops. 1800 Smoke helmets arrived | Wh |
| Locon | 20/6/15 | | Visited Railhead & distributed stores to Troops. 900 Smoke helmets received<br>Received letter from DDOS 1st Army that all smoke helmets that have been worn in contact with gases are to exchanged, & sent to COO Abbeville to be re-impregnated | Wh |

1577 Wt. W10791/1773 500,000 1/15 D. D. & L. A.D.S.S./Forms/C. 2118.

Army Form C. 2118.

Instructions regarding War Diaries and Intelligence Summaries are contained in F. S. Regs., Part II. and the Staff Manual respectively. Title pages will be prepared in manuscript.

# WAR DIARY
*or*
# INTELLIGENCE SUMMARY.
*(Erase heading not required.)*

| Place | Date | Hour | Summary of Events and Information | Remarks and references to Appendices |
|---|---|---|---|---|
| Lacon | 21/6/15 | | Visited Railhead & distributed stores to Troops. Received 1950 Smoke helmets | Wh. |
| Lacon | 22/6/15 | | Visited Railhead & distributed stores to Troops. | Wh. |
| Lacon | 23/6/15 | | Visited Railhead & distributed stores to Troops. Purchased small cart for carrying rations to troops in fighting line, from wagon line | Wh. |
| Lacon | 24/6/15 | | Visited Railhead & distributed stores to Troops. Received 2700 Smoke Helmets also 2 Vickers Machine Guns & Tripods complete with spare part box, for 1/4 Loyal North Lancs Regt. | Wh. |
| Lacon | 25/6/15 | | Visited Railhead & distributed stores to Troops. Received & issued 2 Vickers Machine Guns & Tripod Mountings complete with spare part box for 1/6 Scottish Rifles | Wh. |
| Lacon | 26/6/15 | | Visited Railhead & distributed stores to Troops. Received 4350 Smoke helmets | Wh. |
| Le-Nouveau Monde | 27/6/15 | | Visited Railhead & brought stores to new Divisional Hd Qrs for distribution tomorrow. Divisional H. Qrs moved to Le-Nouveau Monde. Received 10000 respirators for reserve. | Wh. |
| Le Nouveau Monde | 28/6/15 | | Visited Railhead & distributed stores to Troops | Wh. |

1577 Wt. W10791/1773 500,000 1/15 D. D. & L. A.D.S.S./Forms/C. 2118.

Instructions regarding War Diaries and Intelligence Summaries are contained in F. S. Regs., Part II. and the Staff Manual respectively. Title pages will be prepared in manuscript.

# WAR DIARY
*or*
# INTELLIGENCE SUMMARY.
*(Erase heading not required.)*

Army Form C. 2118.

| Place | Date | Hour | Summary of Events and Information | Remarks and references to Appendices |
|---|---|---|---|---|
| Le-Keaveau Monde | 29/6/15 | | Visited Railhead & distributed stores to Troops | Wh. |
| Do | 30/6/15 | | Visited Railhead & distributed stores to Troops. Received instructions to receive 8 Vermoral Sprayers from Meerut Division & 2 from Lahore Division | Wh. |
| | | | The following were purchased today for disinfecting purposes in the trenches &c:- Watering Cans with rose 20 - Garden Syringes 12 - Hooks reaping 76. Sharpening Stones 50 | Wh. |

W Maltby Capt
DADOS
51st Highland Division

2/7/15

1577 Wt. W10791/1773 500,000 1/15 D. D. & L. A.D.S.S./Forms/C. 2118.

51st Division

181/61/9

DADOS. 51st Division

Vol III

Instructions regarding War Diaries and Intelligence Summaries are contained in F. S. Regs., Part II. and the Staff Manual respectively. Title pages will be prepared in manuscript.

# WAR DIARY

~~or~~

~~INTELLIGENCE SUMMARY~~.

*(Erase heading not required.)*

Army Form C. 2118.

| Hour, Date, Place | Summary of Events and Information | Remarks and references to Appendices |
|---|---|---|
| | Confidential. | |
| | War Diary of:- | |
| | D.A.D.O.S. 51st Division. | |
| | (Capt. W. Maltby A.O.D.) | |
| | From:- 1-7-15. | |
| | To:- 31-7-15. | |

(73989) W4141—463. 400,000. 9/14. H.&J.Ltd. Forms/C. 2118/10.

Instructions regarding War Diaries and Intelligence Summaries are contained in F. S. Regs., Part II. and the Staff Manual respectively. Title pages will be prepared in manuscript.

# WAR DIARY
*or*
# INTELLIGENCE SUMMARY.
*(Erase heading not required.)*

1-7-15 To 31-7-15
D.A.D.O.S.
51st Division

Army Form C. 2118.

| Place | Date | Hour | Summary of Events and Information | Remarks and references to Appendices |
|---|---|---|---|---|
| Le Nouveau Monde | 1/7/15 | | Visited Railhead & Distributed Stores to Troops. Received instructions that 4 Portable Machine Gun Mountings were to be issued to 51st (Highland) Division | G.H.Q. Q2804 25/6/15 |
| | | | Demanded by wire 2 - B.L.C. 15 pr Mark I Guns - 1 each for City of Dundee Battery & Forfar Battery - to replace 2 others condemned as beyond local repair by I.O.M. | |
| | | | Purchased a quantity of colourwash & brushes for colouring loopholes in parapets of trenches | Ch. |
| Le Nouveau Monde | 2/7/15 | | Visited Railhead & distributed stores to Troops. Received instructions to purchase locally "Cross breech Rifle" as they are not available at the Base | D.D.O.S. 1st Army Ch. O.S. |
| Le Nouveau Monde | 3/7/15 | | Visited Railhead & distributed stores to Troops. 4 Portable Machine Gun mountings referred to on the 1st inst. received, & issued to Inf. units. | Ch. 7/56 1-7-15 |
| Le Nouveau Monde | 4/7/15 | | Visited Railhead & distributed stores to Troops. 4 pairs of Shoepack boots received for experimental purposes & report. | Ch. |

P.T.O.

Instructions regarding War Diaries and Intelligence Summaries are contained in F. S. Regs., Part II. and the Staff Manual respectively. Title pages will be prepared in manuscript.

# WAR DIARY
*or*
# INTELLIGENCE SUMMARY.
*(Erase heading not required.)*

Army Form C. 2118.

| Place | Date | Hour | Summary of Events and Information | Remarks and references to Appendices |
|---|---|---|---|---|
| Le Nouveau Monde | 5/7/15 | | Visited Railhead & distributed stores to Troops. Received 7 more Portable Machine Gun Mountings & issued to Inf: units. Received 2400 Smoke helmets | See 3rd day remarks [illegible] |
| Do | 6/7/15 | | No stores arrived today at Railhead. 2000 Smoke helmets received. Purchased 12 local pattern sythes for cutting grass in the vicinity of trenches | [illegible] |
| Do | 7/7/15 | | Visited Railhead & distributed stores to troops. | [illegible] |
| Do | 8/7/15 | | No stores arrived today for Troops. Purchased 10 small beer barrels to contain water for troops in earthworks | [illegible] |
| Do | 9/7/15 | | Visited Railhead & distributed stores to troops. Commenced this day to issue the second smoke helmet & completed Infantry units. Respirators released withdrawn. Purchased 4 more syringes (garden pattern) for disinfecting purposes for use of Sanitary Section | [illegible] |
| Do | 10/7/15 | | Visited Railhead & distributed stores to Troops. Issued 5 Vermorel Sprayers each to 153rd & 154th Infantry Brigade | [illegible] |
| Do | 11/7/15 | | Visited Railhead & distributed stores to Troops. Cancelled the issue of 2nd Smoke helmet referred to on the 9th. 2nd smoke helmet not now to be issued until reserve of smoke helmets is complete. | [illegible] 780/2 8-7-15 |

PTO

1577 Wt. W10791/1773 500,000 1/15 D. D. & L. A.D.S.S./Forms/C. 2118.

Instructions regarding War Diaries and Intelligence Summaries are contained in F. S. Regs., Part II. and the Staff Manual respectively. Title pages will be prepared in manuscript.

# WAR DIARY
*or*
# INTELLIGENCE SUMMARY.

(*Erase heading not required.*)

Army Form C. 2118.

| Place | Date | Hour | Summary of Events and Information | Remarks and references to Appendices |
|---|---|---|---|---|
| Le Nouveau Monde | 11/7/15 Entered | | Received 7 Catapults for Bomb Throwing. Issued 1 to Divnl Cyclist Company & 2 to each of 3 Inf: Bde Bomb Schools. for preliminary instruction | Wh |
| Do | 12/7/15 | | Visited Railhead & distributed stores to Troops. Received 2250 Smoke Helmets towards reserve. Purchased 100 tins to contain 8 ozs each of hypo solution for respirators for horses. | Wh HQ 1st Army 1334 |
| Do | 13/7/15 | | No stores arrived at Railhead today. Received 1200 smoke helmets to mat reserve. | Wh AQ 26-6-15 |
| Do | 14/7/15 | | Visited Railhead & distributed stores to Troops. Received 6 Cook Carts from Base for issue to RA units, vide Mob: Table. Purchased locally 10 barrels for storage of water in works of defence also 36 pairs of wire cutters & 36 Spades with narrow blades for use of troops in front line | Wh |
| Do | 15/7/15 | | Visited Railhead & distributed stores to Troops. Received 13 Catapults from Base & issued to Troops according to distribution list received from HQ of Division | Wh |
| Do | 16/7/15 | | Visited Railhead & distributed stores to Troops. The following were approved for issue | |
| | | | General Routine Order 1010 d/ 13/7/15. Battle Sights for Maxim & Vickers Machine Guns - 1 per Gun | |
| | | | " " " 1004 " Lamps Acetylene Field Telegraph. Each Divn'l Signal Co - 5 | |
| | | | " " " 1012 " Pistols Illuminating 1½ inch. Per Inf: Bde - 10 | Wh |

Army Form C. 2118.

# WAR DIARY
*or*
# INTELLIGENCE SUMMARY.

(*Erase heading not required.*)

Instructions regarding War Diaries and Intelligence Summaries are contained in F. S. Regs., Part II. and the Staff Manual respectively. Title pages will be prepared in manuscript.

| Place | Date | Hour | Summary of Events and Information | Remarks and references to Appendices |
|---|---|---|---|---|
| Le Nouveau Monde | 17/7/15 | | Visited Railhead & distributed stores to Troops. Received instructions that all Khaki drill containers for Smoke helmets were to be replaced by Waterproof Containers. 4 Bomb throwers received. Vide H.Q 1st Army OS 53/3. d/ 7-6-15 | |
| | | | Instructions received that last consignment of Vermoral Sprayers were Mark II pattern and that marks of sprayers were to be stated when demanding components for repair. | Wh. |
| Do | 18/7/15 | | No stores arrived at Railhead for Troops. Received memo from D.D.O.S. 1st Army stating that a certain number of pigeon baskets have been obtained & sent to Base & that although organization is not complete indents for such received from Signal Companies are to be passed | 1st Army O.S. 48/177 17.7.15 |
| | | | 1350 Smoke helmets & W.P. containers received. This issue completed the Reserve | Wh. |
| Do | 19/7/15 | | Visited Railhead & distributed stores to Troops | Wh. |
| Do | 20/7/15 | | Visited Railhead & distributed stores to troops. | |
| | | | Received letter reference withdrawal of rifles from H.Q Divn'l Artillery – RFA Batteries & H.Q Bdes – Ammunition Columns of Bdes – Divn'l Ammunition Columns – Divn'l Train – & all personnel Field Ambulances | |

PTO

Instructions regarding War Diaries and Intelligence Summaries are contained in F. S. Regs., Part II. and the Staff Manual respectively. Title pages will be prepared in manuscript.

# WAR DIARY
*or*
# INTELLIGENCE SUMMARY.
*(Erase heading not required.)*

Army Form C. 2118.

| Place | Date | Hour | Summary of Events and Information | Remarks and references to Appendices |
|---|---|---|---|---|
| | Bethune | | | |
| Le Hameau Monde | 20/7/15 | | 10 rifles per battery RFA only to be retained. Bde Ammunition Columns Div'l Ammunition Columns. Div'l Train ASC personnel & Field Ambulances. ASC personnel are to be re-armed with Carbines or Rifles not resighted for Mark VII Ammunition but these are to be ~~supplied~~ issued before arms now in possession are withdrawn. | Wh |
| Do | 21/7/15 | | No stores for troops arrived. | Wh |
| Do | 22/7/15 | | Visited Railhead & distributed stores to troops. Machine demanded for units as under in addition to 2 per Battalion already in possession. 1/7 Black Watch – 2 1/8 Argyle & Sutherland Hdrs – 1 Additional transport also demanded | Wh |
| Do | 23/7/15 | | Visited Railhead & distributed stores to troops. Completed purchase of 15000 local pattern rifle covers at 90 centimes each & distributed to troops Auth. H.Q. 1st Army O.S. 7/56 d/ 1st July 1915 | Wh |
| Do | 24/7/15 | | Visited Railhead & distributed stores to troops. Received instructions to return to Base 4 unserviceable 15 pr guns, before arrival of guns to replace owing to move of Division | |

1577 Wt. W10791/1773 500,000 1/15 D. D. & L. A.D.S.S./Forms/C. 2118.

Instructions regarding War Diaries and Intelligence Summaries are contained in F. S. Regs., Part II. and the Staff Manual respectively. Title pages will be prepared in manuscript.

# WAR DIARY
*or*
# INTELLIGENCE SUMMARY.
*(Erase heading not required.)*

Army Form C. 2118.

| Place | Date | Hour | Summary of Events and Information | Remarks and references to Appendices |
|---|---|---|---|---|
| Le Nouveau Monde | 25/7/15 | | Stores which arrived today for troops were returned to Regulating Station for reconsignment to new Railhead. The 4 unserviceable guns referred to yesterday were returned to Base today. | WL |
| Heilly | 26/7/15 | | No stores arrived for troops. Divisional Hd Qrs moved to Heilly. Railhead Amiens | WL |
| " | 27/7/15 | | No stores arrived for troops. Established office. | |
| " | 28/7/15 | | No stores arrived for troops. Arranged for distribution of stores to troops in new area at refilling points | WL |
| " | 29/7/15 | | Visited Railhead & distributed stores to troops. Received 27 Vermorel Sprayers in part supply of 40 allowed for Division. The 3 Vickers Machine Guns referred to on 22nd instant were received & were re-allotted as follows. One to each 1/6 Black Watch 1/5 Gordon Hdrs 1/7 Gordon Hdrs. | WL |
| " | 30/7/15 | | Visited Railhead & distributed stores to Troops. Wrote letter to D.A.D.O.S 3rd Army asking if "spares" for Catapults could be issued in anticipation of repairs to save delay when repairs were actually necessary (OS/189) | WL |
| " | 31/7/15 | | No stores arrived today for troops. 4 B.L. 6 15 pr Carriages & 2 Limbers replaced, were returned to Base today | WL |

1577 Wt. W10791/1773 500,000 1/15 D. D. & L. A.D.S.S./Forms/C. 2118.

Instructions regarding War Diaries and Intelligence Summaries are contained in F. S. Regs., Part II. and the Staff Manual respectively. Title pages will be prepared in manuscript.

# WAR DIARY
*or*
# INTELLIGENCE SUMMARY.
*(Erase heading not required.)*

Army Form C. 2118.

| Place | Date | Hour | Summary of Events and Information | Remarks and references to Appendices |
| --- | --- | --- | --- | --- |
| Hully | 31/7/15 | | One Vickers gun complete with mounting to be demanded for each of the following units on allotment by DAG 1/6 Scottish Rifles & 1/4 Loyal North Lane's Regt. Necessary transport also indented for. This will complete these units to 3 machine guns per Battalion | Wh |
| | | | 31/7/15 } W Maltby Capt. DADOS 51st Division | |

1577 Wt. W10791/1773 500,000 1/15 D. D. & L. A.D.S.S./Forms/C. 2118.

51st Division

Box 2708

121/6695

DADOS. 51st Division

Vol IV

1 – 31. 8. 15

Instructions regarding War Diaries and Intelligence Summaries are contained in F. S. Regs., Part II. and the Staff Manual respectively. Title pages will be prepared in manuscript.

# WAR DIARY
*or*
# INTELLIGENCE SUMMARY.
*(Erase heading not required.)*

Army Form C. 2118.

| Place | Date | Hour | Summary of Events and Information | Remarks and references to Appendices |
|---|---|---|---|---|
| | | | – Confidential –<br>War. Diary<br>of<br>D.A. D.O.S. 51st Division<br><br>From. 1st Aug: 1915 To 31st Aug: 1915. | |

1577 Wt. W10791/1773 500,000 1/15 D. D. & L. A.D.S.S./Forms/C. 2118.

Instructions regarding War Diaries and Intelligence Summaries are contained in F. S. Regs., Part II. and the Staff Manual respectively. Title pages will be prepared in manuscript.

# WAR DIARY
*or*
# INTELLIGENCE SUMMARY.
*(Erase heading not required.)*

Army Form C. 2118.

| Place | Date | Hour | Summary of Events and Information | Remarks and references to Appendices |
|---|---|---|---|---|
| Heilly | 1/8/15 | | Visited Railhead & distributed stores to Troops. | Wk |
| " | 2/8/15 | | Visited Railhead & distributed stores to Troops. An instance was brought to light today of a unit with a machine gun reported by the unit out of action, but the unit had taken no steps to communicate with the D.A.D.O.S. on the matter. The case is being investigated with a view of ascertaining whether the gun is beyond local repair. | Wk |
| Heilly | 3/8/15 | | From todays date Railhead is at Mericourt. Visited Railhead & distributed stores to troops. Received 13 Vermorel Sprayers which completes establishment of Division viz: 40. Received 2 Vickers Machine Guns complete with tripod mountings & Boxes Spare Parts & issued as follows in accordance with approved allotment 1 to 1/6 Scottish Rifles & 1 to 1/4 Loyal North Lancs Regt. Also received 50 steel helmets for trial. | Wk |
| Heilly | 4/8/15 | | Visited Railhead & distributed stores to troops. Received 4 Vickers Machine Guns complete with tripod mountings & Boxes Spare parts & issued as follows in accordance with approved allotment. 3 – 1/6 A&S Hdrs & 1 – 1/7 Gordon Highlanders | Wk |
| Senlis | 5/8/15 | | Visited Railhead & distributed stores to troops. Divisional HQ moved to Senlis this day | Wk. |

1577 Wt. W10791/1773 500,000 1/15 D. D. & L. A.D.S.S./Forms/C. 2118.

Instructions regarding War Diaries and Intelligence Summaries are contained in F. S. Regs., Part II. and the Staff Manual respectively. Title pages will be prepared in manuscript.

# WAR DIARY
*or*
# INTELLIGENCE SUMMARY.
*(Erase heading not required.)*

Army Form C. 2118.

| Place | Date | Hour | Summary of Events and Information | Remarks and references to Appendices |
|---|---|---|---|---|
| Senlis | 6/8/15 | | Visited Railhead & distributed stores to Troops. Wired for one machine gun for 1/8 Liverpool Regt to replace a converted ·303 in: beyond local repair. 8 Portable Machine Gun mountings received & distributed as follows:- 4 to 2/5 Lancs Fusiliers & 4 to 1/6 Scottish Rifles | |
| Senlis | 7/8/15 | | Visited Railhead & distributed stores to troops | |
| Senlis | 8/8/15 | | — Do — | |
| Senlis | 9/8/15 | | Do Received 1 Maxim ·303 for 1/8 Liverpool Regt in place of the one beyond local repair referred to on 6th instant. | |
| Senlis | 10/8/15 | | Visited Railhead & distributed stores to troops. Wired for Vickers machine Guns with Tripod mountings & Boxes Spare parts also Packsaddlery and necessary transport, as allotted by 10th Corps – 1/5 Seaforth Highlanders 3 – 1/6 Black Watch 2 – 1/7 Gordon Highlanders 1 Total 6. Returned the machine gun beyond local repair referred to on the 6th instant, to Base, after being replaced. | |
| Senlis | 11/8/15 | | Visited Railhead & distributed stores to Troops | |
| Senlis | 12/8/15 | | — Do — | |

Continued overleaf.

1577 Wt. W10791/1773 500,000 1/15 D. D. & L. A.D.S.S./Forms/C. 2118.

Army Form C. 2118

Instructions regarding War Diaries and Intelligence Summaries are contained in F. S. Regs., Part II. and the Staff Manual respectively. Title pages will be prepared in manuscript.

# WAR DIARY
*or*
# INTELLIGENCE SUMMARY.
*(Erase heading not required.)*

| Place | Date | Hour | Summary of Events and Information | Remarks and references to Appendices |
|---|---|---|---|---|
| Lenlis | 13/8/15 | | Visited Railhead & distributed stores to troops. 6 Guns Vickers, with Tripod Mountings complete with spare part boxes arrived & issued to units as follows: 3 – 1/5 Seaforth Highlanders. 2 – 1/6 Black Watch & 1 – 1/7 Gordon Highlanders. The additional transport for these 6 guns is still to be supplied. These guns are issued in part to complete to 4 Machine Guns per Infantry Battalion | Wh. |
| | | | Received amended instructions regarding issue of Smoke helmets & Respirators viz: each officer & man to have 2 Smoke helmets in possession & one per officer & man in Divisional Reserve. On receipt of the 2nd Smoke helmet per officer & man, (now in possession of 1 respirator per officer & man in lieu) all respirators including those in reserve to be wasted. Present situation is as follows:- | |
| | | | — In possession — In Reserve — | |
| | | | Smoke helmets :- 1 per officer & man — 1 per officer & man | |
| | | | Respirators 1 — Do — 1 — Do — | Wh. |
| | | | Continued. | |

1577 Wt. W10791/1773 500,000 1/15 D. D. & L. A.D.S.S./Forms/C. 2118.

Army Form C. 2118.

Instructions regarding War Diaries and Intelligence Summaries are contained in F. S. Regs., Part II. and the Staff Manual respectively. Title pages will be prepared in manuscript.

# WAR DIARY
*or*
# INTELLIGENCE SUMMARY.

*(Erase heading not required.)*

| Place | Date | ~~Hour.~~ | Summary of Events and Information | Remarks and references to Appendices |
|---|---|---|---|---|
| Senlis | | 14 8/15 | Proceeded on leave until the 21st inst. Acting Sub Conductor E. C. Carolan AOC will perform the duties of DADOS temporarily, under supervision of the DA QMG 51st Division | [illegible] |
| Senlis | | 14 8/15 | Visited Railhead & distributed stores to Troops. Received list of stores authorized for issue for repair of No. 7 dial sights. O.C.B. 1485. | [illegible] |
| Senlis | | 15 8/15 | Visited Railhead + distributed stores to Troops. Received further instructions re staining tents &c. O.S.R. 959. | [illegible] |
| Senlis | | 16 8/15 | Visited Railhead + distributed stores to Troops. | [illegible] |
| Senlis | | 17 8/15 | Visited Railhead & distributed stores to Troops. 3 rifles with telescopic sights allotted to 51st Div. 51st (H) Div: No. 514 Q. 550 acid & fire proof suits allotted to 51st Div. Xth Corps No. 73/1 Q. | [illegible] |
| Senlis | | 18 8/15 | Visited Railhead + distributed stores to Troops. | [illegible] |
| Senlis | | 19 8/15 | Visited Railhead + distributed stores to Troops. Received instructions re reports on damaged guns &c. Q. M. G. G.H.Q. No. Q 1854. One telescope 'Micro-Dawson' allotted to 51st Div. for special use of Artillery Commander. DDOS III Army No. 047. Received instructions re demands for cable for artillery units. D 3 Cable to be | [illegible] |

P.T.O.

1577 Wt. W10791/1773 500,000 1/15 D. D. & L. A.D.S.S./Forms/C. 2118.

Instructions regarding War Diaries and Intelligence Summaries are contained in F. S. Regs., Part II. and the Staff Manual respectively. Title pages will be prepared in manuscript.

# WAR DIARY
*or*
# INTELLIGENCE SUMMARY.

(*Erase heading not required.*)

Army Form C. 2118.

| Place | Date | Hour | Summary of Events and Information | Remarks and references to Appendices |
|---|---|---|---|---|
| | | Continued | | |
| Senlis | 19 8/15 | | Economised & D1 issued as far as possible. Q.M.G. Q1401a Issue approved of 50 pairs of gum boots to 51st Div. for use of Field Companies working in mud & water. D.D.O.S. 3rd Army No O42/2. | [illegible] |
| Senlis | 20 8/15 | | Visited Railhead & distributed stores to Troops | [illegible] |
| Senlis | 21 8/15 | | Visited Railhead & distributed stores to Troops. Received instructions re return of leather hoods for Mark IV tripods for machine guns to Base. Xth Corps No 103 Q. | [illegible] |
| Senlis | 22 8/15 | | Visited Railhead. No stores for Troops | [illegible] |
| Senlis | 23 8/15 | | Returned from leave on the morning of the 23rd inst. Visited Railhead & distributed stores to Troops. | Wh. |
| Senlis | 24 8/15 | | Visited Railhead & distributed stores to Troops. One "Harp shaped periscope" allotted to each Artillery Brigade, for trial & report. Aut: DDOS GHQ 30/38 d/ 20-8-15. | Wh. |
| Senlis | 25 8/15 | | Visited railhead & distributed stores to troops. 2 Vickers Machine Guns with Tripod mountings & Boxes Spare Parts to be received for 1/4 Royal Lancs Regt. to complete to 4 per Battalion. | Wh. |
| Senlis | 26 8/15 | | Visited Railhead & distributed stores to Troops. Received an initial supply of 280 Tube pattern | Wh. |
| | | | | Continued |

1577 Wt. W10791/1773 500,000 1/15 D. D. & L. A.D.S.S./Forms/C. 2118.

Army Form C. 2118.

Instructions regarding War Diaries and Intelligence Summaries are contained in F. S. Regs., Part II. and the Staff Manual respectively. Title pages will be prepared in manuscript.

# WAR DIARY
*or*
# INTELLIGENCE SUMMARY.
*(Erase heading not required.)*

| Place | Date | Hour | Summary of Events and Information | Remarks and references to Appendices |
|---|---|---|---|---|
| Senlis | 26/8/15 | | Smoke helmets - Officers & men to be ultimately equipped with one each in addition to the ordinary smoke helmet - 3 Telescopic rifles received | Wh |
| Senlis | 27/8/15 | | Visited Railhead & distributed stores to Troops. Received notification that 24 Guns, Carriages & Limbers QF 18 pr. & 72 Wagons Ammunition & Limbers QF 18 pr will arrive at supply railhead during night of 27th - 28th inst. These are for re-arming the Division. 4 GS Wagons released from the Brigade Ammn Columns to be transferred to the Divisional Ammn Col to take extra weight of 18 pr QF ammunition. Harness for these 4 wagons has been demanded today. BLC 15 pr equipment is to be returned to Base as soon as possible after receipt of the QF 18 pr equipment. | Wh |
| Senlis | 28/8/15 | | Visited Railhead & distributed stores to Troops | Wh |
| Senlis | 29/8/15 | | Visited Railhead & distributed stores to Troops. 6 Vickers Machine Guns complete with spare part boxes & Tripod mountings received & issued as follows:- 3 - 1/6 Liverpool Regt 1 - 1/7 Black Watch. 1 - 1/5 Gordon Highlanders & 1 - 1/6 Argyll & Sutherland Highlanders. Received notification that 4500 "P" respirators will be issued to Division for issue to Infantry not in possession of tube pattern smoke helmets. | Wh |
| | | | Wired for 2 Maxim guns to replace 2 beyond local repair, for 1/7 Black Watch | Wh |

Army Form C. 2118.

Instructions regarding War Diaries and Intelligence Summaries are contained in F. S. Regs., Part II. and the Staff Manual respectively. Title pages will be prepared in manuscript.

# WAR DIARY
*or*
# INTELLIGENCE SUMMARY.

*(Erase heading not required.)*

| Place | Date | Hour | Summary of Events and Information | Remarks and references to Appendices |
|---|---|---|---|---|
| Senlis | | 30/9/15 | Visited Railhead & distributed stores to Troops. Received 1200 "P" pattern respirators referred to on 29th inst. & issued to Infantry. Purchased 1. Handcart with cycle wheels (to avoid noise) for carrying rations to front line trenches; for experimental purposes. Also purchased 40 local pattern stretchers for carrying wounded through narrow trenches. These stretchers allow the patient to sit, leaning against the back of the front bearer. | Wh |
| Senlis | | 31/9/15 | Visited Railhead & distributed stores to Troops. Received instructions that owing to reduction of ammunition to be carried by 5 in: Howitzer Brigades, 8 Ammunition Wagons complete turnouts have to be returned to Advanced Horse Transport Depot ~~Base~~ Wh by ~~4~~ Wh 51st Divnl Ammunition Col. | Wh Wh |

31/8/15 } Whalley Capt DADOS 51st Division

1577 Wt. W10791/1773 500,000 1/15 D. D. & L. A.D.S.S./Forms/C. 2118.

51st Division

121/6902

DADOS. 51st Division

Vol V

September 15.

5203

Instructions regarding War Diaries and Intelligence Summaries are contained in F. S. Regs., Part II. and the Staff Manual respectively. Title pages will be prepared in manuscript.

# WAR DIARY
*or*
# INTELLIGENCE SUMMARY.
*(Erase heading not required.)*

Army Form C. 2118.

| Place | Date | Hour | Summary of Events and Information | Remarks and references to Appendices |
|---|---|---|---|---|
| | | | – Front Sheet – | |
| | | | Confidential | |
| | | | War Diary | |
| | | | of | |
| | | | D.A.D.O.S. 51st Division | |
| | | | From 1-9-15 To 30-9-15. | |
| | | | 30/9/15 Whalley Capt. D.A.D.O.S. 51st Division | |



1577 Wt. W10791/1773 500,000 1/15 D. D. & L. A.D.S.S./Forms/C. 2118.

Instructions regarding War Diaries and Intelligence Summaries are contained in F. S. Regs., Part II. and the Staff Manual respectively. Title pages will be prepared in manuscript.

# WAR DIARY
*or*
# INTELLIGENCE SUMMARY.
*(Erase heading not required.)*

Army Form C. 2118.

| Place | Date | Hour | Summary of Events and Information | Remarks and references to Appendices |
|---|---|---|---|---|
| Senlis | 1/9/15 | | Visited Railhead & distributed stores to Troops. Received 2 Maxim Guns to replace 2 - beyond local repair, for 1/7 Black Watch | Wh. |
| Senlis | 2/9/15 | | Visited Railhead & distributed stores to Troops. Returned to Base all BLC 15 pr equipment released by issue of QF 18 pr equipment. The following were returned:- 24 Guns & Carriages, & limbers - 48 Ammunition Wagons & Limbers - 20 GS. wagons. | Wh. |
| Senlis | 3/9/15 | | Visited Railhead & distributed stores to Troops. Received a further supply of "P" respirators, and issued to troops. Purchased 48 rat traps for troops in trenches | Wh. |
| Senlis | 4/9/15 | | Visited Railhead & distributed stores to Troops | Wh. |
| Senlis | 5/9/15 | | Visited Railhead & distributed stores to Troops. Received 400 P respirators (further supply) | Wh |
| Senlis | 6/9/15 | | Visited Railhead & distributed stores to Troops. Demanded Blanket GS. to complete to 1 per man | Wh |
| Senlis | 7/8/15 | | Visited Railhead & distributed stores to Troops. Took steps to form a Divisional Armourers shop. 2 Armourers per Brigade to be withdrawn, and the 2 left with Brigade to be under the HQ of Bdes & to carry out repairs to rifles &c on charge of all units in the Brigade. In addition to the 2 Armourers per Bde to work in Divisional workshop, each Brigade | |

1577 Wt. W10791/1773 500,000 1/15 D. D. & L. A.D.S.S./Forms/C. 2118.

Army Form C. 2118.

Instructions regarding War Diaries and Intelligence Summaries are contained in F. S. Regs., Part II. and the Staff Manual respectively. Title pages will be prepared in manuscript.

# WAR DIARY
*or*
# INTELLIGENCE SUMMARY.
*(Erase heading not required.)*

| Place | Date | Hour | Summary of Events and Information | Remarks and references to Appendices |
|---|---|---|---|---|
| | | | will provide 2 men for armourers shop, who have been already instructed in the work. The Divisional Armourers Shop will carry out all repairs to bicycles, and such repairs to arms & machine guns which cannot be performed regimentally | Wh |
| Senlis | 8/9/15 | | Visited Railhead & distributed stores to Troops. | Wh |
| Senlis | 9/9/15 | | Visited Railhead & distributed stores to Troops. Issued instructions to units on the subject of economy in cleaning material, owing to the observed tendency of units to increase quantities demanded. | Wh |
| Senlis | 10/9/15 | | Visited Railhead & distributed stores to Troops. Instructions received that hyposcopes for the present are limited to 1 per two Vickers & Maxim Guns, but that Lewis Machine Guns should be equipped with 1 per gun. | Wh |
| Senlis | 11/9/15 | | Visited Railhead & distributed stores to troops. Purchased locally 40 Tubs for use of troops at washing centres | Wh |
| Senlis | 12/9/15 | | Visited Railhead & distributed stores to Troops. Received 1 Maxim Gun for 2/5 Lancashire Fusiliers to replace one beyond local repair. | Wh |
| Senlis | 13/9/15 | | Visited Railhead & distributed stores to Troops. Received 100 tents as first supply for accommodation of troops during Winter months. | Wh |

1577 Wt. W10791/1773 500,000 1/15 D. D. & L. A.D.S.S./Forms/C. 2118.

Army Form C. 2118

Instructions regarding War Diaries and Intelligence Summaries are contained in F. S. Regs., Part II. and the Staff Manual respectively. Title pages will be prepared in manuscript.

# WAR DIARY
*or*
# INTELLIGENCE SUMMARY.
*(Erase heading not required.)*

| Place | Date | Hour | Summary of Events and Information | Remarks and references to Appendices |
|---|---|---|---|---|
| Senlis | 14/9/15 | | Visited Railhead & distributed stores to Troops. Received 10 Ulster Divisional Optical Rifle Sights. Purchased 100 flat irons for ironing lice infected clothing | Wh. |
| Senlis | 15/9/15 | | Visited Railhead & distributed stores to troops | Wh |
| Senlis | 16/9/15 | | Visited Railhead & distributed stores to troops. Received & issued to troops 1 blanket per man | Wh |
| Senlis | 17/9/15 | | Visited Railhead & distributed stores to troops. Received 8 West Bomb Throwers | Wh |
| Senlis | 18/9/15 | | Visited Railhead & distributed stores to troops. Purchased & issued to washing centres 26 more tubs made from wine barrels. | Wh |
| Senlis | 19/9/15 | | Visited Railhead & distributed stores to troops. Sufficient Tube pattern smoke helmets have now been received to equip Infantry, RE & RA. | Wh |
| Senlis | 20/9/15 | | Visited Railhead & distributed stores to troops. Blankets received & issued at the rate of 1 per all ranks other than officers | Wh |
| Senlis | 21/9/15 | | Visited Railhead & distributed stores to troops. | Wh |
| Senlis | 22/9/15 | | Visited Railhead & distributed stores to troops. Purchased flags (224) & Green white American Cloth (9) required by General Staff of Division | Wh. |
| Senlis | 23/9/15 | | Visited railhead & distributed stores to troops. Purchased ~~13~~ 39 Wh boilers for washing centres. | Wh |

1577 Wt. W10791/1773 500,000 1/15 D. D. & L. A.D.S.S./Forms/C. 2118.

Instructions regarding War Diaries and Intelligence Summaries are contained in F. S. Regs., Part II. and the Staff Manual respectively. Title pages will be prepared in manuscript.

# WAR DIARY
*or*
# INTELLIGENCE SUMMARY.
*(Erase heading not required.)*

Army Form C. 2118.

| Place | Date | Hour | Summary of Events and Information | Remarks and references to Appendices |
|---|---|---|---|---|
| Senlis | 24/9/15 | | Visited railhead & distributed stores to troops | Wh |
| Senlis | 25/9/15 | | Visited railhead & distributed stores to troops. Purchased 27 barrels for the making of washing tubs for the troops. | Wh |
| Senlis | 26/9/15 | | Visited Railhead & distributed stores to troops | Wh |
| Senlis | 27/9/15 | | Visited Railhead & distributed stores to troops. Issues completed of 1 blanket each per man. Received & issued 2 sets of fitting for front limber of machine gun limber for experimental purposes, to enable 2 Machine Guns 20 belt boxes of ammunition & other fighting equipment to be carried. Issues of Tube pattern smoke helmets completed today to complete 1 per Officer & man | Wh |
| Senlis | 28/9/15 | | Visited railhead & distributed stores to Troops. 6 pieces of white American Cloth each measuring 15' x 3', for the purposes of indicating where messages are to be dropped by Aeroplanes, demanded today. Distribution 3 to Divisional Hd Qrs 3 to Hd Qrs Divisional Artillery. | Wh<br>Wh |
| Senlis | 29/9/15 | | Visited railhead & distributed stores to Troops. | Wh |
| Senlis | 30/9/15 | | Visited railhead & distributed stores to Troops. Received 400 Knob-Kerries for hand to hand fighting, & issued to troops. All ordinary respirators & P respirators withdrawn from troops & returned to Base on completion of issues of Smoke helmets - 1 per Officer & man | Wh<br>Wh |

W. Whalley Capt
DADOS
51st Division
30/9/15

1577 Wt. W10791/1773 500,000 1/15 D. D. & L. A.D.S.S./Forms/C. 2118.

121/7333

DADOS. 5th Division

Vol VI

Oct 15

Instructions regarding War Diaries and Intelligence Summaries are contained in F. S. Regs., Part II. and the Staff Manual respectively. Title pages will be prepared in manuscript.

# WAR DIARY
*or*
# INTELLIGENCE SUMMARY.
*(Erase heading not required.)*

Army Form C. 2118.

| Place | Date | Hour | Summary of Events and Information | Remarks and references to Appendices |
|---|---|---|---|---|
| | | | – Front Sheet –<br>Confidential<br>War Diary<br>of<br>DADOS 51st Division<br>From 1-10-15 To 31-10-15<br>31/10/15 W Maltby Capt<br>DADOS<br>51st Division | |

1577 Wt. W10791/1773 500,000 1/15 D. D. & L. A.D.S.S./Forms/C. 2118.

Instructions regarding War Diaries and Intelligence Summaries are contained in F. S. Regs., Part II. and the Staff Manual respectively. Title pages will be prepared in manuscript.

# WAR DIARY
*or*
# INTELLIGENCE SUMMARY.
*(Erase heading not required.)*

Army Form C. 21[illegible].

| Place | Date | Hour | Summary of Events and Information | Remarks and references to Appendices |
|---|---|---|---|---|
| Sentis | 1/10/15 | | Visited Railhead & distributed stores to troops. Purchased locally 370 Aprons & 370 pairs of short sleeves for issue to cooks of all units. | Wh |
| Sentis | 2/10/15 | | Visited railhead & distributed stores to troops. Received a further supply of Braziers for use in the trenches. | Wh |
| Sentis | 3/10/15 | | Visited Railhead & distributed stores to troops. Received a further supply of 500 Latrine Buckets for Winter Accommodation & for use in trenches. This completes the 600 allotted to this Division. | Wh |
| Sentis | 4/10/15 | | Visited Railhead & distributed stores to troops. | Wh |
| Sentis | 5/10/15 | | Visited Railhead & distributed stores to troops. Received 11 wire cutters for attaching to rifles | Wh |
| Sentis | 6/10/15 | | Visited Railhead & distributed stores to troops. Received instructions that in future, all horse drawn and mechanical transport vehicles will be painted with approved signs instead of lettering. All lettered markings to be obliterated. Necessary paint demanded. | Wh |
| Sentis | 7/10/15 | | Visited railhead & distributed stores to troops. Issued instructions to RA units on the importance of returning condemned gun & carriage components to the DADOS. Referred especially to the most important items such as, running out springs. These are to be returned to the Base, if they cannot be repaired by the IOM. of the Corps. | Wh |

1577 Wt. W10791/1773 500,000 1/15 D. D. & L. A.D.S.S./Forms/C. 2118.

Instructions regarding War Diaries and Intelligence Summaries are contained in F. S. Regs., Part II. and the Staff Manual respectively. Title pages will be prepared in manuscript.

# WAR DIARY
*or*
# INTELLIGENCE SUMMARY.
*(Erase heading not required.)*

Army Form C. 2[illegible].

| Place | Date | Hour | Summary of Events and Information | Remarks and references to Appendices |
|---|---|---|---|---|
| Senlis | 8/10/15 | | Visited Railhead & distributed stores to troops. Received authority for Winter underclothing | Wh |
| Senlis | 9/10/15 | | Visited Railhead & distributed stores to troops. Purchased 100 handsaws for use of troops in building dug outs to | Wh. |
| Senlis | 10/10/15 | | Visited Railhead & distributed stores to troops. Received a further supply of 150 local pattern braziers made from oil drums, & issued to troops in trenches | Wh. |
| Senlis | 11/10/15 | | Visited Railhead & distributed stores to troops. Arranged for indents to be submitted to complete equipments of Q.F. 18 pr Batteries & Divisional Ammunition Column in accordance with [illegible] G1098-14 F & G1098-181 of September 1915, received today | Wh. |
| Senlis | 12/10/15 | | Visited Railhead & distributed stores to troops. Received 225 pairs of Boots Gum Thigh for issue to Infantry in the trenches | Wh |
| Senlis | 13/10/15 | | Visited Railhead & distributed stores to troops. | Wh. |
| Senlis | 14/10/15 | | Visited Railhead & distributed stores to troops. | Wh |
| Senlis | 15/10/15 | | Visited Railhead & distributed stores to troops. Purchased 10 barrels for making washing tubs for troops. Received Winter Scale of Clothing other than service dress & underclothing. Demanded underclothing for 13 Divisional baths, where men are to bathe and receive a change of underclothing. Arrangements for washing the dirty clothing has been made with a local laundry, and on return will be again distributed to the baths for re-issue | Wh. |

1577 Wt. W10791/1773 500,000 1/15 D. D. & L. A.D.S.S./Forms/C. 2118.

Instructions regarding War Diaries and Intelligence Summaries are contained in F. S. Regs., Part II. and the Staff Manual respectively. Title pages will be prepared in manuscript.

# WAR DIARY
*or*
# INTELLIGENCE SUMMARY.
*(Erase heading not required.)*

Army Form C. 2118.

| Place | Date | Hour | Summary of Events and Information | Remarks and references to Appendices |
|---|---|---|---|---|
| Sailly | 16/10/15 | | Visited railhead & distributed stores to troops. Purchased locally 200 metres of calico for the manufacture of muzzle covers for long rifles as only "covers muzzle" for Short Rifle are being supplied by the Base. Also purchased one Forge & implements for a central Shoeing Smiths Shop which is being established for the manufacture of horse shoes to relieve pressure on the Base for horse shoes. | Wh. |
| Sailly | 17/10/15 | | Visited railhead & distributed stores to troops | Wh |
| Sailly | 18/10/15 | | Visited railhead & distributed stores to troops. Received first supply of winter underclothing. Completed interviewing Qr Mrs of Infantry Units & QM Sergts of other units on the importance of demanding stores only which are actually required. In the case of Machine Guns & other technical stores care should be taken that when components only are required the complete article should not be demanded. | Wh. |
| Sailly | 19/10/15 | | Visited railhead & distributed stores to troops. Commenced to receive clothing at Winter Scales. Received instructions to purchase rat traps & mousetraps at the rate of 50 of each per Infantry Brigade | Wh |
| Sailly | 20/10/15 | | Visited railhead & distributed stores to troops. Purchased rat & mouse traps as above & issued to troops. These have become necessary owing to the prevalence of rats & mice in the trenches | Wh. |

1577 Wt. W10791/1773 500,000 1/15 D. D. & L. A.D.S.S./Forms/C. 2118.

Instructions regarding War Diaries and Intelligence Summaries are contained in F. S. Regs., Part II. and the Staff Manual respectively. Title pages will be prepared in manuscript.

# WAR DIARY
*or*
# INTELLIGENCE SUMMARY.
*(Erase heading not required.)*

Army Form C. 2118.

| Place | Date | Hour | Summary of Events and Information | Remarks and references to Appendices |
|---|---|---|---|---|
| | Continued. | | | |
| Senlis | 20/10/15 | | Telescopic Sights & Rifles approved for Infantry units under General Routine Order 1222 d/ 17/10/15 | |
| | | | Rifles fitted with Telescopic Sights 4 } Demands have been called for from units | |
| | | | Lattey Lens Sights 8 } to complete to this scale | |
| | | | Neills Sights or Martin Sights 8 } | Wh |
| Senlis | 21/10/15 | | Visited Railhead & distributed stores to Troops. | Wh |
| Senlis | 22/10/15 | | Visited Railhead & distributed stores to Troops. Sniperscopes received & issued to troops at the rate of 8 per Infantry Battalion | Wh |
| Senlis | 23/10/15 | | Visited railhead & distributed stores to troops. Owing to several cases of excessive wear to bearings of the West Bomb Thrower, having occurred, had Routine Order published that bearings must be kept lubricated to prevent abnormal wear to bearings. | Wh |
| Senlis | 24/10/15 | | Visited railhead & distributed stores to Troops | Wh |
| Senlis | 25/10/15 | | Visited railhead & distributed stores to troops. Arranged for 2 tailors to repair & make up serviceable puttees from worn or unserviceable puttees | Wh |
| Senlis | 26/10/15 | | Visited Railhead & distributed stores to Troops | Wh |
| Senlis | 27/10/15 | | Visited Railhead & distributed stores to Troops. | Wh |
| Senlis | 28/10/15 | | Visited Railhead & distributed stores to Troops Received instructions to submit indents to | |
| | | | Continued | |

Army Form C. 2118.

Instructions regarding War Diaries and Intelligence Summaries are contained in F. S. Regs., Part II. and the Staff Manual respectively. Title pages will be prepared in manuscript.

# WAR DIARY
*or*
# INTELLIGENCE SUMMARY.
*(Erase heading not required.)*

| Place | Date | Hour | Summary of Events and Information | Remarks and references to Appendices |
|---|---|---|---|---|
| | | | Complete Infantry Units to 2. Infantry Range-Finders per unit. At present Infantry units of this Divn have 1 Infantry Range Finder & 2 sets of Mekometers. | Wh. |
| Senlis | 29 10/15 | | Visited Railhead & distributed stores to troops. 1 Carriage Field BL 5 in: howitzer received to replace another with cracked cradle in possession of 1/1 Renfrew How: Battery | Wh. |
| Senlis | 30 10/15 | | Visited Railhead & distributed stores to Troops | Wh. |
| Senlis | 31 10/15 | | Visited Railhead & distributed stores to Troops. | Wh. |

31 10/15

W Maltby Capt.
D.A.D.O.S.
51st Division

1577 Wt. W10791/1773 500,000 1/15 D. D. & L. A.D.S.S./Forms/C. 2118.

D.A.D.O.S. 5th Dn.

Dec.

Vol. VIII

12/1939

Instructions regarding War Diaries and Intelligence Summaries are contained in F. S. Regs., Part II. and the Staff Manual respectively. Title pages will be prepared in manuscript.

# WAR DIARY
*or*
# INTELLIGENCE SUMMARY.
*(Erase heading not required.)*

Army Form C. 2118.

| Place | Date | Hour | Summary of Events and Information | Remarks and references to Appendices |
|---|---|---|---|---|
| | | | Front Sheet<br>Confidential<br>War - Diary<br>of<br>DADOS 51st Division<br>From 1-12-15 To 31-12-15. | |

1577 Wt. W10791/1773 500,000 1/15 D. D. & L. A.D.S.S./Forms/C. 2118.

Instructions regarding War Diaries and Intelligence Summaries are contained in F. S. Regs., Part II. and the Staff Manual respectively. Title pages will be prepared in manuscript.

# WAR DIARY
*or*
# INTELLIGENCE SUMMARY.
*(Erase heading not required.)*

Army Form C. 2118.

| Place | Date | Hour | Summary of Events and Information | Remarks and references to Appendices |
|---|---|---|---|---|
| Senlis | 1/12/15 | | Visited Railhead & distributed stores to troops. Received 28 stoves Soyers which completes to 50 allowed per Division | Wh. |
| Senlis | 2/12/15 | | Visited Railhead & distributed stores to troops. Purchased 1 combined wringer and mangle for use in Divisional Rest Station. Authority for purchase GOC 51st Divn | Wh |
| ~~Senlis~~ Wh | ~~2/12/15~~ | | ~~Visited Railhead & distributed stores to troops~~ Wh. Mastered this day the balance of winter Service Dress caps with covers, & capes macintosh still due. | Wh |
| Senlis | 3/12/15 | | Visited Railhead & distributed stores to troops. | Wh |
| Senlis | 4/12/15 | | Visited Railhead & distributed stores to troops. Stores for conversion of 2 in: Trench Mortars. reg L.E. Mechanism, arrived | } Wh |
| Senlis | 5/12/15 | | Visited Railhead & distributed stores to Troops. Received initial supply of 300 pairs of short woollen drawers for Highlanders. Received 1 Maxim ·303 in gun for 1/6 Seaforth Highlanders in replacement of one beyond local repair. | Wh |
| Senlis | 6/12/15 | | Visited Railhead & distributed stores to troops. 4 Carriages Ambulance Miller James pattern received | Wh |
| Senlis | 7/12/15 | | Visited railhead & distributed stores to troops. | Wh |
| Senlis | 8/12/15 | | Visited railhead & distributed stores to troops | Wh |

1577 Wt. W10791/1773 500,000 1/15 D. D. & L. A.D.S.S./Forms/C. 2118.

Instructions regarding War Diaries and Intelligence Summaries are contained in F. S. Regs., Part II. and the Staff Manual respectively. Title pages will be prepared in manuscript.

# WAR DIARY
*or*
# INTELLIGENCE SUMMARY.
*(Erase heading not required.)*

Army Form C. 2118.

| Place | Date | Hour | Summary of Events and Information | Remarks and references to Appendices |
|---|---|---|---|---|
| Seales | 9/12/15 | | Visited railhead & distributed stores to troops. Purchased locally 10000 canvas covers for muzzles of long rifles at an average cost of 16 Centimes each. These were purchased as only approved pattern cover for short rifles, & authorized for issue, exist. Received a further allotment of | Wh |
| | | | 300 pairs of boots gum thigh for use in the trenches. | Wh |
| | | | 125 Howell muzzle protectors for short rifles, received for experiment & report. | Wh |
| Seales | 10/12/15 | | Visited railhead & distributed stores to troops. Received a further supply of 504 pairs of "Boots Gum Thigh" for use of troops in trenches. | Wh |
| Seales | 11/12/15 | | Visited railhead & distributed stores to troops. Received 330 pairs of F.S. boots and 270 pairs of Strathcona boots. All for issue to troops where the state of the ground warrants issue, especially in the case of wagon lines | Wh. |
| Seales | 12/12/15 | | Visited Railhead & distributed stores to troops | Wh |
| Seales | 13/12/15 | | Visited Railhead & distributed stores to troops. | Wh. |
| Seales | 14/12/15 | | Visited Railhead & distributed stores to troops. "Bags Trench for carrying Machine Guns" were received today at the rate of 1 per machine gun, as authorized. | Wh |
| Seales | 15/12/15 | | Visited railhead & distributed stores to troops | Wh |
| Seales | 16/12/15 | | Visited railhead & distributed stores to troops | Wh |

1577 Wt. W10791/1773 500,000 1/15 D. D. & L. A.D.S.S./Forms/C. 2118.

Army Form C. 2118.

Instructions regarding War Diaries and Intelligence Summaries are contained in F. S. Regs., Part II. and the Staff Manual respectively. Title pages will be prepared in manuscript.

# WAR DIARY
*or*
# INTELLIGENCE SUMMARY.
*(Erase heading not required.)*

| Place | Date | Hour | Summary of Events and Information | Remarks and references to Appendices |
|---|---|---|---|---|
| Senlis | 17/12/15 | | Visited railhead & distributed stores to troops. 200 steel helmets received as a further supply towards equipping Division at the rate of 1 per Officer & man | Wh. |
| | | | One Oxy-Acetylene Searchlight complete, received for 1/1 Highland Field Company as a first issue. | Wh. |
| Senlis | 18/12/15 | | Visited Railhead and distributed stores to troops. | Wh. |
| Senlis | 19/12/15 | | Visited railhead and distributed stores to troops | Wh. |
| Senlis | 20/12/15 | | Visited railhead and distributed stores to troops. Placed an order locally for the manufacture of 200 "Blocks Brake Field and Transport" as these are not at present available at the Base | Wh. |
| Senlis | 21/12/15 | | Visited Railhead & distributed stores to troops. Demands submitted this day to complete all ranks with 2nd Tube helmet. | Wh. |
| Senlis | 22/12/15 | | Visited railhead & distributed stores to Troops. | Wh. |
| Senlis | 23/12/15 | | Visited railhead and distributed stores to Troops. Received supply of Tube pattern smoke helmet to complete every officer & man to two each. Arrangements will be mad to withdraw the ordinary smoke helmet in possession of troops | Wh. |
| Senlis | 24/12/15 | | Visited railhead & distributed stores to troops. Instructed further WOs of Brigade groups in special duties regarding supply of Ordnance Stores, in the event of multiple refilling points | Wh. |

1577 Wt. W10791/1773 500,000 1/15 D. D. & L. A.D.S.S./Forms/C. 2118.

Instructions regarding War Diaries and Intelligence Summaries are contained in F. S. Regs., Part II. and the Staff Manual respectively. Title pages will be prepared in manuscript.

# WAR DIARY
*or*
# INTELLIGENCE SUMMARY.
*(Erase heading not required.)*

Army Form C. 2118.

| Place | Date | Hour | Summary of Events and Information | Remarks and references to Appendices |
|---|---|---|---|---|
| Senlis | 25/12/15 | | Visited railhead & distributed stores to troops | Wh |
| Senlis | 26/12/15 | | Visited railhead & distributed stores to troops. Made necessary arrangements for refilling of Ordnance stores owing to change of railhead to date from the 27th inst. Gave special instructions to B'de O.O's | Wh |
| Flesselles | 27/12/15 | | Moved to Flesselles on the night of the 26th–27th insts and picked up stores at new railhead viz: Ailly-sur-Somme, and afterwards distributed to troops at refilling points (Q) | Wh |
| Flesselles | 28/12/15 | | Visited railhead, but no stores arrived | Wh |
| Flesselles | 29/12/15 | | Visited railhead and distributed stores to troops. Arrangements for opening baths for troops made. Local purchase authorized for the purchase of 24 boilers portable and 56 tubs for washing purposes. | Wh |
| Flesselles | 30/12/15 | | Visited railhead & distributed stores to troops. Received 12 cups for Mills Bombs for "West Bomb Throwers" First supply | Wh |
| Flesselles | 31/12/15 | | Visited railhead & distributed stores to troops. | Wh |

31/12/15

C. Whalley Capt.
DADOS
51st Division

DADOS. 51st Dn.

Jan

Vol. IX

Army Form C. 2118.

# WAR DIARY

*or*

~~INTELLIGENCE SUMMARY.~~

*(Erase heading not required.)*

Instructions regarding War Diaries and Intelligence Summaries are contained in F. S. Regs., Part II. and the Staff Manual respectively. Title pages will be prepared in manuscript.

| Place | Date | Hour | Summary of Events and Information | Remarks and references to Appendices |
|---|---|---|---|---|
| | | | Front Sheet<br>Confidential<br>War – Diary<br>of<br>D.A.D.O.S. 51st Division<br>From 1-1-16 To 31-1-16. | |

1577 Wt. W10791/1773 500,000 1/15 D. D. & L. A.D.S.S./Forms/C. 2118.

Instructions regarding War Diaries and Intelligence Summaries are contained in F. S. Regs., Part II. and the Staff Manual respectively. Title pages will be prepared in manuscript.

# WAR DIARY
*or*
~~INTELLIGENCE SUMMARY~~.

*(Erase heading not required.)*

Army Form C. 2118.

| Place | Date | Hour | Summary of Events and Information | Remarks and references to Appendices |
|---|---|---|---|---|
| Flesselles | 1/1/16 | | Visited Railhead and distributed stores to troops | WM |
| Flesselles | 2/1/16 | | Visited Railhead and distributed stores to troops. 100 more steel helmets arrived for issue to Infantry | WM |
| Flesselles | 3/1/16 | | Visited railhead & distributed stores to troops<br>1 Observation ladder arrived for Hd Qrs Divl Artillery.<br>2 Vickers Machine Guns arrived, in replacement of unserviceable, 1 each for 1/5 Seaforth Hdrs & 1/4 Royal Lancaster Regt | WM |
| Flesselles | 4/1/16 | | Visited railhead & distributed stores to troops. One Merryweather fire ladder received this day for Hd Qrs Divl Artillery. This ladder is part of the allotment per Division of 1 Durand ladder & 1 Merryweather ladder for Observation purposes. | WM |
| Flesselles | 5/1/16 | | Visited Railhead & distributed stores to troops. Received Issue Order for 4.5 in: Howitzer Equipment for 1/3 Highland Howitzer Brigade, who will return the 5 in Howitzer Equipment on completion of re-arming | WM |
| Flesselles | 6/1/16 | | Visited Railhead & distributed stores to troops | WM |
| Flesselles | 7/1/16 | | Visited railhead & distributed stores to troops. Delivered a lecture to a selected class of officers on the demand & supply of equipment & ordnance stores in the field | WM |

1577 Wt. W10791/1773 500,000 1/15 D. D. & L. A.D.S.S./Forms/C. 2118.

Instructions regarding War Diaries and Intelligence Summaries are contained in F. S. Regs., Part II. and the Staff Manual respectively. Title pages will be prepared in manuscript.

# WAR DIARY
*or*
# ~~INTELLIGENCE~~ SUMMARY.
*(Erase heading not required.)*

Army Form C. 2118.

| Place | Date | Hour | Summary of Events and Information | Remarks and references to Appendices |
|---|---|---|---|---|
| Flesselles | 8/1/16 | | Visited Railhead & distributed stores to troops | Wh |
| Flesselles | 9/1/16 | | Visited Railhead & distributed stores to troops Received notification that 4.5 in Q.F. How: equipment for 1/3 Highland How: Bde would arrive on the 12th inst | Wh. |
| Flesselles | 10/1/16 | | Handed over DADOS to Lt R F Johnson AOD. prior to proceeding to 30th Divn to take over duties of DADOS. | Wh |
| | | | W Maltby Capt D.A.D.O.S. 51st Divn. | |
| | | | Took over duties of D.A.D.O.S. from Capt Maltby, A.O.D. No stores arrived. Instructed quartermasters reference Lewis gun indents and consequent adjustment of transport. | Roy F. Johnson, Lieut. D.A.D.O.S. 51st Divn |
| Flesselles | 11/1/16 | | Visited Railhead & distributed stores to troops. 4.5 in Q.F. How equipment arrived Railhead. Warned units. Battery only sent for equipment and was represented by B. Sergt Major only. Reported Q. Parked remainder in R.T.O's yard under sentry & asked Q to arrange additional guard. Also unloaded additional truck attached 4.5 in how. train, loaded with general Ordnance stores | RFJ. |
| Flesselles | 12/1/16 | | No stores arrived. Sent out indents for Lewis M.G for all battalions of this divn. Arranged formally to distribute 4.5" how equipment tomorrow on arrival of second battery in divl. area. (Informal receipts meanwhile obtained) | RFJ |

1577 Wt. W10791/1773 500,000 1/15 D. D. & L. A.D.S.S./Forms/C. 2118.

Army Form C. 2118.

# WAR DIARY

*or*

# ~~INTELLIGENCE SUMMARY.~~

*(Erase heading not required.)*

Instructions regarding War Diaries and Intelligence Summaries are contained in F. S. Regs., Part II. and the Staff Manual respectively. Title pages will be prepared in manuscript.

| Place | Date | Hour | Summary of Events and Information | Remarks and references to Appendices |
|---|---|---|---|---|
| Hesselles | 13/1/16 | | Visited Railhead & distributed stores to troops. Visited HQ, 1/3 Highland Howitzer Brigade. Distributed 4·5" equipment among batteries & brigade ammn. col., obtained receipt from CO. & sent discrepancy report to Base. Paid 1500f for 1500 long rifle covers and 300 F for 200 brake blocks. 100 trench helmets received. Notified DADOS | RH. |
| Hesselles | 14/1/16 | | Four privates A.O.C. sentenced by Camp Commandant for drunkenness. | RH |
| Hesselles | 15/1/16 | | Visited Railhead & distributed stores to troops. 55 Lewis Machine Guns arrived for distribution to battalions in lieu of Maxim, converted & Vickers guns to be handed over to Brigade Machine Gun Companies | RH. |
| Hesselles | 16/1/16 | | Visited Railhead & distributed stores to troops. 55 Lewis Machine Guns distributed | RH |
| Hesselles | 17/1/16 | | No truck at Railhead. | RH |
| Hesselles | 18/1/16 | | Visited Railhead & distributed stores to troops. Received & despatched 5" how equipment, replaced | RH |
| Hesselles | 19/1/16 | | Visited Railhead & distributed stores to troops. | RH |
| Hesselles | 20/1/16 | | Visited Railhead & distributed stores to troops | RH |
| Hesselles | 21/1/16 | | Visited Railhead & distributed stores to troops. | RH |
| Hesselles | 22/1/16 | | Visited Railhead & distributed stores to troops. Four AOC men arrived to replace 4 prisoners sentenced 14·1·16 who will go to Base on expiration of sentences. | RH |
| Hesselles | 23/1/16 | | Visited Railhead & distributed stores to troops. | RH |
| Hesselles | 24/1/16 | | Visited Railhead & distributed stores to troops. | RH. |

1577 Wt. W10791/1773 500,000 1/15 D. D. & L. A.D.S.S./Forms/C. 2118.

Army Form C. 2118.

Instructions regarding War Diaries and Intelligence Summaries are contained in F. S. Regs., Part II. and the Staff Manual respectively. Title pages will be prepared in manuscript.

# WAR DIARY
*or*
~~INTELLIGENCE SUMMARY.~~
*(Erase heading not required.)*

| Place | Date | Hour | Summary of Events and Information | Remarks and references to Appendices |
|---|---|---|---|---|
| Hesselles. | 25/1/16 | | Visited Railhead & distributed stores ~~to troops~~. | RM |
| Hesselles | 26/1/16 | | To Abbeville for hobnails, urgently required by several units | RM |
| Hesselles | 27/1/16 | | To Railhead distributed stores to troops | RM |
| Hesselles | 28/1/16 | | Visited Railhead & distributed stores to troops | RM. |
| Hesselles | 29/1/16 | | Visited railhead & distributed stores to troops | RM |
| Hesselles | 30/1/16 | | Visited railhead & distributed stores to troops | RM |
| Hesselles | 31/1/16 | | Visited railhead & distributed stores to troops | RM |

2/1/16 } [illegible] Lieut
D.A.D.O.S.
51st Division

1577 Wt. W10791/1773 500,000 1/15 D. D. & L. A.D.S.S./Forms/C. 2118.

Army Form C. 2118.

Instructions regarding War Diaries and Intelligence Summaries are contained in F. S. Regs., Part II. and the Staff Manual respectively. Title pages will be prepared in manuscript.

# WAR DIARY
*or*
# INTELLIGENCE SUMMARY.
*(Erase heading not required.)*

| Place | Date | Hour | Summary of Events and Information | Remarks and references to Appendices |
|---|---|---|---|---|
| | | | Front Sheet<br>Confidential<br>War Diary<br>of<br>D.A.D.O.S. 57th Division<br>From 1/2/16 to 29/2/16.<br>Vol X | |

1577 Wt. W10791/1773 500,000 1/15 D. D. & L. A.D.S.S./Forms/C. 2118.

Army Form C. 2118.

# WAR DIARY

or

~~INTELLIGENCE~~ SUMMARY.

(*Erase heading not required.*)

Instructions regarding War Diaries and Intelligence Summaries are contained in F. S. Regs., Part II. and the Staff Manual respectively. Title pages will be prepared in manuscript.

| Place | Date | Hour | Summary of Events and Information | Remarks and references to Appendices |
|---|---|---|---|---|
| Hesselles | 1/2/16 | | Visited Railhead & distributed stores to troops. | RY |
| Hesselles | 2/2/16 | | Visited Daours and arranged new depot | RY |
| Hesselles | 3/2/16 | | Visited Railhead & distributed stores to troops | RY |
| Hesselles | 4/2/16 | | Visited Railhead & distributed stores to troops; Recd 60 Vermoral sprayers | RY |
| Hesselles | 5/2/16 | | Visited Railhead & distributed stores to troops. Recd 3375 lbs iron for horseshoes | RY |
| Hesselles | 6/2/16 | | Visited Railhead & distributed stores to troops. ~~[illegible]~~ | RY |
| Hesselles | 7/2/16 | | Transferred smoke helmet reserve & to Daours. | RY |
| Daours | 8/2/16 | | Arrived in Daours. Received 100 veils for snipers | RY |
| Daours | 9/2/16 | | Visited Railhead & distributed stores to troops. Recd 4 experimental Hill's magnifying sights | RY |
| Daours | 10/2/16 | | Recd. 3 Miller-James Cav. amb. stretchers, part of 20 allowed for division. 6 Bicycles for artillery brigades & 1000 feet timber deal white for Supply Col | RY |
| Daours | 11/2/16 | | Wired Brig MG Cos to send in tripods for ~~repair~~ rebushing. Recd 4 sets Hill sights. | RY |
| Daours | 12/2/16 | | Distributed stores to troops | RY |
| Daours | 13/2/16 | | 1 Max. 303 (153 Brig) exchanged for 1 Vickers from temporary stock. Maxim sent to 30th Divn | RY |
| Daours | 14/2/16 | | Recd. 1440 magazines for Lewis Guns | RY |
| Daours | 15/2/16 | | Exchanged 7 Vickers guns for 7 .303 Maxim from 153 Bde | RY |

1577 Wt. W10791/1773 500,000 1/15 D. D. & L. A.D.S.S./Forms/C. 2118.

Instructions regarding War Diaries and Intelligence Summaries are contained in F. S. Regs., Part II. and the Staff Manual respectively. Title pages will be prepared in manuscript.

# WAR DIARY
or
~~INTELLIGENCE SUMMARY.~~
(Erase heading not required.)

Army Form C. 2118.

| Place | Date | Hour | Summary of Events and Information | Remarks and references to Appendices |
|---|---|---|---|---|
| Daours | 16/7/16 | | Completed 153 Brigade with 8 Vickers & 8·303 Maxim guns; 152 Brigade with 16 Vickers: 154 Brigade with 16 Vickers. All surplus maxims to Base. Went to Etinehem to arrange new Ordnance ~~of~~ dump | RJ |
| Daours | 17/7/16 | | Distributed stores to troops | RJ |
| Daours | 18/7/16 | | Received 167 non resighted rifles per Supply Col. Sent in report on rifle sights | RJ |
| Daours | 19/7/16 | | Received stores & distributed to troops | RJ |
| Daours | 20/7/16 | | Distributed stores to troops | RJ |
| Daours | 21/7/16 | | Distributed stores to troops | RJ |
| Daours | 22/7/16 | | Distributed stores to troops | RJ |
| Daours | 23/7/16 | | Distributed stores to troops | RJ |
| Daours | 24/7/16 | | Distributed stores to troops. | RJ |
| Daours | 25/7/16 | | Sent off M.G., Lewis magazine & Personnel returns | RJ |
| Daours | 26/7/16 | | Distributed stores to troops | RJ |
| Daours | 27/7/16 | | Distributed stores to troops | RJ |
| Daours | 28/7/16 | | Ordered to move to Flesselles. Suspended despatch of stores from Base | RJ |
| Flesselles | 29/7/16 | | Arrived Flesselles. Removed suspension | RJ |

Robt. Johnson Lieut
D.A.D.O.S. 51st Division

1577 Wt. W10791/1773 500,000 1/15 D. D. & L. A.D.S.S./Forms/C. 2118.

Instructions regarding War Diaries and Intelligence Summaries are contained in F. S. Regs., Part II. and the Staff Manual respectively. Title Pages will be prepared in manuscript.

# WAR DIARY
*or*
# INTELLIGENCE SUMMARY
*(Erase heading not required.)*

Army Form C. 2118

51

| Place | Date | Hour | Summary of Events and Information | Remarks and references to Appendices |
|---|---|---|---|---|
| | | | SECRET.<br>Front Sheet<br>Confidential<br>War Diary<br>of<br>D.A.D.O.S. 51st (H) Division<br>from 1/3/16 to 31/3/16.<br>Vol XI | |

1875 Wt. W593/826 1,000,000 4/15 J.B.C. & A. A.D.S.S./Forms/C. 2118.

Instructions regarding War Diaries and Intelligence Summaries are contained in F. S. Regs., Part II. and the Staff Manual respectively. Title Pages will be prepared in manuscript.

# WAR DIARY
*or*
# INTELLIGENCE SUMMARY
*(Erase heading not required.)*

Army Form C. 2118

| Place | Date | Hour | Summary of Events and Information | Remarks and references to Appendices |
|---|---|---|---|---|
| Hesselle | 1 3/16 | | Distributed stores to troops | RH |
| do | 2 3/16 | | Distributed stores to troops | RH |
| do | 3 3/16 | | Distributed stores to troops | RH |
| do | 4 3/16 | | Distributed stores to troops | RH |
| do | 5 3/16 | | Issued one PH helmet per officer & man in lieu of 1 P helmet returned to Base. Also 2 extra Lewis M Guns per battn making 6 per battn | RH |
| do | 6 3/16 | | Distributed stores to troops | RH |
| Beauval | 7 3/16 | | Moved store to Doullens. | RH |
| Beauval | 8 3/16 | | Went to Hermaville & chose site for store | RH |
| Frévent | 9 3/16 | | Moved store to Hermaville. Indented for trench stores to full scale. | RH |
| do | 10 3/16 | | nothing to report | RH |
| Frevent | 11 3/16 | | Visited stores. Lifted trench stores for 154 Bde from Boquemaison Reconsigned remainder to Aubigny | RH |
| Frevent | 12 3/16 | | Visited stores. | RH |
| Hermaville | 13 3/16 | | Moved my office to Hermaville. Stores mentioned on 11th arrived at Aubigny | RH |
| Hermaville | 14 3/16 | | Distributed stores to troops | RH |
| Hermaville | 15 3/16 | | Distributed stores to troops | RH |
| Hermaville | 16 3/16 | | Distributed stores to troops. | RH |
| Hermaville | 17 3/16 | | Distributed stores to troops Fire broke out in Hermaville 2 a.m. attended personally. | RH |
| " | 18 3/16 | | Distributed stores to troops | RH |
| " | 19 3/16 | | Distributed stores to troops | RH |
| " | 20 3/16 | | Distributed stores to troops | RH |

1875 Wt. W593/826 1,000,000 4/15 I.B.C. & A. A.D.S.S./Forms/C 2118.

Army Form C. 2118

Instructions regarding War Diaries and Intelligence Summaries are contained in F. S. Regs., Part II. and the Staff Manual respectively. Title Pages will be prepared in manuscript.

# WAR DIARY
*or*
# INTELLIGENCE SUMMARY

*(Erase heading not required.)*

| Place | Date | Hour | Summary of Events and Information | Remarks and references to Appendices |
|---|---|---|---|---|
| Hermaville | 21st | | DDOS. Third Army visited Depot. Attended Conference at ADOS. 17th Corps. | RH |
| " | 22 | | Distributed stores to Troops. | RH |
| " | 23 | | Distributed stores to Troops | RH |
| " | 24 | | Distributed stores to Troops | RH |
| " | 25. | | Gen Harper made inspection of Depot. 456 Respty Towers recd. Distbtd stores to Troops. | RH |
| " | 26 | | Trench mortar burst. Demanded stores 3" to replace. | RH |
| " | 27. | | Distributed Stores to Troops. | PB |
| " | 28 | | Received 17000 SH Helmets to complete 2 per Officer & man. Distributed stores to Troops. | PB |
| " | 29 | | Distributed stores to Troops. | PB |
| " | 30 | | Distributed stores to Troops. | PB |
| " | 31 | | 2" Trench Mortar burst. Demanded one to replace. Distributed stores to Troops. | PB |

R[illegible] Lieut
DADOS
51 (H) Dn.

1875 Wt. W593/826 1,000,000 4/15 J.B.C. & A. A.D.S.S./Forms/C. 2118.

67

Dados 51 Div

Vol XII

# WAR DIARY
*or*
# INTELLIGENCE SUMMARY
*(Erase heading not required.)*

Instructions regarding War Diaries and Intelligence Summaries are contained in F. S. Regs., Part II. and the Staff Manual respectively. Title Pages will be prepared in manuscript.

Army Form C. 2118

D.A.D.O.S.
51st H Division

| Place | Date | Hour | Summary of Events and Information | Remarks and references to Appendices |
|---|---|---|---|---|
| Hermaville. | 1/4/16 | | Distributed stores to Troops | RH |
| " | 2 | | Distributed stores to Troops. | RH |
| " | 3 | | Distributed stores to Troops | RH |
| " | 4 | | Distributed stores to Troops | RH |
| " | 5 | | Distributed stores to Troops. Winter Clothing: Undercoats fur returned from 152 Bde | RH |
| " | 6 | | 4 Stokes Trench Mortars received & issued. Distributed stores to Troops. | RH |
| " | 7 | | Distributed stores to Troops. Undercoats fur returned from 153 Bde | RH |
| " | 8 | | Distributed stores to Troops. " " " " 154 " | RH |
| " | 9 | | Distributed stores to Troops. Stokes Trench Mortar (153/1 Bty) burst; new one demanded. " " " " H.Q. Units | RH |
| " | 10 | | Distributed stores to Troops. | RH |
| " | 11 | | Lewis Gun out of action damaged by Shell fire (1/6th Argylls) new one demanded to replace. Distributed stores to Troops. 1st Consignment of Winter clothing returned to Railhead | RH |
| " | 12 | | Distributed stores to Troops. Stokes Trench Mortar Gun issued to 153/1 Bty. | RH |
| " | 13 | | Distributed stores to Troops. 2nd consignment Winter Clo: to Railhead. | RH |
| " | 14 | | Distributed stores to Troops. | RH |
| " | 15 | | Distributed stores to Troops | RH |
| " | 16 | | Distributed stores to Troops. | RH |
| " | 17 | | 1/2 Aberdeen Bty had 18 pdr out of action. Gun demanded from Base. Distributed stores to Troops | RH |
| " | 18 | | Distributed stores to Troops | RH |
| " | 19 | | Distributed stores to Troops | RH |
| " | 20 | | Distributed stores to Troops. New 18 pdr issued to 1/2 City Aberdeen Bty. | RH |
| " | 21 | | Distributed stores to Troops | RH |
| " | 22 | | Distributed stores to Troops | RH |
| " | 23 | | Distributed stores to Troops. | RH |

1875 Wt. W593/826 1,000,000 4/15 J.B.C. & A. A.D.S.S./Forms/C. 2118.

Instructions regarding War Diaries and Intelligence Summaries are contained in F. S. Regs., Part II. and the Staff Manual respectively. Title Pages will be prepared in manuscript.

# WAR DIARY
*or*
# INTELLIGENCE SUMMARY
*(Erase heading not required.)*

Army Form C. 2118

| Place | Date | Hour | Summary of Events and Information | Remarks and references to Appendices |
|---|---|---|---|---|
| Hermaville | 24 | | Distributed Stores to Troops | RY |
| " | 25 | | Distributed stores to Troops attended Conference at ADOS XVII Corps. | RY. |
| " | 26 | | Distributed stores to Troops. | RY |
| " | 27 | | Distributed stores to Troops | RY |
| " | 28 | | D.D.O.S inspected Depot. Distributed stores to Troops. | RY |
| " | 29 | | Distributed Stores to Troops. 700 Spicer Anti Gas Goggles received for reserve. | RY |
| " | 30 | | Distributed Stores to Troops. (Sr. Cardam W.O on duty.) Trench Mortar 2" Burst X/51 Bty. sent to I.O.M for examination | RY |

51

Army Form C. 2118

Instructions regarding War Diaries and Intelligence Summaries are contained in F. S. Regs., Part II. and the Staff Manual respectively. Title Pages will be prepared in manuscript.

# WAR DIARY
*or*
# INTELLIGENCE SUMMARY
*(Erase heading not required.)*

| Place | Date | Hour | Summary of Events and Information | Remarks and references to Appendices |
|---|---|---|---|---|
| | | | Vol 13<br><br>Front Sheet<br>SECRET<br>Confidential<br><br>War Diary<br>of<br>D.A.D.O.S. 57th (Highland) Division<br>from 1.V.16 to 30.V.16. | |

1875 Wt. W593/826 1,000,000 4/15 J.B.C. & A. A.D.S.S./Forms/C. 2118.

Army Form C. 2118

Instructions regarding War Diaries and Intelligence Summaries are contained in F. S. Regs., Part II. and the Staff Manual respectively. Title Pages will be prepared in manuscript.

# WAR DIARY
*or*
# INTELLIGENCE SUMMARY
*(Erase heading not required.)*

| Place | Date | Hour | Summary of Events and Information | Remarks and references to Appendices |
|---|---|---|---|---|
| Hermaville | 1 5/16. | | Distributed Stores to Troops. | |
| " | 2 | | Distributed Stores to Troops. Attended Conference ADOS XVII Corps. 2345 Pte FARQUHAR, J. 5 Gordons, found in store marquee & charged with theft of 4 prs boots. Remitted by O.C. Convalescent Coy to F.G.C.M. | |
| | 3 | | Received 1000 Trench Helmets | RJJ |
| " | 4 5/16 | | Received 15190 "PH" Smoke Helmets as reserve 1 per Officer and man. Distributed Stores to Troops | RJJ |
| " | 5 5/16. | | Distributed stores to Troops. Received 1780 Drill Helmets for 10% Troops. | RJJ |
| " | 6 5/16. | | Received 600 Trench Helmets. | RJJ |
| " | 7 5/16 | | Cond. Fishwick W.O. on duty. ADOS visited Depot. inspected Lewis Gun. 4.5 Howitzer put out of action belonging to R Bty 1/3 How Bde. New one demanded to replace | RJ |
| " | 8 5/16. | | Distributed stores to Troop. Journeyed to Railhead to check new 18 pdr for new Batteries & BAC. received 12 QF 18 pr with carriages & limbers and 36 Amn Wagons & limbers | RJJ |
| " | 9 5/16 | | Distributed Stores to Troops. 700 Trench Helmets received | RJJ |

1875 Wt. W593/826 1,000,000 4/15 J.B.C. & A. A.D.S.S./Forms/C. 2118.

Army Form C. 2118

Instructions regarding War Diaries and Intelligence Summaries are contained in F. S. Regs., Part II. and the Staff Manual respectively. Title Pages will be prepared in manuscript.

# WAR DIARY
*or*
# INTELLIGENCE SUMMARY
*(Erase heading not required.)*

| Place | Date | Hour | Summary of Events and Information | Remarks and references to Appendices |
|---|---|---|---|---|
| Hermaville | 10 5/16 | | Distributed Stores to Troops 273 Trench Helmets received. | RH |
| " | 11 5/16 | | Distributed stores to Troops. 300 Trench Helmets received | RH |
| " | 12 5/16 | | One Ordnc QF 4.5" How: with fittings received for R Bty. 1/3 How Bde. | RH |
| " | 13 5/16 | | Distributed stores to Troops. | RH |
| " | 14 5/16 | | 1 Mess Cart + 4 Water Carts received at Railhead for Btys. also one 60 pdr Field carriage for 16th Heavy Bty. S/Cndr Carolan on duty. | RH |
| " | 15 5/16 | | First consignment of 2nd Satchel for Smoke Helmets received. (4500) | RH |
| " | 16 5/16 | | Distributed stores to Troops. Y/51 Trench Mortar out of action mechanism broken retd to Bde Armrs Shop. 1 Evans Mounting received. | RH |
| " | 17 5/16 | | 100 Trench Helmets received. Distributed stores to Troops. | RH |
| " | 18 5/16 | | Distributed stores to Troops. 152/1 TM Bty gun out of action | RH |
| | 19 5/16 | | Demanded new gun (3" Stokes) for 152/1 TM Bty. Distributed stores to Troops | RH |

1875 Wt. W593/826 1,000,000 4/15 J.B.C. & A. A.D.S.S./Forms/C. 2118.

Army Form C. 2118

Instructions regarding War Diaries and Intelligence Summaries are contained in F. S. Regs., Part II. and the Staff Manual respectively. Title Pages will be prepared in manuscript.

# WAR DIARY
*or*
# INTELLIGENCE SUMMARY
*(Erase heading not required.)*

| Place | Date | Hour | Summary of Events and Information | Remarks and references to Appendices |
|---|---|---|---|---|
| Hermaville | 20/5/16 | | Received - 1000 Satchels for Smoke Helmets & 120 Box Respirators. D.D.O.S inspected Depot & A.D.O.S inspected books | RH |
| " | 21/5/16 | | Distributed Stores to Troops. | RH |
| " | 22/5/16 | | Distributed Stores to Troops. | RH |
| " | 23/5/16 | | Distributed Stores to Troops. | RH |
| " | 24/5/16 | | 26 Lewis Guns & Magazines recd. 2 issued to each Infy Btn. | RH |
| " | 25/5/16 | | 24 Vermoral Sprayers 12 Carts Hand & 2 No.24 Periscopes recd. | RH |
| " | 26/5/16 | | 1 Trench Mortar 2" received for X/51 T.M. Bty. | RH |
| " | 27/5/16 | | Distributed Stores to Troops. | RH |
| " | 28/5/16 | | 504 Box Respirators received also 700 Trench Helmets. Distributed Stores to Troops. | RH |

1875 Wt. W593/826 1,000,000 4/15 J.B.C. & A. A.D.S.S./Forms/C. 2118.

Instructions regarding War Diaries and Intelligence Summaries are contained in F. S. Regs., Part II. and the Staff Manual respectively. Title Pages will be prepared in manuscript.

# WAR DIARY
*or*
# INTELLIGENCE SUMMARY
*(Erase heading not required.)*

Army Form C. 2118

| Place | Date | Hour | Summary of Events and Information | Remarks and references to Appendices |
|---|---|---|---|---|
| Hermaville | 29 5/16 | | One 18 Pdr QF destroyed by shell fire belonging to "A" 157 Bde. RFA new one demanded. Distributed stores to Troops. | RJ |
| " | 30 5/16 | | Distributed Stores to Troops. | RJ |
| " | 31 5/16 | | Distributed stores to Troops. | RJ |

31 5/16

R.J. Johnson Lt
D.A.D.O.S.
57th (H) Divn

1875 Wt. W593/826 1,000,000 4/15 J.B.C. & A. A.D.S.S./Forms/C. 2118.

Army Form C. 2118

Instructions regarding War Diaries and Intelligence Summaries are contained in F. S. Regs., Part II. and the Staff Manual respectively. Title Pages will be prepared in manuscript.

# WAR DIARY
*or*
# INTELLIGENCE SUMMARY

*(Erase heading not required.)*

| Place | Date | Hour | Summary of Events and Information | Remarks and references to Appendices |
|---|---|---|---|---|
| | | | SECRET | |

1875 Wt. W593/826 1,000,000 4/15 J.B.C. & A. A.D.S.S./Forms/C. 2118.

Army Form C. 2118 51

Instructions regarding War Diaries and Intelligence Summaries are contained in F. S. Regs., Part II. and the Staff Manual respectively. Title Pages will be prepared in manuscript.

# WAR DIARY
or
# INTELLIGENCE SUMMARY
*(Erase heading not required.)*

Vol 14

| Place | Date | Hour | Summary of Events and Information | Remarks and references to Appendices |
|---|---|---|---|---|
| | | | SECRET<br>ORIGINAL<br>Front Sheet<br>Confidential<br>War Diary of<br>D.A.D.O.S. 51st H Division<br>From 1/6/16 to 30/6/16<br>R H Johnson Capt<br>D.A.D.O.S.<br>51st (H) Div | |

1875 Wt. W593/826 1,000,000 4/15 J.B.C. & A. A.D.S.S./Forms/C. 2118.

Instructions regarding War Diaries and Intelligence Summaries are contained in F. S. Regs., Part II. and the Staff Manual respectively. Title Pages will be prepared in manuscript.

# WAR DIARY
*or*
# INTELLIGENCE SUMMARY
*(Erase heading not required.)*

Army Form C. 2118

| Place | Date | Hour | Summary of Events and Information | Remarks and references to Appendices |
|---|---|---|---|---|
| Hermaville | 1/6/16 | | Distributed Stores to Troops. 1650 Trench Helmets received. 948 Box Respirators received. | RH |
| " | 2/6/16 | | Trench mortar belonging to 152/1 destroyed by shell fire new one demanded. | RH |
| " | 3/6/16 | | Distributed stores to Troops. 400 Box Respirators received | RH |
| " | 4/6/16 | | Distributed Stores to Troops | RH |
| " | 5/6/16 | | Distributed Stores to Troops | RH |
| " | 6/6/16 | | 4 Lewis Guns received for 1/6th Gordon Hrs. One 18pdr limber carriage recd for B Battery 258 Bde<br>1 Maltese cart received for D.A.C. | RH |
| " | 7/6/16 | | Distributed Stores to Troops 1000 Trench Helmets received | RH |
| " | 8/6/16 | | Distributed Stores to Troops 130 Box Respirators received. | RH |
| " | 9/6/16 | | 2-2" Trench Mortars received for Z/51 TM Bty. & 2-3" Stokes mortars for 152/1 T.M. Bty. | RH |
| " | 10/6/16 | | Distributed Stores to Troops 1000 Trench Helmets received. 728 PHG Helmets recd. | RH |
| " | 11/6/16 | | Distributed Stores to Troops. | RH |

1875 Wt. W593/826 1,000,000 4/15 J.B.C. & A. A.D.S.S./Forms/C. 2118.

Instructions regarding War Diaries and Intelligence Summaries are contained in F. S. Regs., Part II. and the Staff Manual respectively. Title Pages will be prepared in manuscript.

# WAR DIARY
or
# INTELLIGENCE SUMMARY
*(Erase heading not required.)*

Army Form C. 2118

| Place | Date | Hour | Summary of Events and Information | Remarks and references to Appendices |
|---|---|---|---|---|
| Hermaville | 12/6/16 | | Distributed Stores to Troops | RH |
| " | 13/6/16 | | Distributed Stores to Troops. | RH |
| " | 14/6/16 | | Distributed Stores to Troops Trench Mortar destroyed by shell fire belonging to X51 T.M.Bty | RH |
| " | 15/6/16 | | Distributed Stores to Troops. | RH |
| " | 16/6/16 | | D.D.O.S. 3rd Army inspected Depot Chief Inspector of Armourers arrived for inspection of Shop. Distributed stores to Troops. | RH |
| " | 17/6/16 | | Chief Inspector of Armourers left. Distributed stores to Troops. | RH |
| " | 18/6/16 | | Distributed stores to Troops. | RH |
| " | 19/6/16 | | 800 Short Rifles received also 204 No9 Periscopes and 456 Prs Gum Boots Thigh. Distributed Stores to Troops. | RH |
| " | 20/6/16 | | 1200 Short Rifles received Trench Mortar received for 51/K T.M.Bty also 420 Vigilant Periscopes Stores Distributed to Troops | RH |
| " | 21/6/16 | | 409 Rifles received from 46th Divn. Stores distributed to Troops. | RH |

1875 Wt. W593/826 1,000,000 4/15 J.B.C. & A. A.D.S.S./Forms/C. 2118.

Instructions regarding War Diaries and Intelligence Summaries are contained in F. S. Regs., Part II. and the Staff Manual respectively. Title Pages will be prepared in manuscript.

# WAR DIARY
or
# INTELLIGENCE SUMMARY
*(Erase heading not required.)*

Army Form C. 2118

| Place | Date | Hour | Summary of Events and Information | Remarks and references to Appendices |
|---|---|---|---|---|
| Fermaville | 22/6/16 | | Stores Distributed to Troops | RJJ |
| " | 23/6/16 | | Distributed stores to Troops. | RJJ |
| " | 24/6/16 | | 8 Vickers Guns received, to replace 8 Maxims in possession of 153 M. G. Coy. Distributed Stores to Troops | RJJ |
| " | 25/6/16 | | West Bomb Thrower reported out of action by 153 Bde Distributed Stores to Troops. | RJJ |
| " | 26/6/16 | | Parts for West Bomb Thrower sent up & put in Action Distributed Stores to Troops. | RJJ |
| " | 27/6/16 | | Received 36000 Safety Pins for Smoke Helmets. Distributed Stores to Troops. 24 Shields for Bombers received | RJJ |
| | | | | RJJ |
| " | 28/6/16 | | Distributed Stores to Troops | RJJ |
| " | 29/6/16 | | Distributed Stores to Troops. | RJJ |
| " | 30/6/16 | | Distributed Stores to Troops. | |

R F Johnson
Capt
D.A.D.O.S.
57th (H) Division

1875 Wt. W593/826 1,000,000 4/15 J.B.C. & A. A.D.S.S./Forms/C. 2118.

Instructions regarding War Diaries and Intelligence Summaries are contained in F. S. Regs., Part II. and the Staff Manual respectively. Title Pages will be prepared in manuscript.

# WAR DIARY
or
# INTELLIGENCE SUMMARY
*(Erase heading not required.)*

CONFIDENTIAL. No 3092A HIGHLAND DIVISION.

Army Form C. 2118

| Place | Date | Hour | Summary of Events and Information | Remarks and references to Appendices |
|---|---|---|---|---|
| | | | Vol 15<br>Confidential.<br>War Diary<br>of<br>D.A.D.O.S. 51st H Division<br>from 1st July. '16 to 31st July '16<br>R Johnson Capt<br>D.A.D.O.S.<br>51 (H) Division | |

1875 Wt. W593/826 1,000,000 4/15 J.B.C. & A. A.D.S.S./Forms/C. 2118.

Instructions regarding War Diaries and Intelligence Summaries are contained in F. S. Regs., Part II. and the Staff Manual respectively. Title Pages will be prepared in manuscript.

# WAR DIARY

~~or~~

~~INTELLIGENCE SUMMARY~~

*(Erase heading not required.)*

CONFIDENTIAL. No HIGHLAND DIVISION.

Army Form C. 2118

| Place | Date | Hour | Summary of Events and Information | Remarks and references to Appendices |
|---|---|---|---|---|
| Hermaville | 1/7/16 | | Distributed Stores to Troops. | RY |
| " | 2/7/16 | | Distributed Stores to Troops | RY |
| " | 3/7/16 | | Distributed Stores to Troops | RY |
| " | 4/7/16 | | Distributed Stores to Troops. | RY |
| " | 5/7/16 | | Distributed Stores to Troops. | RY |
| " | 6/7/16 | | One Vickers Gun received & issued to 153 Bde M.G. Coy 3000 PH Helmets received. | RY |
| " | 7/7/16 | | Received 8 Spare part boxes for Vickers Gun 153 Bde Machine Gun Coy. | RY |
| " | 8/7/16 | | D.D.O.S visited Depot Distributed Stores to Troops. | RY |
| " | 9/7/16 | | Distributed Stores to Troops. | RY |
| " | 10/7/16 | | Distributed Stores to Troop. | RY |
| " | 11/7/16 | | Distributed Stores to Troops | RY |
| " | 12/7/16 | | Distributed Stores to Troops. | RY |
| " | 13/7/16. | | Distributed Stores to Troops. | RY |

1875 Wt. W593/826 1,000,000 4/15 J.B.C. & A. A.D.S.S./Forms/C. 2118.

Instructions regarding War Diaries and Intelligence Summaries are contained in F. S. Regs., Part II. and the Staff Manual respectively. Title Pages will be prepared in manuscript.

# WAR DIARY

~~or~~

~~INTELLIGENCE SUMMARY~~

*(Erase heading not required.)*

Army Form C. 2118

| Place | Date | Hour | Summary of Events and Information | Remarks and references to Appendices |
|---|---|---|---|---|
| Hermaville | 14/7/16 | | Moved whole of stores to new area Villers Chatel. 18pdr belonging to C/256 Bty out of action new gun demanded | RY |
| Villers Chatel | 15/7/16 | | Loaded stores for removal to Doullens. | RY |
| Doullens | 16/7/16 | | Started refilling system for Ordnance Stores. | RY |
| " | 17/7/16 | | Distributed stores to Troops at Refilling point. Packed up stores & removed to Ribeaucourt. Vickers gun reported out of action belonging to 152 Bde Machine Gun Coy. | RY |
| Ribeaucourt | 18/7/16 | | 18 pr Gun received from Base & issued C/256 Battery R.F.A. Visited Railhead | RY |
| " | 19/7/16 | | Issued stores to Troops at Refilling Point. Visited Railhead. New Vickers gun demanded for 152 Bde Machine Gun Coy. | RY |
| | 20/7/16 | | Distributed stores at Refilling Point | RY |
| " | 21/7/16 | | Office removed to Supply Col. Heilly. D.A.D.O.S went to Méaulte with Hd Qrs. Vickers Gun received & issued to 152 Bde M G Co | RY |
| | ~~22/7/16~~ | | | |
| Heilly & Méaulte | 22/7/16 | | 1920 Trench Helmets received & issued to Units. Distributed Stores at Refilling Point | RY |
| " | 23/7/16 | | Distributed stores at Refilling Point | RY |

1875 Wt. W593/826 1,000,000 4/15 J.B.C. & A. A.D.S.S./Forms/C. 2118.

Instructions regarding War Diaries and Intelligence Summaries are contained in F. S. Regs., Part II. and the Staff Manual respectively. Title Pages will be prepared in manuscript.

# WAR DIARY
~~or~~
~~INTELLIGENCE SUMMARY~~

*(Erase heading not required.)*

Army Form C. 2118

| Place | Date | Hour | Summary of Events and Information | Remarks and references to Appendices |
|---|---|---|---|---|
| Heilly & Méaulte | 24/7/16 | | Distributed Stores to Troops. | RJ |
| " | 25/7/16 | | Distributed stores to Troops | RJ |
| " | 26/7/16 | | Mess cart received for D Bty 80th Bde. 2 Water carts & Travelling Kitchen received for 7th A & S Hrs | RJ |
| " | 27/7/16 | | One Vickers Gun received for 154 Bde M.G. Coy | RJ |
| " | 28/7/16 | | Distributed Stores to Troops. | RJ |
| " | 29/7/16 | | One 18 pdr received for C/256 Bty RFA. 258 Bde report 3-18 pdrs out of action. 12 Handcarts for Lewis Guns received & issued. | RJ |
| " | 30/7/16 | | Vickers Gun reported out of action. New Gun demanded to replace. | RJ |
| " | 31/7/16 | | Distributed Stores to Troops at Refilling Point. | RJ |

R. F. Johnson Capt
DADOS
51 (H) Division

31/7/16.

1875 Wt. W593/826 1,000,000 4/15 J.B.C. & A. A.D.S.S./Forms/C. 2118.

Instructions regarding War Diaries and Intelligence Summaries are contained in F. S. Regs., Part II. and the Staff Manual respectively. Title Pages will be prepared in manuscript.

# WAR DIARY
*or*
# INTELLIGENCE SUMMARY
*(Erase heading not required.)*

Army Form C. 2118



| Place | Date | Hour | Summary of Events and Information | Remarks and references to Appendices |
|---|---|---|---|---|
| | | | ORIGINAL<br>SECRET<br>Confidential<br>War Diary of<br>DADOS 51st H Division<br>From 1st August to 31st Aug. 1916<br>[signature] Capt.<br>DADOS 51st H Division | Vol 16 |

1875 Wt. W593/826 1,000,000 4/15 J.B.C. & A. A.D.S.S./Forms/C. 2118.

Instructions regarding War Diaries and Intelligence Summaries are contained in F. S. Regs., Part II. and the Staff Manual respectively. Title Pages will be prepared in manuscript.

# WAR DIARY
*or*
# INTELLIGENCE SUMMARY
*(Erase heading not required.)*

Army Form C. 2118



| Place | Date | Hour | Summary of Events and Information | Remarks and references to Appendices |
|---|---|---|---|---|
| Heilly & Meaulte | 1/8/16 | | Received 1 Travelling Kitchen for 8th A&SH & Water Cart for 2/1 Fd Ambl. Distributed stores to Troops | RY |
| " | 2/8/16 | | Received G.S. Wagon for Divl Train, also 33 Handcarts. Distributed Stores to Troops. | RY |
| " | 3/8/16 | | Received 2 Water carts one for 1/6 Gordons & 1 for 1/255 Bty " " " " | RY |
| " | 4/8/16 | | Distributed Stores to Troops. | RY |
| " | 5/8/16 | | " " " | RY |
| " | 6/8/16 | | " " " | RY |
| " | 7/8/16 | | Received 4 Lewis Guns. Distributed stores to Troops | RY |
| " | 8/8/16 | | Distributed Stores to Troops | RY |
| " | 9/8/16 | | Removed to Pont Remy. | RY |
| Pont Remy | 10/8/16 | | 2 - 18 pdr guns demanded for | RY |
| " | 11/8/16 | | Removed to Reniscure. | RY |
| Reniscure | 12/8/16 | | No Stores up. | RY |
| " | 13/8/16 | | Distributed stores to Troops. | RY |

1875 Wt. W593/826 1,000,000 4/15 J.B.C. & A. A.D.S.S./Forms/C. 2118.

Army Form C. 2118

Instructions regarding War Diaries and Intelligence Summaries are contained in F. S. Regs., Part II. and the Staff Manual respectively. Title Pages will be prepared in manuscript.

# WAR DIARY
*or*
# INTELLIGENCE SUMMARY
*(Erase heading not required.)*

| Place | Date | Hour | Summary of Events and Information | Remarks and references to Appendices |
|---|---|---|---|---|
| Remisure | 14/8/16 | | Distributed Stores to Troops. | RY |
| " | 15/8/16 | | Distributed Stores to Troops | RY |
| L'Hallé O'Bean | 16/8/16 | | Removed to L'Hallé O'Bean. arranged depot. | RY |
| " | 17/8/16 | | Received one Q.F. 18 pdr for C/Bty 255 Bde F.A. Distributed stores to Troops. | RY |
| " | 18/8/16 | | Distributed stores to Troops. Sergt Milliken (Shoemaker) recalled to his Unit. | RY |
| " | 19/8/16 | | Received one QF 18pdr for B/255 Battery F.A. ADOS 2/Anzac visited Depot. Distributed Stores to Troops. | RY |
| " | 20/8/16 | | Distributed stores to Troops. Interviewed T.M. Bty Officers re deficiencies after handing over stores to N.Z. T.M. Btys. | RY |
| " | 21/8/16 | | Distributed Stores to Troops. | RY |
| " | 22/8/16 | | Distributed Stores to Troops | RY |
| " | 23/8/16 | | Distributed Stores to Troops | RY |
| " | 24/8/16 | | Attended Conference at ADOS. 10 am. Distributed stores to Troops. | RY |
| " | 25/8/16 | | Distributed Stores to Troops. | RY |

1875 Wt. W593/826 1,000,000 4/15 J.B.C. & A. A.D.S.S./Forms/C. 2118.

Instructions regarding War Diaries and Intelligence Summaries are contained in F. S. Regs., Part II. and the Staff Manual respectively. Title Pages will be prepared in manuscript.

# WAR DIARY
*or*
# INTELLIGENCE SUMMARY
*(Erase heading not required.)*

Army Form C. 2118

| Place | Date | Hour | Summary of Events and Information | Remarks and references to Appendices |
|---|---|---|---|---|
| L'Halle o Beau | 26/8/16 | | Distributed stores to Troops Received 10730 PHG Helmets | RH |
| " | 27/8/16 | | ADOS inspected Depot. Distributed stores to Troops. Received 6150 PHG Helmets. | RH |
| " | 28/8/16 | | Removed shops to new area. | RH |
| Steenwerck | 29/8/16 | | Removed whole of Stores to New Area. Distributed stores to Troops. Received 50 Tents from Second Corps Troops | RH |
| " | 30/8/16 | | Distributed stores to Troops. | RH |
| " | 31/8/16 | | Received 800 French Helmets. Distributed stores to Troops | RH |

RHarrison Capt
DADOS 51st H Division

1875 Wt. W593/826 1,000,000 4/15 J.B.C. & A. A.D.S.S./Forms/C. 2118.

Instructions regarding War Diaries and Intelligence Summaries are contained in F. S. Regs., Part II. and the Staff Manual respectively. Title Pages will be prepared in manuscript.

# WAR DIARY
*or*
# INTELLIGENCE SUMMARY

*(Erase heading not required.)*

Army Form C. 2118

Vol 17

| Place | Date | Hour | Summary of Events and Information | Remarks and references to Appendices |
|---|---|---|---|---|
| | | | 51st (H) Division<br>D.A.D.O.S.<br>War Diary<br>September, 1916. | |
| | | | Secret<br>[illegible] Capt.<br>D.A.D.O.S. 51(H) Division | |



1875 Wt. W593/826 1,000,000 4/15 J.B.C. & A. A.D.S.S./Forms/C. 2118.

Instructions regarding War Diaries and Intelligence Summaries are contained in F. S. Regs., Part II. and the Staff Manual respectively. Title Pages will be prepared in manuscript.

# WAR DIARY
*or*
# INTELLIGENCE SUMMARY

*(Erase heading not required.)*

Army Form C. 2118

| Place | Date | Hour | Summary of Events and Information | Remarks and references to Appendices |
|---|---|---|---|---|
| Steenwerck | 1/9/16 | | Distributed stores to Troops. | MJ |
| " | 2/9/16 | | Distributed stores to Troops. Received 1 water cart for 4 Co: Train. 2 pontoon wagons for 2/2 Fd. Co: R.E. 1 Vickers gun for 153 Inf. Co: | MJ |
| " | 3/9/16 | | Distributed stores to Troops. 66 bicycles received and distributed. | MJ |
| " | 4/9/16 | | Distributed stores to Troops. Received 1 kitchen travelling limber for 1/6 Black Watch. | MJ |
| " | 5/9/16 | | Received and issued 2300 blankets – first consignment to bring up to one per all ranks. Distributed stores to Troops. | MJ |
| " | 6/9/16 | | Distributed stores to Troops. | MJ |
| " | 7/9/16 | | Distributed stores to Troops. Received 1 wagon limbered R.E. body for Divl: Signal Co; also 700 Trench helmets from base and 142 from R.O.O. Latest Infy. drafts completed and remainder distributed to various units. 2000 blankets received and issued. | MJ |
| " | 8/9/16 | | Distributed stores to Troops. Received 4000 small box respirators which were distributed under instructions from Q. 51(H)D. | MJ |
| " | 9/9/16 | | Distributed stores to Troops. 1 G.S. wagon for H.Q. Co: Train + 1 cart water tank for 6th Rl. Hrs, received, also 300 trench helmets. | MJ |
| " | 10/9/16 | | Distributed stores to Troops. Received 14 bicycles for Inf: Co: R.E., and 2300 blankets. | MJ |
| " | 11/9/16 | | Distributed stores to Troops. Received 1000 small box respirators; 1 Lewis gun for 1/8 A + S. Hrs; 1 kitchen travelling body for 1/8 Arg. Hrs, + 1 cart for 1/4 Sea: Hrs + 1/9 Rl. Scots. | MJ |

1875 Wt. W593/826 1,000,000 4/15 J.B.C. & A. A.D.S.S./Forms/C. 2118.

Instructions regarding War Diaries and Intelligence Summaries are contained in F. S. Regs., Part II. and the Staff Manual respectively. Title Pages will be prepared in manuscript.

# WAR DIARY
*or*
# INTELLIGENCE SUMMARY
*(Erase heading not required.)*

Army Form C. 2118

| Place | Date | Hour | Summary of Events and Information | Remarks and references to Appendices |
|---|---|---|---|---|
| Steenwerck | 12.9.16 | | Distributed stores to Troops. Received 2150 blankets. | MJ |
| " | 13.9.16 | | Distributed stores to Troops. Received and distributed, Blankets G.S. 2150, Carts hand T.M. 22, Box respirators small No. 3, 4000, Trench helmets 59; 1 gun Vickers ·303" for 152 M.G. Co. | MJ |
| " | 14.9.16 | | Distributed stores to Troops. Received and distributed 3000 blankets G.S. 500 No. 2 small box respirators. | MJ |
| " | 15.9.16 | | Distributed stores to Troops. Received 7 marquees for Divisional Schools. Kitchens travelling boxes 1 for 1/8 A&S. Hrs. + 1 for 1/7 A&S. Hrs. 1 Q.M.L. 3" Trench Howzr. Stokes for 152 M.G. Co. also Blankets G.S. 2100. | MJ |
| " | 16.9.16 | | Distributed stores to units. Received 2100 blankets, 1199 Lewis magazines (this completes to 64 per gun); 18 Stewart horse clipping machines – 1 per Rgt. R.F.A. + 4 to D.A.C. 2 to Train + 1 to Mob. Vet. Section. No. 1659 Ar. S. Sgt. Franklin A.O.C. tried by F.G.C.M. for ~~refusing to obey an order~~ insubordinate language to his superior officer. | MJ |
| " | 17.9.16 | | Distributed stores to Troops. Sentence on S. Sgt. Franklin promulgated i.e. reduction to rank of Sergt. | MJ |
| " | 18.9.16 | | Distributed stores to Troops. Received one 3" Stokes Trench Howzr. and two mark II Stokes mountings for 152 T.M. Batty. Received 61 Tents C.S.L. from 2nd Army area. | MJ |
| " | 19.9.16 | | Received 1 kitchen travelling box for 1/9 Re. Scots. | MJ |
| " | 20.9.16 | | Distributed stores to Troops. Received 1 Vickers ·303" gun for 152 M.G. Co.; 300 caps comforters for hatless wounded soldiers (100 for each ambulance); 60 sponges running out 18 per. for D.A.C.; 8 sprayers knapsack for 1/6 Gor: Hrs; 9 containers food for 152 Infy. Bde.; 600 box respirators small No. 2; 1080 Trench helmets; Carts trench 25. | MJ |

1875 Wt. W593/826 1,000,000 4/15 J.B.C. & A. A.D.S.S./Forms/C. 2118.

Instructions regarding War Diaries and Intelligence Summaries are contained in F. S. Regs., Part II. and the Staff Manual respectively. Title Pages will be prepared in manuscript.

# WAR DIARY
*or*
# INTELLIGENCE SUMMARY
*(Erase heading not required.)*

Army Form C. 2118

| Place | Date | Hour | Summary of Events and Information | Remarks and references to Appendices |
|---|---|---|---|---|
| Steenwerck | 21.9.16 | | Distributed stores to Troops. Received box respirators small No. 3, 4800; Handcarts Lewis gun 25; Wagon limb. G.S. complete 1 for 154 Mg. Co.; O.M.L. 2" Trench Howzr. Boxes silencer large 3, small 3; Springs running out Q.F. 4.5" Howr. wound right 1, left 1 for 2 Sec: D.A.C.; left 1 for 4 Sec: D.A.C. | My |
| " | 22.9.16 | | Distributed stores to Troops. Received 20 large box respirators for emergency parties (five to each Section D.A.C.); also 2 mark II mountings for 3" Stokes Howzrs. | My |
| " | 23.9.16 | | Distributed stores to Troops. Received 1135 prs. Shoepack & I.S. boots, 25% of strength of mounted men of Division. | My |
| " | 24.9.16 | | Distributed stores to Troops. | My |
| " | 25.9.16 | | Distributed stores to Troops. Received 1 Vickers gun for 153 Mg. Co.; 1 Lewis gun for 6th RL. Hrs and 1 Lewis gun for 5th Gr: Hrs. | My |
| " | 26.9.16 | | Distributed stores to Troops. | My |
| " | 27.9.16 | | No stores received from Base. Armr. Sergt: Franklin recalled to his unit (1/6 Sea: Hrs). | My |
| " | 28.9.16 | | Distributed stores to Troops. Received 1 mess cart for 9th RL. Scots. | My |
| " | 29.9.16 | | No stores received from Base. | My. |
| " | 30.9.16 | | Moved stores to new area Bus-les-artois. | |

R.H. Johnson Capt
DADOS
51(H) Div

1875 Wt. W593/826 1,000,000 4/15 J.B.C. & A. A.D.S.S./Forms/C. 2118.

Army Form C. 2118.

# WAR DIARY
*or*
# INTELLIGENCE SUMMARY

*(Erase heading not required.)*

Instructions re[a]rding War Diaries and Intelligence Summaries [a]re contained in F. S. Regs., Part II. and the St[a]ff Manual respectively. Title Pages will be pr[ep]ared in manuscript.

Vol 18

| Place | Date | Hour | Summary of Events and Information | Remarks and references to Appendices |
| --- | --- | --- | --- | --- |



51st (H) Division

D.A.D.O.S.

War Diary

October, 1916.

Secret.

M Johnson Capt.
D.A.D.O.S. 51 (H) Division

2449 Wt. W14957/M90 750,000 1/16 J.B.C. & A. Forms/C.2118/12.

Army Form C. 2118

Instructions regarding War Diaries and Intelligence Summaries are contained in F. S. Regs., Part II. and the Staff Manual respectively. Title Pages will be prepared in manuscript.

# WAR DIARY
*or*
# INTELLIGENCE SUMMARY
*(Erase heading not required.)*

| Place | Date | Hour | Summary of Events and Information | Remarks and references to Appendices |
|---|---|---|---|---|
| Bus-les-Artois | 1.10.16 | | Opened new depot. | MY |
| —"— | 2.10.16 | | No stores received. | MY |
| —"— | 3.10.16 | | Distributed stores to Troops. 20 T.M.s Stokes 3" with Fowlers adaptor received from 48th Division and 24 3" Stokes T.M.s ordinary handed over to 48th Division in exchange. | MY |
| —"— | 4.10.16 | | Distributed stores to Troops. Issued 20 T.M.s Stokes 3" with Fowlers adapters — 8 to 152 T.M.B. 8 to 153 T.M.B.; 4 to 154 T.M.B. 26 Lewis guns received to complete 13 battns. to 10 guns each. 18 magazines only received for each gun; remainder demanded from Base. Pte. Yule 1st Gordon Hrs. evacuated to Base (sick). | MY |
| —"— | 5.10.16 | | Distributed stores to Troops. | MY |
| —"— | 6.10.16 | | Distributed stores to Troops. Received 1000 trench ~~[illegible]~~ shelters from 13 Corps. Received one 18 pdr. for B 256 Bty. R.F.A also 108 periscopes No. 9. Pte. Kerr AOC evacuated to Base with D.A.H. | MY |
| —"— | 7.10.16 | | Distributed stores to Troops. Received 1 Gun 18 pdr. (5480) & Carriage (38975) for B256 Bty. | MY |
| —"— | 8.10.16 | | Distributed stores to Troops. Received 1 Carriage 18 pr. (64348) for A 260 Bty. | MY |
| —"— | 9.10.16 | | Distributed stores to Troops. Received 60 tents C.S.L. from Corps (XIII) | MY |
| —"— | 10.10.16 | | Distributed stores to Troops. Received 1 Carriage 18 pr. (64344) for A 260 Bty. | MY |
| —"— | 11.10.16 | | Distributed stores to Troops. Received 1 gun 18 pr. (5705) and 1 Carriage 18 pr. (63672) for B 260 Bty. Taken over by A/248 Bty. R.F.A. | MY |

1875 Wt. W593/826 1,000,000 4/15 J.B.C. & A. A.D.S.S./Forms/C. 2118.

# WAR DIARY
*or*
# INTELLIGENCE SUMMARY
*(Erase heading not required.)*

Instructions regarding War Diaries and Intelligence Summaries are contained in F. S. Regs., Part II. and the Staff Manual respectively. Title Pages will be prepared in manuscript.

Army Form C. 2118.

| Place | Date | Hour | Summary of Events and Information | Remarks and references to Appendices |
|---|---|---|---|---|
| Bus-les-Artois | 12·10·16 | | Distributed stores to Troops. ~~[illegible]~~ | [initials] |
| — " — | 13-10-16 | | Distributed stores to Troops. Received one 18 pr. gun (2726) and one carriage 18 pdr. (29392) for A/256 Bty. R.F.A. and one 18 pdr. gun (5416) and one carriage 18 pdr. for A/255 Bty. R.F.A. | [initials] |
| — " — | 14·10·16 | | Distributed stores to Troops. ~~[illegible]~~ | [initials] |
| — " — | 15·10·16 | | Distributed stores to Troops. | [initials] |
| — " — | 16-10-16 | | Distributed stores to Troops. ~~Received~~ Received 2310 prs Boots F.S. | [initials] |
| — " — | 17-10-16 | | Distributed stores to Troops | [initials] |
| Leatvillers | 18-10-16 | | Opened new Depot. Distributed Stores to Troops. Received 178 Pairs Boots F.S. 13800 Cap Comforters and 12360 Waistcoats Cardigan. | [initials] |
| — " — | 19·10·16 | | Distributed stores to Troops. | [initials] |
| — " — | 20-10-16 | | Distributed stores to Troops. Received 2 Carriages Field QF 18 Pdr Nos 27619 & 64376 for A/260. Also 17088 Vests Woollen & Flannel and 11298 Prs Soles inner for Boots Ankle. | [initials] |
| — " — | 21-10-16 | | Distributed stores to Troops Received 1000 Pairs Boots Gum Thigh from V Corps | [initials] |
| — " — | 22-10-16 | | Distributed stores to Troops. 300 Trench shelters received from V Corps | [initials] |
| — " — | 23-10-16 | | Distributed stores to Troops 200 Trench shelters received from V Corps. | [initials] |
| — " — | 24-10-16 | | Distributed stores to Troops. Received 2 Mess Carts for A/256 R.F.A. Bde & HQrs 255 Bde R.F.A. ~~[illegible]~~ & QF 4·5 How. complete for D/255 F. A. Bde. | [initials] |

2449 Wt. W14957/M90 750,000 1/16 J.B.C. & A. Forms/C.2118/12.

Instructions regarding War Diaries and Intelligence Summaries are contained in F. S. Regs., Part II. and the Staff Manual respectively. Title Pages will be prepared in manuscript.

# WAR DIARY
or
~~INTELLIGENCE SUMMARY~~
(Erase heading not required.)

Army Form C. 2118.

| Place | Date | Hour | Summary of Events and Information | Remarks and references to Appendices |
|---|---|---|---|---|
| Lealvillers | 25/10/16 | | Distributed stores to Troops. | My |
| — " — | 26/10/16 | | Distributed stores to Troops. | My |
| — " — | 27/10/16 | | Distributed stores to Troops. Received 360 Helmets French completing Divn. to 1 per man. | My |
| — " — | 28/10/16 | | No stores received. | My |
| — " — | 29/10/16 | | Distributed stores to Troops. | My |
| — " — | 30/10/16 | | No stores received. | My |
| — " — | 31/10/16 | | Distributed stores to Troops Received Ordnance 18 Pr without ~~Mounting~~ Carriage or Breech Mechanism Regd. number 371 for A/260 Bde R.F.A. and 3500 Blankets being first issue of 2nd blanket. | |
| | | | No 7177 Pte (Local A/L'Cpl.) Ahelock F. J. left for duty at No 5 OMW (Heavy) as Foreman of Stores Authority D.D.O.S., Fifth Army 0/10/2 dated 31/10/16. | My |

R H Johnson
Capt
DADOS
57 (W) Div

Army Form C. 2118.

Instructions regarding War Diaries and Intelligence Summaries are contained in F. S. Regs., Part II. and the Staff Manual respectively. Title Pages will be prepared in manuscript.

# WAR DIARY
*or*
# ~~INTELLIGENCE SUMMARY~~
*(Erase heading not required.)*

Vol 19

| Place | Date | Hour | Summary of Events and Information | Remarks and references to Appendices |
|---|---|---|---|---|
| | | | 51st (H) DIVISION.<br>D. A. D. O. S.<br>War Diary.<br>NOVEMBER 1916.<br>SECRET. | |

CONFIDENTIAL
No 21/A
HIGHLAND DIVISION.

R Johnson Capt
D.A.D.O.S.
51st (H) Division

2449 Wt. W14957/M90 750,000 1/16 J.B.C. & A. Forms/C.2118/12.

Instructions regarding War Diaries and Intelligence Summaries are contained in F. S. Regs., Part II. and the Staff Manual respectively. Title Pages will be prepared in manuscript.

# WAR DIARY
~~or~~
~~INTELLIGENCE SUMMARY~~
*(Erase heading not required.)*

Army Form C. 2118.

| Place | Date | Hour | Summary of Events and Information | Remarks and references to Appendices |
|---|---|---|---|---|
| LEALVILLERS | 1/11/16. | | 65 Tents sent to FORCEVILLE. | RH |
| " | 2/11/16. | | To AMIENS for local purchases | RH |
| " | 3/11/16 | | Q.M.G letter received saying that Bagpipes could not be supplied from Public funds. | RH |
| " | 4/11/16 | | Received new local pattern rifle cover which can be worn while rifle is slung. | RH |
| " | 5/11/16 | | Demonstrated Lewis handcart at Army Headquarters. | RH |
| " | 6/11/16 | | Units told to camouflage tents with mud pending discovery of a paint which does not cause them to let water. | RH |
| " | 7/11/16 | | Distributed stores to troops. | RH |
| " | 8/11/16 | | Capt Johnson A.O.D. D.A.D.O.S 51st (H) Division proceeded on leave, to England | RH |
| " | 9/11/16 | | Distributed stores to troops. Signal shutters received from 5 A.A.P. 5 Lewis handcarts issued to 1/6 Black Watch + 2 to 1/4 A.&S.Hdrs. | RH |
| " | 10/11/16 | | Distributed stores to troops. 16. T.M. handcarts issued to this Division by Base in error. Disposed of under instructions from A.D.O.S. V Corps. | RH |
| " | 11/11/16 | | No stores received from Base. Received 500 pr Gum Boots thigh from V Corps Troops. | RH |
| " | 12/11/16 | | Gum boot experts gave instructions to shoemakers in repair of gum boots. | RH |
| " | 13/11/16 | | Distributed stores to troops. Received O.Q.F. 18 Pdr without B.M. No 5409 for A/256 Bde. 153 M.G.Co. report 1 Vickers lost. 153 T.M. Batty report 5 Stokes guns out of action. | RH |
| " | 14/11/16 | | Distributed stores to troops. | RH |
| " | 15/11/16 | | Distributed stores to troops. 152 Bde report following Lewis guns lost 1/6 Seaforths 2, 1/5 Seaforths 5, 1/8 A.&S.Hdrs 1. | RH |

Instructions regarding War Diaries and Intelligence Summaries are contained in F. S. Regs., Part II. and the Staff Manual respectively. Title Pages will be prepared in manuscript.

# WAR DIARY
*or*
# ~~INTELLIGENCE SUMMARY~~
*(Erase heading not required.)*

Army Form C. 2118.

| Place | Date | Hour | Summary of Events and Information | Remarks and references to Appendices |
|---|---|---|---|---|
| LEALVILLERS | 16/11/16 | | No stores received. Ord. QF 18pdr No 2146 on charge of A/255 + No 3282 of C/255 condemned by I.O.M. V Corps for scoring. Recovered Lewis gun No 3202, property of 1/6 Black Watch, from Salvage Dump. 2 Lewis guns withdrawn from 1/8 Royal Scots Nos 3509 + 17805. | M |
| " | 17/11/16 | | Distributed stores to troops. Lewis gun No 5215 on charge of 1/5 Gordon Hdrs returned to Depot by Salvage Coy. Issued 2 Lewis guns Nos 3509 and 17805 to 1/6 Seaforths. Received 2,300 Blankets (2nd Blanket) Ord QF 18pdr without B.M. on charge of B/255 No 3132 and Ord QF 18pdr No 2613 on charge of A/255 condemned by I.O.M V Corps for scoring. 153 M.G. Coy report recovery of Vicker's gun reported lost on 13/11/16 154 M.G. Coy Vicker's gun No L. 414 condemned by Arm S.S. Brown as beyond local repair. | M |
| " | 18/11/16 | | No stores received. | M |
| " | 19/11/16 | | No stores received. | M |
| " | 20/11/16 | | Distributed stores to troops. Received 5 Stokes 3" T.M for 153 T.M.B. 1 Vicker's for 154 M.G.Co. 5 Rifle Batteries, 3 Lewis gun handcarts for 1/4 Seaforth Hdrs. 9 trucks of stores due from Base. Capt Johnson. A.O.D. returned from leave. | M |
| " | 21/11/16 | | Distributed stores to troops | M |
| " | 22/11/16 | | Distributed stores to troops. | M |
| " | 23/11/16 | | Distributed stores to troops. Received 7 Ord QF 18 pdrs without B.M. for B/255. No 2722. A/260, 1281. A/255 No 2864 + 4419. C/255 No 279, C/317 No 4992 + A/315 No 5333. Carts water tank 2 for 1/5 Seaforth Hdrs + A/256 Bde R.F.A. and 1 Kitchen travelling body for 1/4 Black Watch. | M |

2449 Wt. W14957/M90 750,000 1/16 J.B.C. & A. Forms/C.2118/12.

Instructions regarding War Diaries and Intelligence Summaries are contained in F. S. Regs., Part II. and the Staff Manual respectively. Title Pages will be prepared in manuscript.

# WAR DIARY

*or*

~~INTELLIGENCE SUMMARY~~

*(Erase heading not required.)*

Army Form C. 2118.

| Place | Date | Hour | Summary of Events and Information | Remarks and references to Appendices |
|---|---|---|---|---|
| LEALVILLERS | 22/11/16 | | Distributed stores to troops | RJ |
| " | 23/11/16 | | Distributed stores to troops. Received 7 Ord QF 18 pdrs without B.M for B/255 No 2122, A/260 No 1281 A/255 No 2864 + 4419, C/255 No 249, C/314 No 4992 and A/315 No 5333. Carts water tank, 2 for 1/5 Seaforth Hdrs and A/256 Bde R.F.A. and 1 Kitchen travelling body for 1/4 Black Watch | RJ |
| " | 24/11/16 | | Railhead changed to AVELUY. | RJ |
| " | 25/11/16 | | No stores received. | RJ |
| " | 26/11/16 | | Distributed stores to troops. | RJ |
| " | 27/11/16 | | Moving depot. Distributed stores to troops. Received Ord QF 18 pdr without B.M No 2949 for B/255 F.A. Bde + Ord QF 4.5 How with B.M. for D/317 Bde. | RJ |
| BOUZINCOURT | 28/11/16 | | Opened new Depot. Distributed stores to troops. Took over from 4 Canadn Divn. dumps of braziers and packsaddles. | RJ |
| " | 29/11/16 | | Distributed stores to troops. Received 2 L. gun Handcarts for 1/7 Gordon Hdrs and 6 for 1/4 Gordon Hdrs. | RJ |
| " | 30/11/16 | | Distributed stores to troops. 5 Truck loads received. 50 sets Tent Bottoms received. Made 40 sets ropes for pulling men out of mud in the trenches | RJ |

R H Johnson Capt
D.A.D.O.S
51st (H) Division

Instructions regarding War Diaries and Intelligence Summaries are contained in F. S. Regs., Part II. and the Staff Manual respectively. Title Pages will be prepared in manuscript.

# WAR DIARY
*or*
# INTELLIGENCE SUMMARY
*(Erase heading not required.)*



Army Form C. 2118.

Vol 20

| Place | Date | Hour | Summary of Events and Information | Remarks and references to Appendices |
|---|---|---|---|---|
| | | | 51ST (HIGHLAND) DIVISION<br>D. A. D. O. S.<br>WAR DIARY<br>DECEMBER, 1916<br><br>SECRET<br><br>R H Johnson Capt<br>D.A.D.O.S.<br>51(H) Div. | |

2449 Wt. W14957/M90 750,000 1/16 J.B.C. & A. Forms/C.2118/12.

Instructions regarding War Diaries and Intelligence Summaries are contained in F. S. Regs., Part II. and the Staff Manual respectively. Title Pages will be prepared in manuscript.

# WAR DIARY
or
# INTELLIGENCE SUMMARY
*(Erase heading not required.)*

Army Form C. 2118.

| Place | Date | Hour | Summary of Events and Information | Remarks and references to Appendices |
|---|---|---|---|---|
| BOUZINCOURT | 1916 Dec. 1 | | Improvised packsaddlery: 4 ammunition carriers received for trial and issued. 63rd Div. Ordnance Staff, attached to administer 63rd Div. Arty., left. Wired Base that if nosebags were not forthcoming at once they would be purchased. (These were issued a few days later). Lorry broke down. | |
| " | " 2 | | Received: 18-pounder for A/260. S/Condr. FISHWICK went on leave. Issued packs for carrying daily supply of dry socks to trenches. | |
| " | " 3 | | Twenty extra men employed cleaning rifles salved in clearance of battlefield. First consignment received of new green (second) identity discs. Lorry broke down. | |
| " | " 4 | | Conference, IV Corps. Received 668 capes mackintosh from Corps. Base having referred officers indenting for clothes &c to Fifth Army Officers' shop, DOULLENS, wrote pointing out that this was 23 miles away. (Base subsequently agreed to supply) Lorry broke down. | |
| " | " 5 | | Trousers issued in lieu of kilts to lessen exposure in the trenches — 3000 pairs, also 6000 prs. braces, body-bands & drawers. | |
| " | " 6 | | A.D.O.S. IV Corps inspected depot. | |
| " | " 7 | | Improvised packsaddlery: received pin-bags for trial and 50 emergency ammunition carriers: also 50 hot food containers. G.O.C. decided not to issue these at present as they could not be got up to the trenches. | |
| " | " 8 | | 50 more hot food containers received: also 21 Soyer stoves & 32 trench mortar handcarts. Enemy on this front reported to respect Red Cross, so made and issued (1 per battalion and 1 per battery) red cross flags to enable wounded to be brought in by day. Lorry broke down. | |
| " | " 9 | | No stores at railhead. 6 Arbuthnot kettles received for trial. 2 chaffcutters received. To Amiens for local purchase. | |
| " | " 10 | | Received 1736 pairs of gum-boots thigh from IV Corps, and delivered to Gum Boot store. Lorry broke down at Pozieres. | |
| " | " 11 | | Further 1553 pairs of gumboots received from Corps, and 1503 mackintosh capes from Base. To Amiens to buy a wringer for Baths, to facilitate drying of daily supply of dry socks to trenches. | |
| " | " 12 | | 55th Supply Column lorries left & 51st. D.S.C. lorries joined. 82 camp kettles & 15 hot food retainers received from Corps. No stores at railhead | |

2449 Wt. W14957/M90 750,000 1/16 J.B.C. & A. Forms/C.2118/12.

Instructions regarding War Diaries and Intelligence Summaries are contained in F. S. Regs., Part II. and the Staff Manual respectively. Title Pages will be prepared in manuscript.

# WAR DIARY
*or*
# INTELLIGENCE SUMMARY
*(Erase heading not required.)*

Army Form C. 2118.

| Place | Date | Hour | Summary of Events and Information | Remarks and references to Appendices |
|---|---|---|---|---|
| | 1916 | | | |
| BOUZINCOURT | Dec 13 | | B Coy 2nd Bn South African Native Labour Battalion attached for Ordnance. Instructed second-in-command in methods of obtaining stores &c. + sent a warrant officer to do the same for the Q.M.S. 5 Store tents received from Corps. | |
| " | " 14 | | Supply of tent bottoms, ultimately one per tent, began. | |
| " | " 15 | | Issued all remaining trench shelters to 8 Royal Scots (50) + 7th Cavalry Pioneer Battalion. To VIGNACOURT to order 1000 bayonets, Base reporting none available. 18-pdr no 4115 of B/256 condemned for prematures. Evidence received of units' dislike of cleaned clothing, now issued as about 30% of total supply. · Requested Div. H.Q. to order all units to accept this. | |
| " | " 16 | | 18-pdr no 5737 of A/255 condemned. Issued store tent to 255 + 260 Bdes R.F.A. Requested Base to undertake repair of officers' gumboots on payment, which they agreed to do. Called attention of Base to serious position regarding Strombos Horns, Gas Officer declaring 10 to be the minimum of safety. 21 were demanded. Issue began in January. | |
| " | " 17. | | Issued store tent to H.Q. R.A. | |
| " | " 18 | | Conference with A.D.O.S. IV Corps. Drew attention to serious shortage of siege lamps. Authority requested for purchase or issue of tape, for distinguishing marks for battalions. 7th Cavalry Pioneer Battalion attached for Ordnance | |
| " | " 19 | | To Amiens for local purchase. Called attention of Div. H.Q. to practice of carrying rations, books &c in anti-gas satchel. This was then forbidden by D.R.O. | |
| " | " 20 | | Recd. 18-pdrs no 188 for A/255, no 5795 for B/256 + misc carts for B/255 + C/256. 226 Field Co RE moved to 63rd Div. | |
| " | " 21 | | Issued 2 Lewis guns, making 12 in all, to all battalions except Pioneers. L/Cpl Reeves A.O.C. left for II Corps Troops on promotion to Sergeant. | |

2449 Wt. W14957/M90 750,000 1/16 J.B.C. & A. Forms/C.2118/12.

Army Form C. 2118.

Instructions regarding War Diaries and Intelligence Summaries are contained in F. S. Regs., Part II. and the Staff Manual respectively. Title Pages will be prepared in manuscript.

# WAR DIARY
*or*
# INTELLIGENCE SUMMARY
*(Erase heading not required.)*

| Place | Date | Hour | Summary of Events and Information | Remarks and references to Appendices |
|---|---|---|---|---|
| | 1916 | | | |
| BOUZINCOURT | Dec 22 | | To POUCHVILLERS for supply of new Lewis dummy cartridges and to DDOS Fifth Army for YUKON pack for trial. | |
| " | " 23 | | To AMIENS for local purchase | |
| " | " 24 | | Nothing to report | |
| " | " 25 | | 3rd Field Co RE (from 63rd Div) attached for Ordnance. Improvised packsaddles – 300 ration bags made from old ground-sheets received | |
| " | " 26 | | 18-pdr received for B/255. Signal shutters received (344) to complete under G.R.O. 1944. Complete supply of bayonets received and issued. Called attention of Base to serious delay in supplying R.A. stores. | |
| " | " 27 | | 18-pdr no 5791 received for B/256 and carriage 4.5 how. for C/260 also G.S. wagon each for No 2 + 4 section D.A.C, and ambulance wagon for 1/2 (H) Field Amb[ce] | |
| " | " 28 | | no stores at railhead. Dumps at refilling points completed. Called attention of Base to delay in issuing stores to D.A.C. | |
| " | " 29. | | Recd. + issued 2 handcarts per battalion (except Pioneers) for last two Lewis guns. 20 (Labour) Battn, Notts + Derby Regt, attached for Ordnance. | |
| " | " 30 | | Base refused to issue dirks. for pipers, stating sword bayonets must be accepted in lieu. | |
| " | " 31 | | Received 4 Lewis handcarts to replace unserviceable: also carriage, 18 pdr, for C/255 | |
| | | | GENERAL During the month a reserve was accumulated, under Corps orders, of a week's supply of boots, oil, flannelette and other necessities, in case of all traffic being stopped after a frost. Intermittent shortages during the month of nosebags, bayonets, leather and refills for | |

2449 Wt. W14957/M90 750,000 1/16 J.B.C. & A. Forms/C.2118/12.

Instructions regarding War Diaries and Intelligence Summaries are contained in F. S. Regs., Part II. and the Staff Manual respectively. Title Pages will be prepared in manuscript.

# WAR DIARY
*or*
# INTELLIGENCE SUMMARY
*(Erase heading not required.)*

Army Form C. 2118.

| Place | Date | Hour | Summary of Events and Information | Remarks and references to Appendices |
|---|---|---|---|---|
| | | | torches. During the month about 144 tons of unserviceable, salvaged or surplus stores were received, sorted, repaired when possible, & sent to Base, including 1221 rifles, 22 cycles & 33 handcarts. | |
| | | | R.F. Johnson, Capt A.O.D. D.A.D.O.S. 51 (H) Div. | |

2449 Wt. W14957/M90 750,000 1/16 J.B.C. & A. Forms/C.2118/12.

Instructions regarding War Diaries and Intelligence Summaries are contained in F. S. Regs., Part II. and the Staff Manual respectively. Title Pages will be prepared in manuscript.

# WAR DIARY
*or*
# INTELLIGENCE SUMMARY
*(Erase heading not required.)*



Army Form C. 2118.

Vol 21

| Place | Date | Hour | Summary of Events and Information | Remarks and references to Appendices |
|---|---|---|---|---|

51ST (HIGHLAND) DIVISION

D. A. D. O. S.

## — WAR DIARY —

JANUARY 1917.

SECRET.

R Johnson
Capt. A.O.D.
DA.D.O.S. 51(H) DIV.

2449 Wt. W14957/M90 750,000 1/16 J.B.C. & A. Forms/C.2118/12.

Instructions regarding War Diaries and Intelligence Summaries are contained in F. S. Regs., Part II. and the Staff Manual respectively. Title Pages will be prepared in manuscript.

# WAR DIARY
*or*
# INTELLIGENCE SUMMARY
*(Erase heading not required.)*



Army Form C. 2118.

| Place | Date | Hour | Summary of Events and Information | Remarks and references to Appendices |
|---|---|---|---|---|
| BOUZINCOURT | 1917 JAN 1 | | Recd. 2400 Lumbermen's socks for Batts, and issued one complete set of underclothing + towels to Div Artillery (all units) | |
| " | - 2 | | To new area. Arranged to take over from 18th Division their reserve of P.H. helmets. Recd. large Consignment of naves + wheels: 4 Lewis handcarts for 5th Gordons. | |
| " | - 3 | | To Amiens for local purchase. | |
| " | - 4 | | Drew attention of H.Q. Div. Artillery to neglect of bicycles. Moved 7th Cavalry Pioneer Battalion to V Corps Troops for Ordnance. Suspended issue of dial sights and warned DADOS 2nd Div (who are taking over the guns) re shortages. Dial sights will be indented for by 51st Div. Arty when they take over their new guns from 2nd Div. No truck recd. | |
| " | - 5 | | "Tyreoid" tested + approved, nail being driven through tyre & pulled out without much loss of air. 18-pdr received for B/260. (no 5427) G.S. wagon for H.Q. Train, Lim. Wag. G.S. (fore) for 6 Gordons, Cart Water Tank for B/255. Moved 2 Div Artillery to 51 Div for Ordnance. | |
| " | - 6 | | Suspended issue of Strombos Horns, as no opportunity yet offers of placing them usefully in the line (A.D.O.S. instructions) | |
| " | - 7 | | Sent all gum boots to gum boot store at POZIÈRES | |
| " | - 8 | | Nothing special to report. | |

Army Form C. 2118.

# WAR DIARY
*or*
# INTELLIGENCE SUMMARY
*(Erase heading not required.)*

Instructions regarding War Diaries and Intelligence Summaries are contained in F. S. Regs., Part II. and the Staff Manual respectively. Title Pages will be prepared in manuscript.

| Place | Date | Hour | Summary of Events and Information — 2nd Sheet | Remarks and references to Appendices |
|---|---|---|---|---|
| BOUZINCOURT | 1917 JAN 9 | | moved 51 Sanitary Section, B Co, 2 SANLC and 20th Notts + Derby Lab. Bn to 2nd Division. Suspended all issues. moved 2 Div Arty to 2 Div from 12.1.17. Stopped taking in salvage. | |
| " | – 10 | | Ar. Sr. Sjt ASH left, with armourers and shoemakers, to prepare new depot. RA stores also sent. 3 compasses for observation posts received. Handed to 2 Div. Ordnance representative. Moved 3rd Field Company to 63rd Division | |
| " | – 11 | | DADOS. 2nd Div arrived and took over following stores: one week's supply of boots oil, horseshoes, grindery + flannellette: complete antigas reserve: 65 camp kettles: 1440 field dressings: 54 brayers: 400 body shields + necklets: 72 food containers and 249 sets of packsaddlery including 94 improvised. | |
| " | – 12 | | S/Condr. FISHWICK left with entire detachment and records. Handed over to 2nd Div. 163 Lewis handcarts, 2571 shovels G.S. 2067 axes pick heads, 1935 helves + other tools. | |
| MARIEUX | – 13 | | DADOS moved with Div H.Q. Returned YUKON pack to OO 4 Corps Troops. | |
| BERNAVILLE | – 14 | | DADOS moved with Div H.Q. | |
| BUIGNY ST MACLOU | – 15 | | DADOS arrived and took over new depot. 152 LEWIS HANDCARTS, left by 18th Div, taken over. | |
| " | – 16 | | Truck at ABBEVILLE but unapproachable. No truck at St ~~Riequier~~ RIQUIER. moved 18 Div School to me for Ordnance. S/Condr Carolan inspected entire stores of A/255 battery and adjusted indents | |
| " | – 17 | | Detachment examined for SCABIES. 4 cases noted. Truck at ABBEVILLE still unapproachable. No truck at St R. S/Condr. Carolan inspected entire stores of B/255 battery and adjusted indents. | |
| " | – 18 | | Cleared following trucks from St R. 40522 jerkins, clo &c: 41902, oil grease &c: 210311 boots &c: 470076 oil &c. 17309 Limber 18 pdr wagon for H.Q. 51 Div Arty(?) Limber 18 pdr wagon for 2 DAC. Visited no 8 Ord Depot + St R. Base stated supply of paint now ample. S/Condr. Carolan inspected entire stores of C/255 battery + adjusted indents. | |
| " | – 19 | | Trucks recd: 132532 with paillasses + G.S. paint: 27254, with carr. 4.5 how for D/255 no 85780; 16836 with GS wagons for 4 Sec DAC, Cart W.T. for 7 Gordons + cart men for A/260: 5632 with wag G.S for 4 Sec DAC. 7495 with GS wag for 4 Sec DAC | |
| " | – 20 | | No truck at railhead. | |
| " | – 21 | | Truck 76415 with picketing gear recd. Office closed for half a day. | |

2449 Wt. W14957/M90 750,000 1/16 J.B.C. & A. Forms/C.2118/12.

Instructions regarding War Diaries and Intelligence Summaries are contained in F. S. Regs., Part II. and the Staff Manual respectively. Title Pages will be prepared in manuscript.

# WAR DIARY
*or*
# INTELLIGENCE SUMMARY
*(Erase heading not required.)*

Army Form C. 2118.

| Place | Date | Hour | Summary of Events and Information | Remarks and references to Appendices |
|---|---|---|---|---|
| BUIGNY | 1917 JAN 22 | | Trucks 18990 with clothing = 471072 with necessaries. Collected 1000 bayonets, local purchase, from THUILLIER-BURIDARD, VIGNACOURT. | |
| " | JAN 23 | | Truck 33708 with smoke helmets. Visited COO Abbeville & borrowed 1000 blankets | |
| " | " 24 | | Truck 132293 with boots: 56790 with 802 blankets | |
| " | " 25 | | No Truck | |
| " | " 26 | | No truck. | |
| " | " 27 | | Truck 52133 with horse shoes. | |
| " | " 28 | | Truck 56483 with oil & grease.. unable to close office. | |
| " | " 29 | | No Truck. Inspected 153 Bde Transport with IOM no 30 workshop, Abbeville. Office closed for half a day. | |
| " | " 30 | | 5 trucks & one extra consignment — 66359 with clothing: 1463 with jerkins & necessaries = 29966, blankets, bayonets & horse rugs: 200760 general & 40 cases body armour (left at railhead) 65756 with 1000 box respirators & 40 bales blankets. Borrowed 4 lorries from columns & shifted over 40 tons of stores. Inspected transport of 152 Bde with IOM no 30 workshop & wagons of 255 & 256 Bdes with IOM no 28 workshop. To Abbeville to purchase stuff for flags. | |
| " | " 31 | | 200 flags for training made in depot. No truck. Moved 8 R. Scots & 1/1 & 1/2 Field Companies to 6th Corps Troops & cancelled all indents for billet stores. | |
| | | | GENERAL:- During the latter half of this month, while the Division has been "at rest", the whole of the guns except 2 have been overhauled by IOM. The entire gun stores, tools &c of each ~~unit~~ artillery unit have been inspected in detail by a W.O. from this depot. The transport of 2 out of 3 brigades had been inspected and a | |

2449 Wt. W14957/M90 750,000 1/16 J.B.C. & A. Forms/C.2118/12.

Army Form C. 2118.

Instructions regarding War Diaries and Intelligence Summaries are contained in F. S. Regs., Part II. and the Staff Manual respectively. Title Pages will be prepared in manuscript.

# WAR DIARY
*or*
# INTELLIGENCE SUMMARY
*(Erase heading not required.)*

| Place | Date | Hour | Summary of Events and Information | Remarks and references to Appendices |
|---|---|---|---|---|
| | | | large number of repairs & changes made. Returns have been secured showing how each battalion, M.G. Company, T.M. Battery & Field Company stood with regard to important stores & indent for all deficiencies passed. Since arrival in present area nearly 200 tons of stores have been distributed and nearly a thousand detailed indents have been examined and passed, many of them comprising several score of items. During the month 117 tons of Ordnance stores, surplus and unserviceable, were sorted packed and returned to Base. The outstanding feature of the month has been the improvement in the supply of artillery stores. | |
| | | | 1/2/17 | |
| | | | R Johnson<br>Capt A.O.D.<br>D.A.D.O.S. 57 (H) Div. | |

2449 Wt. W14957/M90 750,000 1/16 J.B.C. & A. Forms/C.2118/12.

D. A. D. O. S.,
51st (HIGHLAND)
DIVISION.
No. J.B/220.
Date 2/3/17.

SECRET.

Headquarters "Q"
51st (H) Division

Herewith please war diary for the month of February.

[signature]

Capt.
D.A.D.O.S.
51st (H) Division

Instructions regarding War Diaries and Intelligence Summaries are contained in F. S. Regs., Part II. and the Staff Manual respectively. Title Pages will be prepared in manuscript.

# WAR DIARY
*or*
~~INTELLIGENCE SUMMARY~~
*(Erase heading not required.)*

Army Form C. 2118.

Vol 22

| Place | Date | Hour | Summary of Events and Information | Remarks and references to Appendices |
|---|---|---|---|---|
| | | | 51st (HIGHLAND) DIVISION.<br>D.A.D.O.S.<br>WAR DIARY<br>FEBRUARY 1917<br>SECRET<br>R.H. Johnson Capt A.O.D.<br>DADOS 51(H) Div | |

2449 Wt. W14957/M90 750,000 1/16 J.B.C. & A. Forms/C.2118/12.

Instructions regarding War Diaries and Intelligence Summaries are contained in F. S. Regs., Part II. and the Staff Manual respectively. Title Pages will be prepared in manuscript.

# WAR DIARY
*or*
# ~~INTELLIGENCE SUMMARY~~
*(Erase heading not required.)*

Army Form C. 2118.

| Place | Date | Hour | Summary of Events and Information | Remarks and references to Appendices |
|---|---|---|---|---|
| ~~[illegible]~~ BUIGNY | 1917 FEB. 1 | | Truck 148893 oil + grease. 3178 boots. Total 26 tons. | |
| " | " 2 | | Truck 96243 with 24 Lewis guns making 14 per battalion, and horse shoes. Gas officer reports 5% of box respirators issued before 1/1/17 useless. Wired 5 Seaforths & 6 Gordons to change forthwith & released indent for 5000. Moved 18th Div. School to Fourth Corps Troops. Wired Havre & Rouen to cease supply at once and Calais to begin on 8th except for box respirators wanted on 7th. | |
| " | " 3 | | No Truck. 86 Lewis handcarts (6 per Bn. except 5 Seaforths, who returned 12 and 8 R. Scots who returned 8) returned to COO. Abbeville. Artillery changes completed. No 3 Section DAC. ceases to exist; also HQ 260. D/260 is split between D/255 & D/256 who now have 6 howitzers each. A/260 becomes C/315, B/260 becomes C/86 & D/260 becomes D/82. Vehicles rendered surplus returned to A.H.T.D. Abbeville. Reported 6700 pairs of boots repaired monthly ~~[illegible]~~ in Division. | |
| " | " 4 | | Altered move of F. Coy & 8 R Scots (see Jan 31) to 17 Corps Troops. Moved three surplus batteries as above (Feb 3) to 4th Corps Troops. Armourers & Box Respirator left in 2 trucks for new area. | |
| BRAILLY | " 5 | | DADOS moved with Div HQ office left behind | |
| FROHEN-LE GRAND. | " 6 | | DADOS moved with Div. HQ. Office staff proceeded by lorry direct to TINCQUES. Altered moves of batteries (see Feb 3 & 4) to 31 Div. Moved 18 Div School (see Feb 2) to 31 Div. ~~[illegible]~~ Moved 51 Am. Sub. Park to this Div from 4th Corps Troops | |
| ROELLECOURT | " 7 | | DADOS moved with Div. H.Q. Office stayed at TINCQUES, as billets which were to have been ~~available~~ available (under 17 Corps Q orders) by noon on 6th were not available. | |
| MINGOVAL | " 8 | | DADOS moved to new area, office joining | |
| " | " 9 | | Trucks 19646 & 85660 with box respirators urgently required for 152 Bde (theirs having been condemned by Gas officer) discovered to be stuck at ABBEVILLE, tho' had arranged with CALAIS for them to be at new railhead (LIGNY ST FLOCHEL) by 7th. DADRT Abbeville unable to guarantee | |

2449 Wt. W14957/M90 750,000 1/16 J.B.C. & A. Forms/C.2118/12.

Instructions regarding War Diaries and Intelligence Summaries are contained in F. S. Regs., Part II. and the Staff Manual respectively. Title Pages will be prepared in manuscript.

# WAR DIARY
*or*
# ~~INTELLIGENCE SUMMARY~~

*(Erase heading not required.)*

Army Form C. 2118.

| Place | Date | Hour | Summary of Events and Information | Remarks and references to Appendices |
|---|---|---|---|---|
| | FEB 9 (contd) | | time of delivery. Therefore sent 2 lorries at 1 a.m to Abbeville where they were joined by 2 borrowed from 5 Auxiliary Petrol Coy. Whole cargo reached this depot. Moved 51 Supply Col. & Am. Sub. Park to 17th Corps Tps. Moved 51 San Sec from 2 Div to this Div. | |
| MINGOVAL | " 10 | | 152 Bde completed with new box respirators. 152 wired to collect. Armourers arrived at railhead. Also Truck 32003 (clo. & blankets) & 1530, with blankets. All surplus blankets diverted to C.O.O. Abbeville in return for loan. 2000 condemned box respirators returned to Base. ~~Gun~~ 18 pdr demanded for A/256 to replace no 1253 (delayed owing to condemnation certificate being received only today from IOM). Vickers no L1298 of 152 MGC condemned: demand to replace. | |
| " | " 11 | | No truck. Armourers shop set up. | |
| " | " 12 | | Capt R.F. Johnson left for Boulogne for local purchase and to begin leave. Tape purchased for battalion markings. Truck 51915 with blankets. Only 678 now required owing to borrowings but DADRT, Third Army, said truck must be cleared. S/Condr. FISHWICK therefore wired Infantry Bdes & Field Ambulances to indent to complete to establishment. Entire truckload used up & 1000 required to complete. These are due in second truck, not yet received (Not received during month. Probably returned to Base). 2/Lieut RICH, Black Watch, to answer for DADOS wagon ammn. QF 18 pdr no 46897 recd. for No 2. Sec D.A.C. to replace Mark I | |
| " | " 13 | | Ord, 2nd Div wired that 18 pdr no 3400 had been salved. Could we identify? Wired particulars. Trucks 52017 & 47825 recd. with one mess cart each for C/255, C/256 & D/256, one wagon G.S. for C/255, one travelling kitchen complete for 6 Seaforths one wagon G.S. for 4 Sec DAC: also truck 37621 with details. | |
| " | " 14 | | Truck 692 with 18 pdr no 2264 II N/O B.M. for A/256 428 Trench helmets & 100 necklets & body shields. Recd. 670 steel helmets with visors, 7 Stirling cradles (loaned to 152 Bde for Trial) & 1 improvised ("Rough & ready") hot food container, all from Corps. | |

2449 Wt. W14957/M90 750,000 1/16 J.B.C. & A. Forms/C.2118/12.

Instructions regarding War Diaries and Intelligence Summaries are contained in F. S. Regs., Part II. and the Staff Manual respectively. Title Pages will be prepared in manuscript.

# WAR DIARY
*or*
# INTELLIGENCE SUMMARY
*(Erase heading not required.)*

Army Form C. 2118.

| Place | Date | Hour | Summary of Events and Information | Remarks and references to Appendices |
|---|---|---|---|---|
| MINGOVAL | 1917 FEB 15 | | Trucks 59457 + 148557 with 7960 box respirators. Sent Stokes 3" TM No. 2161 (from 152 TMB) to 10M No 6 workshop, who reported "no damage that cannot be repaired apparently." AA & QMG inspected shops | |
| " | " 16 | | No stores received. Railhead changed from LIGNY to TINCQUES. | |
| " | " 17 | | No stores received. Stokes TM no 2161 returned from 10M | |
| " | " 18 | | Trucks 47609, 17745, 28017 + 12410 received with one cart W.T. for 6 Gordons, 4 wagons lim. G.S. for 1 Sec DAC, one for 6 Seaforths, 1 wagon lim. G.S. (hind part) for 152 M.G.C 1 maltese cart for 4 Seaforths, one wagon L. G.S. and three wagons ambulance for 2/1 Highland Field Ambulance. Also truck 156610, with clothing + horse shoes. Road precautions in force from 7 a.m. Arranged with Q for 5 G.S. wagons from R.A to clear urgent stores. Remainder rest at railhead under guard. A.D.O.S. XVII Corps visited depot. | |
| " | " 19 | | Trucks 60319 + 22245 with oil equipment + picketing gear. Vickers no 6378 for 152 M.G.C. 5 more G.S. loads removed from Railhead. Stokes TM no 2161 issued to 152 TMB | |
| " | " 20 | | No stores received. No transport available for removal of stores from railhead. | |
| " | " 21 | | Truck 58287 recd. with 9 tons of stable necessities, boots, gumboots + clothing. Recd permission for 4 lorries to run. Stores stacked in barn borrowed from Town Major. Railhead completely cleared. Received 1000 pairs gum boots from 6th Corps Troops. 154 Bde to draw 300 + 8 R. Scots 200 (Q wire) | |
| " | " 22 | | DAC report 28 inner running out springs + 26 outer required. Reported to ADOS. | |
| " | " 23 | | Trucks 150750 + 412 with horse shoes and underclothing. Q obtained permission for units to draw from depot by horse transport. | |

2449 Wt. W14957/M90 750,000 1/16 J.B.C. & A. Forms/C.2118/12.

Army Form C. 2118.

Instructions regarding War Diaries and Intelligence Summaries are contained in F. S. Regs., Part II. and the Staff Manual respectively. Title Pages will be prepared in manuscript.

# WAR DIARY
*or*
# INTELLIGENCE SUMMARY

*(Erase heading not required.)*

| Place | Date | Hour | Summary of Events and Information | Remarks and references to Appendices |
|---|---|---|---|---|
| | 1917 | | | |
| MINGOVAL | FEB 24 | | Spring Rfs for DAC demanded from Base, by Corps permission. Hitherto they have been obtainable only from workshops & no spares have been carried. | |
| " | 25 | | No stores received | |
| " | " 26 | | No truck received. 1 [illegible] & bottoms from 17 Corps Troops & two 3" stokes & one 2" TM from Third Army School. 2" sent to DOTM, the 3" with 153 TMB & one 3" in shop. Q ordered body shields & necklets distributed as follows:- 152 Bde -134, 153 Bde 133, 154 Bde 133. No one reported sick this day - the first clean day for a considerable time. Road precautions ended. | |
| " | " 27 | | Railhead changed from TINCQUES to AUBIGNY. No trucks. | |
| " | " 28 | | No trucks. Distribution of stores at Refilling Point resumed. DADOS returned from leave | |
| | | | Issues were again above the average, owing mainly to the completion of indents submitted during refitting. Considerable credit is due to Acting Sub-Conductor FISHWICK, O. A.O.C. for the negotiation, with a minimum of confusion, of the difficulties of the longest period of road precautions yet experienced by the Division, in the absence of the D.A.D.O.S. | |
| | | | R Johnson Capt A.O.D.<br>D.A.D.O.S. 51st (H) Division | |
| | | | 1/3/17. | |

2449 Wt. W14957/M90 750,000 1/16 J.B.C. & A. Forms/C.2118/12.

Instructions regarding War Diaries and Intelligence Summaries are contained in F. S. Regs., Part II. and the Staff Manual respectively. Title Pages will be prepared in manuscript.

# WAR DIARY
*or*
# INTELLIGENCE SUMMARY
*(Erase heading not required.)*

Army Form C. 2118.

Vol 23

| Place | Date | Hour | Summary of Events and Information | Remarks and references to Appendices |
|---|---|---|---|---|

51st (HIGHLAND) DIVISION.

D. A. D. O. S.

# WAR DIARY

MARCH, 1917

SECRET.

RHJohnson
Capt. A.O.D.
D.A.D.O.S
51st (H) Division

2449 Wt. W14957/M90 750,000 1/16 J.B.C. & A. Forms/C.2118/12.

Army Form C. 2118.

Instructions regarding War Diaries and Intelligence Summaries are contained in F. S. Regs., Part II. and the Staff Manual respectively. Title Pages will be prepared in manuscript.

# WAR DIARY
*or*
~~INTELLIGENCE SUMMARY~~

(Erase heading not required.)

SHEET 1.

| Place | Date 1917 | Hour | Summary of Events and Information | Remarks and references to Appendices |
|---|---|---|---|---|
| MINGOVAL | MAR 1. | | Truck 150575 with boots clothing and box respirators: 148626 with timber. Divisional Heavy Trench Mortar Battery received its first pieces – four 9.45" mortars – from XVII Corps. | |
| " | " 2 | | Battalions (less Pioneers) raised to 16 LEWIS guns each, 24 arriving in Truck 147132. Received from Corps 30 basket carriers for 9.45" T.M. ammunition and 5 tarpaulins for Grenade Dump. | |
| " | " 3 | | Borrowed 4 Soyer Stoves from XVII Corps & issued to 2 Co., Train for Soup Kitchen. | |
| " | " 4 | | Truck 23413 at TINCQUES with picketing gear. | |
| " | " 5 | | Trucks 4073, with 3500 mackintosh capes (not now required), and 1192 with camp equipment. No leather bend received. 1624 lbs now due, none having been received since Feb. 10. Wired to Base pointing out that if leather was not forthcoming demands for boots would be heavier owing to cessation of repairs. Bought seven ladies' longcloth nightgowns to enable last night's raiding party to try and find a missing and wounded officer in snow-covered "No Man's Land." | |
| " | " 6 | | No stores received | |
| " | " 7 | | Transport surplus from HQ 260 Bde., R.F.A. (ceasing to exist) returned to Depot, viz:- one wagon G.S., one cable wagon, one maltese cart and one cook's cart. Truck 621156 with 44 wheels, and 16848 with picketing gear. | |
| " | " 8 | | Maltese cart (see Mar. 7) issued to 139 Heavy Bde., R.G.A., and G.S. wagon to 2 Co., Train. No stores received. | |
| " | " 9 | | Stokes mortars with FOULIS adapters replaced by 12 new Stokes mortars in Truck 88289: this also contained 260 sets packsaddlery = 20 per battalion. Also Truck 11012 with clothing and 2523 with limbered wagon for 7th A.&S.H. | |
| " | " 10 | | No stores received. | |
| " | " 11 | | 3520 paillasses in Truck 1044: also 54623 with G.S. wagon for 2 Co., Train: transferred (see March 8) to 2 Sec., D.A.C.; and water cart for 400 Field Co. 26474 with limbered wagon for 154 M.G.C. and R.E. lim. wagon (body) for Div. Signal Co. | |
| " | " 12 | | Timber arrived (Truck 102450) for water-carriers for G.S. wagons. Also Truck 99791 with paint &c, and 25021 with horseshoes and full issue of leather, sole bend (see Mar 5). Sub-Condr. FISHWICK to Amiens to buy cycle and carriage lamps for use as extempore siege lamps, 88 being long outstanding to R.A units. | |
| " | " 13 | | Conference with A.D.O.S. XVII Corps. To St. POL to complete purchase of cycle lamps: also bought cardboard for 400 discs for special operations. | |
| " | " 14 | | 64th Army F.A. Bde moved from 9th Div. Made pattern Lewis gun sling, for firing from the hip, for Corps. | |

2449 Wt. W14957/M90 750,000 1/16 J.B.C. & A. Forms/C.2118/12.

Instructions regarding War Diaries and Intelligence Summaries are contained in F. S. Regs., Part II. and the Staff Manual respectively. Title Pages will be prepared in manuscript.

# WAR DIARY
*or*
# ~~INTELLIGENCE SUMMARY~~

*(Erase heading not required.)*

Army Form C. 2118.

SHEET 2

| Place | Date 1917 | Hour | Summary of Events and Information | Remarks and references to Appendices |
|---|---|---|---|---|
| MINGOVAL | MAR 15 | | Truck 52283 with boots and 150 braziers (50 repaid to Corps Troops): 76483 with water cart for 8th A & S.H and limbered wagon for 9th the Royal Scots: 75712 with kitchen travelling (body) for 5th Gordons and water cart for 9th the Royal Scots: 48026 with 24 sets of packsaddlery for R.A., 100 latrine pails and 8 dial sights (one spare per battery) for D.A.C., this at length completing the Division with dial sights. | |
| " | " 16 | | Sub-Condr. ELLIS to Boulogne for purchases. Ar. St. Sgt ASH to Heavy Mobile Workshops for steel &c. Truck 131896 with horse shoes. | |
| " | " 17 | | V/63 and Y/2 Trench Mortar Batteries moved to this Division. | |
| " | " 18 | | Ar. St. Sgt ASH appointed acting Armourer Sgt Major (W.O. 1st class) without pay & allowances, while in charge of Divisional Armourer's shop. No stores received. | |
| " | " 19 | | Wrote XVII Corps giving examples of the delay in trucks. Truck 210466 with oil, picketing gear &c. | |
| " | " 20 | | To St POL for local purchases. | |
| " | " 21 | | Boxes tin for LEWIS magazines received to complete to 22 per 4 guns, in Truck 147626; also 20 Soyer Stoves. Vickers gun of 153 M.G.C. destroyed by shell-fire. To BOULOGNE for "10 complete ration" labels. | |
| " | " 22 | | Returned from Boulogne. Vickers gun of 154 M.G.C. condemned. | |
| " | " 23 | | Truck 96310 with boots &c. | |
| " | " 24 | | Wrote XVII Corps complaining of inaccuracy of accounts rendered by Regimental Paymaster, Departmental Corps & Remounts. Truck 33813 with horse shoes &c. Sub-Condr Fishwick to Boulogne for thermos box fittings &c. | |
| " | " 25 | | First supply of 7500 rubber sponge goggles, towards one per man, received in truck 40305 | |
| " | " 26 | | No stores received | |
| " | " 27 | | Trucks 1598, 350, 136561 and 77057 with two G.S. wagons for 4 Sec. D.A.C, trav. kitchen for 4th Gordons, water cart for 1/3 Field Ambce, mess cart for C/256 Batt., limbered wagon for 2 Sec, D.A.C limbered wagon (hind) for 154 Bde & (fore) for 152 Trench Mortar Battery: (fore) for 404 Field Co: also pontoon wagon for 404 Field Co & water cart for D/64 Batt | |
| " | " 28 | | V/62 Trench Mortar Battery and 34, 84 & 315 Army F.A. Brigades moved to this Division. Truck 180316 with winter clothing & 2 Newton 2" T. Mortar beds. | |

2449 Wt. W14957/M90 750,000 1/16 J.B.C. & A. Forms/C.2118/12.

Instructions regarding War Diaries and Intelligence Summaries are contained in F. S. Regs., Part II. and the Staff Manual respectively. Title Pages will be prepared in manuscript.

# WAR DIARY
*or*
# ~~INTELLIGENCE SUMMARY~~
*(Erase heading not required.)*

Army Form C. 2118.

SHEET 3

| Place | Date 1917 | Hour | Summary of Events and Information | Remarks and references to Appendices |
|---|---|---|---|---|
| MINGOYAL | MAR 29 | | Truck 223916 with Boots & 5 Soyer Stoves (4 returned to 00 Corps Troops to repay loan) | |
| " | " 30 | | No stores received from Base. Twenty-two tarpaulins from Corps | |
| " | " 31 | | Truck 9581 with horse shoes. | |

## GENERAL

During the month 1346 indents, comprising from one to 130 items each, were checked and sent forward. These included 118 for officers, on payment.

Shortages were experienced in LEATHER SOLE BEND, HAYNETS, MINERAL OIL, siege lamps, wagon parts & certain small sizes of F.S. boots. The supply of leather reverted to normal about the middle of the month. The other shortages continue.

WORK OF THE SHOPS: 2008 pairs of boots were examined by the shoemakers and 284 repaired. In the tailor's shop 606 flags were made for manoeuvre area, 905 armbands for special operations, and 13 garments & 173 pairs of puttees were repaired. Among the articles that passed through the Armourer's Shop were: Rifles 417, machine guns 7. 1405 identity discs were stamped & issued: 37 cycles were repaired: 150 candle lamps designed & made from old biscuit tins: 100 tin plates & 400 cardboard discs prepared for operations: and 4 preliminary samples made of a new Lewis gun sling, for firing from the hip.

The most remarkable feature of the month is the response made by units to the recent calls for the return of unserviceable stores.

Twenty four truck loads (about 120 tons) of new stores were distributed to units. 27 lorry loads (about 81 tons) of repairable &c. stores were returned to Base. 24776 articles were "conditioned", recorded in detail, packed labelled & despatched. About 90% of this amount came direct from units through Refilling Points – i.e. only one-tenth was left lying in the area, to be removed by the Salvage Company. The entire work of loading, sorting, packing & recording this salvage was done by three men. In addition to these figures, the Divisional Baths returned to Base direct 1261 unserviceable articles up to March 22, when this was undertaken by Corps Laundry.

There is still room for greater care, however, in the return of certain articles e.g. ground sheets (818 issued, 75 returned) boots (3122 issued, 1510 returned) pantaloons (996 issued, 344 returned) & P.H. helmets (2455 issued, 1216 returned)

Issues of water bottles, mess tins, ground sheets, lubricating oil, mineral jelly & lubricating grease were above normal but the demands were evenly distributed and it is not clear to what the excess is due.

R.H. Munson Capt. A.O.D., D.A.D.O.S., 51st (Highland) Division

2449 Wt. W14957/M90 750,000 1/16 J.B.C. & A. Forms/C.2118/12.

Instructions regarding War Diaries and Intelligence Summaries are contained in F. S. Regs., Part II. and the Staff Manual respectively. Title Pages will be prepared in manuscript.

# WAR DIARY
*or*
# INTELLIGENCE SUMMARY
*(Erase heading not required.)*

Army Form C. 2118

Vol 24

| Place | Date | Hour | Summary of Events and Information | Remarks and references to Appendices |
|---|---|---|---|---|
| | | | 51[ST] (HIGHLAND) DIVISION<br>D. A. D. O. S<br>— WAR DIARY —<br>APRIL - 1917.<br>SECRET<br>R H Johnson, Capt, A.O.D.,<br>D.A.D.O.S 51 (H) DIV. | |

D. A. D. O. S., 51st (HIGHLAND) DIVISION.
No. J5/44
Date 9/5/17.

1875 Wt. W593/826 1,000,000 4/15 J.B.C. & A. A.D.S.S./Forms/C. 2118.

Army Form C. 2118.

# WAR DIARY
*or*
# INTELLIGENCE SUMMARY.
*(Erase heading not required.)*

Instructions regarding War Diaries and Intelligence Summaries are contained in F. S. Regs., Part II. and the Staff Manual respectively. Title pages will be prepared in manuscript.

| Place | Date 1917 | Hour | Summary of Events and Information | Remarks and references to Appendices: Miles | Tons |
|---|---|---|---|---|---|
| MINGOVAL. | April 1. | | Truck 56210 with 194 sets of packsaddlery to complete to 24 per battalion. Also received from railhead 5 water carts, with harness for reserve. Arranged plans for operations with salvage officer. | 60. | 12 |
| " | " 2. | | Truck arrived at railhead at 3-30 pm. but R.O.O. said it would not be in position for off loading until 7 a.m. to-morrow. Soyer stove, 125 tents (from Corps) + 500 paillasses, returned from 1/8 Royal Scots, issued to T.M. BRAY: also 22 tarpaulins to R.A. units. Each battalion's shoemaker finished making 8 new pattern Lewis gun slings for firing from the hip. Tailor finished 200 red armbands for R.A. runners. Recd 5 more water carts to complete to reserve of 10. | 102. | 20 |
| " | " 3 | | To St Pol to buy hobnails (1000 lbs due + supply at a standstill) and 34 carriage lamps for issue as siege lamps after painting in shops. Borrowed 150 gals of lubricating oil from Corps M.T. units to issue to Batteries in lieu of buffer oil. Truck 69599 with oil grease and picketing gear: 52719 with wagon G.S for B/64 Batty. | 102. | 23. |
| " | " 4 | | Third limbered wagon per battn for carriage of Lewis guns arrived, but not through A.O.D. Received truck No 664 with stable necessaries + 4 5 how. No 2045 without breech mechanism, for 56th Battery 34th Bde. Received and issued 112 mechanisms for T.M. Batteries (2") | 129. | 14. |
| " | " 5 | | No TRUCK | 138. | 17 |
| " | " 6. | | Truck 1363 with one wagon G.S. for 8 A.&S.H. | 100. | 13. |
| " | " 7. | | Truck 863 with 7 tons boots etc: 17935, with 2 wagons ammunition 18-pdr and one limber 18 pdr wagon for B/64 A.F.A Bde: and 8 dial sights (4 surplus + 4 to complete guns taken over without these = an enquiry is proceeding re this = papers delivered this day to D.D.O.S. Third army) for C/315 A.F.A. Bde = also 4 clinometers sight, 4 carriers dial sight + 4 sighting telescopes. | 115. | 18. |
| " | " 8. | | Trucks 144620 with horseshoes oil + grease = 15 with clothing and grindery (6 tons) = 5781 with limber G.S wagon for 2 Sect. D.A.C. watercart for 2/1 Field Ambulance + A/64 Bde. Lorry to Gun Park for gun for C/356 and carriage 56 Batty 34 A.F.A. Bde | 196. | 30 |

Instructions regarding War Diaries and Intelligence Summaries are contained in F. S. Regs., Part II. and the Staff Manual respectively. Title pages will be prepared in manuscript.

# WAR DIARY
*or*
# INTELLIGENCE SUMMARY.
*(Erase heading not required.)*

Army Form C. 2118.

| Place | Date | Hour | Summary of Events and Information | Remarks and references to Appendices |
|---|---|---|---|---|
| | | | for A/256 | LORRIES MILES TONS |
| MINCOVAL | APRIL 9. | | Truck 52413 with picketing gear (16 tons) special refill to clear R.A. units. 18 pdr without Breech mechanism collected from 3rd army Gun Park and also 18 pdr without breech mechanism for B/315 A.F.A. Bde. | 150. 16. |
| " | " 10. | | Truck 16237 with stable necessaries & 21 sets packsaddlery (about 8 tons) no vouchers in truck. | 176. 19. |
| " | " 11. | | Lorry to third army Ordnance Gun Park, FREVENT for 4.5" How carriage for 56 Batty 34 Bde. 18 pdr without breech mechanism for B/255 Bde and 18 pdr without breech mechanism for B/315 A.F.A. Bde | 221. 29. |
| " | " 12. | | Lorry to Gun Park for Lewis Gun for 1/9 R. Scots, 4.5" How. without breech mechanism for 56 Batty 34th Bde. Visited all battalions and sent w/o's to see QMS to consult about refitting. | 153. 18. |
| " | " 13. | | Lorry to Gun Park for Lewis Gun for 1/9 R. Scots Lewis guns each for 1/4 Gordons 1/6 Seaforths & 1/8 A & S. Hdrs | 225. 6 |
| " | " 14. | | Truck 201152 clothing 9 tons: 4305 clothing 9 tons; 146729 Horseshoes 15 tons. Lorries started working night & day to clear winter clothing. | 210. 33 |
| " | " 15 | | Truck 160997 3" Stokes for 153 T.M.B. 5 tons picketing gear & 5654 with wagons G.S. for 2 Section D.A.C. Lorry to Gun Park for machine Gun each for 152 & 154 M.G. Coy. 1. 3" Stokes for 154 T.M.B & 2" for 51/2 T.M.B received. | 204. 25 |
| | " 16 | | Delivered 5 lorry loads of Stores to 2nd Division for attached R.A. | 251. 27 |
| ACQ | " 17 | | Moved Echelon A. Truck 15010 with stable necessaries 3 tons. Railhead moved to AUBIGNY. | 225. 33 |
| " | " 18. | | Moved Echelon B to ACQ. Truck 5936 boots & necessaries 3 tons. Received 1. 3" Stokes for 152 T.M.B | 140. 21 |
| " | " 19 | | Sent to ARRAS for 1 load Stores. Moved carts water tank to ACQ. Truck 21543 equipment &c. Received 2 T.M.'s for 154 T.M.B. & 2 - 2" T.M's for 51/2 T.M.B. | |
| " | " 20 | | Nothing to report. | |

Instructions regarding War Diaries and Intelligence Summaries are contained in F. S. Regs., Part II. and the Staff Manual respectively. Title pages will be prepared in manuscript.

# WAR DIARY
*or*
# INTELLIGENCE SUMMARY.
*(Erase heading not required.)*

Army Form C. 2118.

| Place | Date | Hour | Summary of Events and Information | Remarks and references to Appendices |
|---|---|---|---|---|
| ACQ. | APRIL 21. | | 3 Vickers guns collected from Gun Park for 152 M.G. Co. Railhead moved to ARRAS. | |
| " | 22. | | Collected from Gun Park Lewis Guns 1 each for 1/7 A&S. Hdrs, 1/9 R. Scots, 1/5 Gordons, and Vickers for 153 M.G. Co. Truck No 660 Box respirators + horseshoes. Truck 4091 bulk S.D. clothing 17316 wagon G.S. for B Ech: DAC, 37912 Carts mess for C/255 + 54995 Pontoon Bipartite for 400 Field Co RE. | |
| " | 23 | | Lorry to Gun Park for 18 pdr for C/255 Bde, 2-18 pdrs for B/255, 18 pdr carriage for A/256 1 Lewis Guns for 1/8 A&S. Hdrs. 2 T.M.s for 152 T.M.B. Truck 98593 Picketing gear, oil, and stable necessaries Truck 1228 with G.S wagon for 'B' Echelon D.A.C. | |
| " | 24 | | Railhead moved to Grand Place, ARRAS. Visited all Brigades and sent W.O.s to QMs to consult re refitting. | |
| " | 25 | | Received 9.45" for V/51 T.M.B (Collected from XVII Corps Troops) Railhead moved to TINQUES. | |
| " | 26 | | Truck 466658 bulk tube helmets, equipment soap + 11 wheels: 37995 2 wagons ammunition for B/256 Bde. Collected from Gun Park 3 - 18 pdrs for A/256 Bde + 1-18 pdr carriage for A/256 Bde. | |
| " | 27 | | Truck 55562 necessaries &c: 24070 general stores Collected 7 Vickers guns from Gun Park for 152 Machine Gun Co. To Boulogne for local purchases. Returned 9 carts water tank (reserve) to XVII Corps Troops. | |
| " | 28 | | Truck 137785 clothing 8 tons. Collected following Lewis guns from Gun Park 1/5 Gordons (1) 1/7 A&S Hdrs (10), 1/4 Gordons (5) 1/4 Seaforths (1) 1/9 Royal Scots (8) 1/6 Gordons (2) 1/6 Black Watch (3) 9 Vickers for 154 M.G. Co + 4.5 How carr: for D/256 Bde. Lewis gun issued to 1/6 Seaforths from Salvage. Detained in Boulogne by car breaking down | |
| " | 29 | | Returned from Boulogne. | |
| " | 30 | | Trucks 8491 - 2 wagons G.S for 1 Sect. D.A.C. + B. Ech D.A.C. 55002 Picketing gear | |

A5834 Wt. W4973 M687 750,000 8/16 D. D. & L. Ltd. Forms/C.2118/13.

Instructions regarding War Diaries and Intelligence Summaries are contained in F. S. Regs., Part II. and the Staff Manual respectively. Title pages will be prepared in manuscript.

# WAR DIARY
*or*
# INTELLIGENCE SUMMARY.
*(Erase heading not required.)*

Army Form C. 2118.

| Place | Date | Hour | Summary of Events and Information | Remarks and references to Appendices |
|---|---|---|---|---|
| General | | | During the month 1115 indents were checked and sent forward. | |
| | | | Few shortages were observable. Supply of lamps electric torch was slow, but batteries, which had been scarce for some months, resumed normal, as did hobnails, supply of which last month was very poor. | |
| | | | Return of winter clothing began this month. Amongst the articles sent to Base were 16738 blankets, 1321 capes mackintosh, 1769 undercoats fur & 4448 leather jerkins. | |
| | | | In all 111 tons of winter clothing were sorted and returned. The bulk of this was not brought into depot by units, as in previous years: owing to the demands on their transport, it was decided to allow the majority of units to dump and their stores were collected by Ordnance lorries. | |
| | | | Salvage figures for the month again show considerable efforts towards economy on the part of units. Roughly 160 tons of new stores were issued, excluding guns & vehicles. 126 tons of unserviceable stores were returned to base. On the other hand the demands for bulk stores (clothing &c) were remarkably low, having in view the active operations in which the Division has been engaged. | |
| | | | The return of winter clothing, the double refitting of the divisions and the necessity of drawing stores from the Gun Park involved very heavy pressure on the depot. For about a fortnight it was only possible to cope with this by working lorries continuously night and day, the men taking 12 hour shifts. During the month the lorries covered a ~~[illegible]~~ gross mileage of 11215, carrying 636 tons gross. | |

A5834 Wt. W4973 M687 750,000 8/16 D. D. & L. Ltd. Forms/C.2118/13.

Instructions regarding War Diaries and Intelligence Summaries are contained in F. S. Regs., Part II. and the Staff Manual respectively. Title pages will be prepared in manuscript.

# WAR DIARY
*or*
# INTELLIGENCE SUMMARY.
*(Erase heading not required.)*

Army Form C. 2118.

| Place | Date | Hour | Summary of Events and Information | Remarks and references to Appendices |
|---|---|---|---|---|
| | | | Work of Shops. More than 1200 rifles + 35 machine guns were overhauled: also 33 cycles. 64 siege lamps were made from carriage lamps: 2000 burial plates made according to 17 Corps pattern (sheet of tin hung on a hook of wire, other end of wire being plunged into the ground). 4000 identity discs were stamped. About 210 pairs of boots were repaired: 350 pairs of puttees made up from old ones: 225 armlets + 105 medal ribbons (for presentation in the field) were made up. Owing to the necessity of employing all available men for clearing urgent stores, work on the shops, unless urgent, was frequently held up. | |
| | | | 2/5/17. R Hutchinson [signature] Capt A.O.D. D.A.D.O.S. 57 (H) Div | |

A5834 Wt. W4973 M687 750,000 8/16 D. D. & L. Ltd. Forms/C.2118/13.

Instructions regarding War Diaries and Intelligence Summaries are contained in F. S. Regs., Part II. and the Staff Manual respectively. Title pages will be prepared in manuscript.

# WAR DIARY
*or*
# INTELLIGENCE SUMMARY.
*(Erase heading not required.)*

Army Form C. 2118.





| Place | Date | Hour | Summary of Events and Information | Remarks and references to Appendices |
|---|---|---|---|---|

Vol 25

51st (HIGHLAND) DIVISION

D. A. D. O. S.

WAR DIARY

MAY - 1917

SECRET.

R Munson [signature]
Capt A.O.D
D.A.D.O.S.
51st (H) DIVISION

A5834 Wt. W4973 M687 750,000 8/16 D. D. & L. Ltd. Forms/C.2118/13.

Instructions regarding War Diaries and Intelligence Summaries are contained in F. S. Regs., Part II. and the Staff Manual respectively. Title pages will be prepared in manuscript.

# WAR DIARY
*or*
# INTELLIGENCE SUMMARY.
*(Erase heading not required.)*

Army Form C. 2118.

| Place | Date | Hour | Summary of Events and Information | Remarks and references to Appendices |
|---|---|---|---|---|
| ACQ | 1/5/17. | | To Thrid Army Ord. Gun Park, collected 3 - 18pdrs for C/255 Bde. R.F.A. | |
| " | 2/5/17. | | Truck No 1651 Received with hind-part limb, wagon for 154 M.G.Co, mess cart for B/256 Bde, R.F.A, R.E. limb, wagon body for 400th Field Co. and kitchen body for 1/6 Gordon Highlanders. Truck No 96134 with 2 Stokes for 153 T.M.Batty, paint and 12 cycles. Truck 59091 - clothing - 4 tons. To Thrid Army Ord. Gun Park collected 1 - 18pdr and carriage for C/255 Bde. R.F.A. | |
| " | 3/5/17. | | Truck 91610, bulk, box respirators dubbin oil &c | |
| " | 4/5/17. | | To Thrid Army Ord. Gun Park, collected 1120 L.G. magazines. | |
| " | 5/5/17 | | Truck 13120 - 18pdr ammun wagon for B/256 Bde R.F.A, 1 water cart for No 1 Sect. 51 D.A.C. and 1 pontoon for 404th Field Co. R.E. Truck 86546 - clothing - 4 tons. to BOULÔGNE for local purchases. | |
| " | 6/5/17 | | To Gun Park for L.G. magazines (640) + Lewis guns for 1/7 Gordons. Truck 147102 - General Stores. | |
| " | 7/5/17 | | No Stores. | |
| " | 8/5/17. | | Truck 43426 1 wagon G.S for No 1 Sect. 51 D.A.C. | |
| " | 9/5/17 | | Truck 8491 - 2 G.S. wagons. Truck 43426, 1 G.S. wagon. Truck 51450 including 1194 P.H. Helmets Truck 73491 - clothing - 3 tons. (1 wagon G.S. for 1 Sect. 51 D.A.C, 1 for 'B' Echelon 51 DAC + 1 for B/255 Bde R.F.A.) Carts' Officers' messes also received for 153 M.G. Co. | |
| " | 10/5/17 | | Truck 8865 - dubbin &c - 6 tons. | |

A5834 Wt. W4973 M687 750,000 8/16 D. D. & L. Ltd. Forms/C.2118/13.

Instructions regarding War Diaries and Intelligence Summaries are contained in F. S. Regs., Part II. and the Staff Manual respectively. Title pages will be prepared in manuscript.

# WAR DIARY
*or*
# INTELLIGENCE SUMMARY.
*(Erase heading not required.)*

Army Form C. 2118.

| Place | Date | Hour | Summary of Events and Information | Remarks and references to Appendices |
|---|---|---|---|---|
| ACQ | 11/5/17 | | Truck 8535 - Horseshoes &c - 9 tons. | |
| " | 12/5/17 | | To Third Army Ord Gun Park collected mountings (Vickers) &c. delivered 16 tents to 401st Field Co RE St NICHOLAS. Railhead changed to AGNES - LES - DUISANS | |
| " | 13/5/17 | | Truck 65107 - clothing - 3 tons. | |
| " | 14/5/17 | | To Third Army Ordnance Gun Park, collected L.G. magazines and other stores. Truck 24494 - respirators - 9 tons also general stores. | |
| " | 15/5/17 | | Lorry to Heavy Mobile Workshops with wheels and collected 18pdr for A/255 Bde RFA from Third Army Ord. Gun Park, also 18pdr for 9255 Bde, 18pdr for F Batty 14 A.H.A Bde + 1 Vicker's for 152 M.G. Co | |
| " | 16/5/17 | | Moved depot to Sheet 51 B Point G. 13 D ARRAS - St POL Road | |
| SHEET 51 B Point G 13 D | " | | Truck No 98646, Box respirators and stable necessaries. | |
| " | 17/5/17 | | Truck No 47222, necessaries. Lorry to Third Army Ord Gun Park and collected 18 pdr for D/256 Bde R.F.A. Truck No 136053, 2 G.S. wagons - 1 for HQ. Co 51 Divl Train and 1 for "B" Echelon 51 D A C. | |
| " | 18/5/17 | | Truck No 163619 oil grease and equipment. Lorry to Third Army Ord, Gun Park & collected 3 Vickers Guns for 152 M.G. Co, and 2 Vicker's for 153 M.G. Co and an 18 pdr carriage for "C" Batty 23rd A.F.A Bde | |
| " | 19/5/17 | | Truck 22900, Horseshoes &c. Lorry to Third Army Ord, Gun Park and collected 4.5" How. carriage for D/255 Bde, R.F.A, 18pdr for 108 Batty 23rd A.F.A. Bde. 7 Lewis Guns for 1/8 A&S. Hdrs + 7 for 1/7 Gordons | |

A5834 Wt. W4973 M687 750,000 8/16 D. D. & L. Ltd. Forms/C.2118/13.

Instructions regarding War Diaries and Intelligence Summaries are contained in F. S. Regs., Part II. and the Staff Manual respectively. Title pages will be prepared in manuscript.

# WAR DIARY
*or*
# INTELLIGENCE SUMMARY.
*(Erase heading not required.)*

Army Form C. 2118.

| Place | Date | Hour | Summary of Events and Information | Remarks and references to Appendices |
|---|---|---|---|---|
| Sheet 51 B Point G. 13 D. | 20/5/17 | | Lorry to Third Army Ord. Gun Park collected 18pdr for 'C' Batty 14 A.H.A Bde & 18pdr for C/23 AFA Bde | |
| | 21/5/17 | | Truck 6190 - general stores - 6 tons. 2 Lorries to Third Army Ord. Gun Park and collected Vickers for 152 M.G. Co. Lewis Gun for 1/6 Seaforths, 6 Lewis Guns for 1/5 Seaforths, 4.5" How. carriage for D/255 Bde R.F.A and 18 pdr with carriage for 107 Batty 23rd A.F.A Bde, | |
| | 22/5/17 | | Truck 3942 - Horseshoes - 6 tons. | |
| | 23/5/17 | | Truck 25574, 1 G.S. wagon for 1 Sect. 51 D.A.C. and 1 for 1/5 Seaforths. Truck 42106 - stable necessaries - 3 tons. Truck 3492 - horseshoes 6 tons. | |
| | 24/5/17 | | Truck 80277 - clothing &c - 6 tons. | |
| | 25/5/17 | | Truck 146170 - 71 cases Goggles anti-gas and Stokes mortar for 153 T.M. Batty. | |
| | 26/5/17 | | No stores. | |
| | 27/5/17 | | Truck 7101, 1 water cart each for 23rd A.F.A. B.A.C., C/255 Bde, R.F.A, 1/4 Gordons, 1 wagon limb. REfr 400th Field Co RE. | |
| | 28/5/17 | | Truck 67731, General stores & respirators. Truck 52658 - 3. 18pdr Ammn wagons for 107 Batty 23rd AFA Bde | |
| | 29/5/17 | | No stores received, | |

A5834 Wt. W4973 M687 750,000 8/16 D. D. & L. Ltd. Forms/C.2118/13.

Army Form C. 2118.

# WAR DIARY
*or*
# INTELLIGENCE SUMMARY.
*(Erase heading not required.)*

Instructions regarding War Diaries and Intelligence Summaries are contained in F. S. Regs., Part II. and the Staff Manual respectively. Title pages will be prepared in manuscript.

| Place | Date | Hour | Summary of Events and Information | Remarks and references to Appendices |
|---|---|---|---|---|
| Sheet 51B Point G13D | 30/5/17 | | Truck 2217, Carts mess for D/255 Bde. R.F.A. Wagon limb. G.S. limb for 51 Div. Signal Co, Kitchen travelling body 1/7 Black Watch. Truck 91349 - equipment & saddlery - 6 tons, Lorry to Third Army Ord Gun Park & collected Carriage OF 18pdr for A/256 Bde R.F.A. | |
| | 31/5/17 | | Truck 37832, Wagon G.S. for 'B' Echelon 51st D.A.C. Truck 35566 - oil and grease - 8 tons. Truck 4693 - carts water tank - 1 each for C/256 Bde R.F.A. D/255 Bde R.F.A. and wagon ambulance for 1/3 (H) Field Ambulance. Truck 67709 - boots & necessaries - 3½ tons. Truck 29654 Carts tool 4 for 401st Field Co RE. Moved 23 Bde A.F.A and 51 Divl Arty with 1/1st Co 51 Divl Train to 9th Div. 51st Sanitary Section & 31st Light Railway Co to XVII Corps Troops. | |
| | | | General. | |
| | | | During the month about 160 tons of new stores were received excluding guns and vehicles. About 180 tons of old stores were sent to Base. The latter included 50 tons of winter clothing, 120 tons of salvage and 10 tons of wheels. Demands for bulk stores were about normal. Clothing was slightly heavier than usual, owing to active operations. | |
| | | | During the month the lorries covered a gross mileage of 2856, carrying 552 tons gross. | |

A5834 Wt. W4973 M687 750,000 8/16 D. D. & L. Ltd. Forms/C.2118/13.

Instructions regarding War Diaries and Intelligence Summaries are contained in F. S. Regs., Part II. and the Staff Manual respectively. Title pages will be prepared in manuscript.

# WAR DIARY
*or*
# INTELLIGENCE SUMMARY.
*(Erase heading not required.)*

Army Form C. 2118.

| Place | Date | Hour | Summary of Events and Information | Remarks and references to Appendices |
|---|---|---|---|---|
| | | | Work of the shops. | |
| | | | Boots repaired during month 179 pairs. | |
| | | | Puttees made up 175 pairs | |
| | | | Bicycles repaired 35. | |
| | | | Identity discs stamped 2566. | |
| | | | Rifles overhauled. 895. | |
| | | | Machine Guns overhauled 28. | |
| | | | 13/6/17. | |
| | | | [signature] Capt A.O.D. D.A.D.O.S. 51st (H) Division. | |

A5834 Wt. W4973 M687 750,000 8/16 D. D. & L. Ltd. Forms/C.2118/13.

Instructions regarding War Diaries and Intelligence Summaries are contained in F. S. Regs., Part II. and the Staff Manual respectively. Title pages will be prepared in manuscript.

# WAR DIARY
*or*
# INTELLIGENCE SUMMARY.
(*Erase heading not required.*)

Army Form C. 2118.

Vol 26

| Place | Date | Hour | Summary of Events and Information | Remarks and references to Appendices |
|---|---|---|---|---|
| | | | 51st (HIGHLAND) DIVISION.<br>D. A. D. O. S.<br>WAR DIARY.<br>JUNE 1917.<br>SECRET. | |

Lieut for Capt
D.A.D.O.S.
51st (H) Division

A5834 Wt. W4973 M687 750,000 8/16 D. D. & L. Ltd. Forms/C.2118/13.

Instructions regarding War Diaries and Intelligence Summaries are contained in F. S. Regs., Part II. and the Staff Manual respectively. Title pages will be prepared in manuscript.

# WAR DIARY
*or*
# INTELLIGENCE SUMMARY.
*(Erase heading not required.)*

Army Form C. 2118.

Sheet 1.

| Place | Date | Hour | Summary of Events and Information | Remarks and references to Appendices |
|---|---|---|---|---|
| Roellecourt | 1/6/17. | | Depot moved to Roellecourt. Truck No 155391 - 7 tons - Horseshoes and tube helmets. | |
| " | 2/6/17. | | Truck No 63813 - 3 tons - Clothing. Base asked to suspend issue of stores. | |
| " | 3/6/17. | | Armourers left with stores and anti-gas reserve by rail to WATTEN. | |
| Pernes. | 4/6/17. | | Left Roellecourt for Pernes. | |
| Boney | 5/6/17 | | Left Pernes for Boney. Railhead changed to Lillers. | |
| " | 6/6/17. | | Nothing to report. | |
| Eperlecques | 7/6/17. | | Left Boney for Eperlecques. Lorry to Frevent to Third Army Ordnance Gun Park to collect machine gun parts. | |
| " | 8/6/17 | | Railhead changed to Watten. New Base - Calais. Truck No 210754 - 4 tons - general stores. Truck 93422 with 1 G.S. limbered wagon for 153 M. Gun Co. also 24285 & 21324 with 240 bales shirts & socks. Armourers rejoin. | |
| " | 9/6/17. | | Truck No. 55381 - 5 tons - clothing. Truck 52439 with 1 travelling kitchen complete for 1/5 Seaforth Highlanders. | |
| " | 10/6/17 | | Truck No. 35508 received 7 tons - clothing and picketing gear. | |
| " | 11/6/17 | | Lorry to Caestre collected 10 tents. Truck No 35522 - 3 tons - equipment. | |
| " | 12/6/17 | | No stores. | |
| " | 13/6/17. | | Truck 46791 - 6 tons - general stores | |
| " | 14/6/17. | | No stores | |

A5834 Wt. W4973 M687 750,000 8/16 D. D. & L. Ltd. Forms/C.2118/13.

Instructions regarding War Diaries and Intelligence Summaries are contained in F. S. Regs., Part II. and the Staff Manual respectively. Title pages will be prepared in manuscript.

# WAR DIARY
*or*
# INTELLIGENCE SUMMARY.

*(Erase heading not required.)*

Army Form C. 2118.

Sheet 2[illegible]

| Place | Date | Hour | Summary of Events and Information | Remarks and references to Appendices |
|---|---|---|---|---|
| Esperlecques | 15/6/17 | | Truck No 201166 - 5 tons - general stores. Lorry to Calais and collected 3 Lewis guns for 1/7 Gordons also Rifles. | |
| " | 16/6/17. | | No stores received. | |
| " | 17/6/17. | | Truck No 91347 - 6 tons - general stores. | |
| " | 18/6/17. | | D.A.D.O.S. to Ordnance Depot Calais with Quartermasters of Division. | |
| " | 19/6/17. | | Truck No 84192 - 5 tons - general stores. | |
| " | 20/6/17 | | No stores received. | |
| " | 21/6/17 | | Truck No 164575 - 6 tons - general stores. Truck No 29836, 48 wheels. Lorry to Calais and collected equipment for 1/5 Gordons. 153 Infantry Brigade including 1/3 (H) Field Ambulance and 1/3 Coy 51st Divisional Train moved to Ordnance Officer XVIII Corps Troops. Sconder Byrne A.O.C with clerk, storeman & lorry load of stores left to join XVIII Corps Troops to administer 153 Infantry Bde. | |
| " | 22/6/17 | | Moving 51st Divisional Shops to Lederzeele. | |
| Lederzeele | 23/6/17 | | Railhead changed to ARNEKE. Truck No 7993 - 5 tons - general stores. Lorry load of stores left for 51st Divisional Artillery to catch refill on 24/6/17. | |
| " | 24/6/17 | | No stores received. | |
| " | 25/6/17. | | Truck No 201051 - 3 tons - general stores. Truck No 25692 - 70 boxes belt ammunition, 30 belts and [illegible] sets packsaddlery. ~~Truck 96107 - 3 tons - general stores~~ | |
| " | 26/6/17 | | Truck 96107 - 3 tons - general stores | |

A5834 Wt. W4973 M687 750,000 8/16 D. D. & L. Ltd. Forms/C.2118/13.

Instructions regarding War Diaries and Intelligence Summaries are contained in F. S. Regs., Part II. and the Staff Manual respectively. Title pages will be prepared in manuscript.

# WAR DIARY
*or*
# INTELLIGENCE SUMMARY.
*(Erase heading not required.)*

Army Form C. 2118.

Sheet 3/

| Place | Date | Hour | Summary of Events and Information | Remarks and references to Appendices |
|---|---|---|---|---|
| Ledezeele | 27/5/17 | | No Stores received. | |
| " | 28/5/17 | | Truck No 56390 - 2 tons - general stores. | |
| " | 29/5/17 | | D.A.D.O.S. left for 10 days leave to United Kingdom. Lorry to Steelhock with stores for 153 Bde including 100 Steel helmets for 1/5 Gordon Hdrs. | |
| " | 31/5/17 | | Truck 52400 - 5 tons - general stores, 51st Divl Artillery moved from 9th Divn to 51st Divn. | |
| | | | General. - During the month about 98 tons of new stores were received excluding vehicles and about 60 tons of old stores returned to Base. | |
| | | | Demands for bulk stores were about normal. Service colour paint was not obtainable from Base. | |
| | | | During the month the lorries covered a gross mileage of 2907 , carrying 479 tons gross | |
| | | | Work of the Shops. | |
| | | | 35 Bicycles were repaired during the month, 43 identity discs were stamped 2 Pistols Webley, 2 Revolvers 20 machine guns and 125 Rifles were overhauled and repaired during the month in Divl Armourer's Shops. In the Tailor's Shops 21 red and 18 blue armbands "D" were made up, also 16 pairs puttees. 151 pairs of boots were repaired in Shoemakers shops during the month. | |
| | | | J Rich Lieut for Capt. D.A.D.O.S. 51st (H) Division | |

A5834 Wt. W4973 M687 750,000 8/16 D. D. & L. Ltd. Forms/C.2118/13.

Instructions regarding War Diaries and Intelligence Summaries are contained in F. S. Regs., Part II. and the Staff Manual respectively. Title pages will be prepared in manuscript.

# WAR DIARY
*or*
# INTELLIGENCE SUMMARY.
(*Erase heading not required.*)

Army Form C. 2118.

Vol 27

| Place | Date | Hour | Summary of Events and Information | Remarks and references to Appendices |
|---|---|---|---|---|
| | | | 51st (HIGHLAND) DIVISION. | |
| | | | — D. A. D. O. S. — | |
| | | | WAR DIARY | |
| | | | — JULY - 1917 — | |
| | | | SECRET. | |
| | | | R Wimsey [signature] Capt. D.A.D.O.S. 51st (H) DIVISION | |

A5834 Wt. W4973 M687 750,000 8/16 D. D. & L. Ltd. Forms/C.2118/13.

Army Form C. 2118.

Instructions regarding War Diaries and Intelligence Summaries are contained in F. S. Regs., Part II. and the Staff Manual respectively. Title pages will be prepared in manuscript.

# WAR DIARY
~~or~~
~~INTELLIGENCE SUMMARY.~~

*(Erase heading not required.)*

| Place | Date | Hour | Summary of Events and Information | Remarks and references to Appendices |
|---|---|---|---|---|
| LEDERZEELE | 1/7/17. | | Nothing to report. | |
| " | 2/7/17. | | Truck 35810 - 5 tons - general stores. Moved 152 Infantry Brigade from 51st Division to XVIII Corps Troops. | |
| " | 3/7/17. | | Truck 148914 - 5 tons - general stores. S/Condr Cholan left for XVIII Corps Troops with lorry load of stores and personnel to administer 152 Infantry Brigade. Moved 153 Infantry Brigade from XVIII Corps Troops to 51st Division. | |
| " | 4/7/17. | | Moved 51st Divisional Artillery from 51st Division to 39th Division under instructions from A.D.O.S. XVIII Corps. | |
| " | 5/7/17. | | Truck 305914 - 5 tons - general stores. Sergt Hold A.O.C. left for 39th Division with lorry load of stores and personnel to administer 51st Divisional Artillery. Lorry load of stores to XVIII Corps Troops for 152 Infantry Brigade. Returned with Stores for 153 Brigade. | |
| " | 6/7/17. | | No Stores. | |
| " | 7/7/17. | | Truck No 144666 - 6 tons - general stores. | |
| " | 8/7/17. | | Moved 154 Infantry Brigade to XVIII Corps Troops. | |
| " | 9/7/17. | | No Stores received. 152 Infantry Bde moved from XVIII Corps Troops to 51st Division. D.A.D.O.S. returned from leave. Lorry left for Divisional Artillery and 154 Infantry Bde. S/Condr Ellis & personnel left to administer 154 Infantry Bde. | |
| " | 10/7/17 | | Truck 200361 - 5 tons - general stores. | |
| " | 11/7/17. | | Lorry to XVIII Corps Troops, with stores for 154 Infantry Brigade. | |

A5834 Wt. W4973 M687 750,000 8/16 D. D. & L. Ltd. Forms/C.2118/13.

Army Form C. 2118.

# WAR DIARY
*or*
## ~~INTELLIGENCE~~ SUMMARY.
*(Erase heading not required.)*

*Instructions regarding War Diaries and Intelligence Summaries are contained in F. S. Regs., Part II. and the Staff Manual respectively. Title pages will be prepared in manuscript.

| Place | Date | Hour | Summary of Events and Information | Remarks and references to Appendices |
|---|---|---|---|---|
| LEDERZEELE | 12/7/17 | | 51st Divisional Artillery moved from 39th Division to 51st Division. 154 Infantry Bde moved from XVIII Corps Troops to 51st Division. Truck 9746 - 4 tons - general stores. Received Vickers Gun for 152 Machine Gun Co. Conference at 153 Brigade Headquarters attended by Staff Captain, Battalion Quartermasters and Trench Mortar Batty + M.G.Co. QM Ss. | |
| " | 13/7/17 | | Conference with 152 Infantry Bde attended by Battalion Quartermasters, Trench Mortar Btty + M.G.Co. Q.M.Ss. Dump and Office moved from Lederzeele to Sheet 27 F27 B.8.8. POPERINGHE - PROVEN Road. Truck 6920 - 3 KT bodies received for 1/6 Seaforth Highlanders. Received 18-pdr for C/256 Bde R.F.A. | |
| SHEET 27 F27 B.8.8 | 14/7/17 | | 201070 - 6 tons - general stores. 2 Lorries to Back area with stores for 152 + 153 Infantry Brigades. | |
| " | 15/7/17 | | Received 200 Petrol tin carriers for water and issued 60 to each Infantry Brigade and 20 to Divisional Machine Gun Officer. | |
| " | 16/7/17 | | Received for B/256 Brigade, R.F.A. 2 - 18 pdrs. For A/256 Brigade R.F.A. 1 - 18 pdr. Truck 69208 and 35316 - 5 tons - general stores. | |
| " | 17/7/17 | | Truck 5077 - 6 tons - general stores. 3 Lorries to Back area with stores for 152 and 153 Infantry Bdes. Received 50 sets Packsaddlery. S/Cond^r Carolan broke leg cycling + was evacuated to Base. | |
| " | 18/7/17 | | Received Vickers gun for 154 Machine Gun Co. Truck 42942 - one G.S. fore for 1/4 Gordons and wheels. Lorry to back area with stores for 152 and 153 Infantry Bdes. Received 100 additional petrol tin carriers. | |
| " | 19/7/17 | | Truck 24366 - 8 tons - general stores. | |
| " | 20/7/17 | | Received 1 Vickers Gun for 154 M.G.Co. Truck 1136 - 1 cart water tank for 2/1st (H) Field Ambulance | |
| " | 21/7/17 | | Truck 22782 - 5 tons - general stores. Truck 58489 - 20,400 Extensions for Box Respirators. Received 4 watercarts - 1/7 A & S. Hdrs - 1 — 1/5 Gordon Hdrs 1 — 1/5 Seaforth Hdrs 1, (from 39th Division) + 400th Field Co 1. (from XVIII Corps Troops. | |

A5834 Wt. W4973 M687 750,000 8/16 D. D. & L. Ltd. Forms/C.2118/13.

Instructions regarding War Diaries and Intelligence Summaries are contained in F. S. Regs., Part II. and the Staff Manual respectively. Title pages will be prepared in manuscript.

# WAR DIARY
*or*
# INTELLIGENCE SUMMARY.
*(Erase heading not required.)*

Army Form C. 2118.

| Place | Date | Hour | Summary of Events and Information | Remarks and references to Appendices |
|---|---|---|---|---|
| SHEET 27 F27 B.8.8 | 21/7/17 | (Cont'd) | Conference with 154 Infantry Bde. Staff Capt, Battalion Quartermaster, Inv. Bty + M.G. Co QMS's attended. Conference with A.D.O.S. XVIII Corps. | |
| " | 22/7/17 | | Truck 3262 – one wagon G.S. for Headquarters 51st D.A.C. Conference, QMS's of Batteries + Brigades R.F.A. attended. | |
| " | 23/7/17 | | Truck 165013 – 8 tons – general stores. Truck 1130 – 1 wagon G.S. – for 1/6 Gordons. Received watercarts for 1/2 (H) Field Ambulance and 1/6 Black Watch, one each. Received 150 special ammunition carriers M.G. belt and issued 40 each to 152 – 3 + 4 M.G. Coys + 30 to 232 M.G. Co. Representatives with 152 + 153 Bdes. returned from Back area to Depot. Received 8 Carts water tank as reserve. Issued 2 per Inf. Bde. | |
| " | 24/7/17 | | Truck 57516 – 5 tons – general stores. Truck 8575 – one cart maltese – for 1/ A.T.S. Hdrs. 60 Hot food containers drawn from XVIII Corps Troops and issued 30 to 152 Infantry Brigade and 30 to 153 Bde. Collected 800 Belts ammunition from Fifth Army Gun Park for distribution 200 to each division. Received 4 chaffcutters and issued to 51 D.A.C. | |
| " | 25/7/17 | | Truck No 313 1 cart water tank in repayment for 1 from XVIII Corps Troops. Received 50 additional Yukon packs + issued 20 each to 152 and 153 Infantry Bdes + 10 to 154 Bde. Recd. 2 water carts to complete reserve to 10. | |
| " | 26/7/17 | | Truck 24068 – 7 tons – general stores. | |
| " | 27/7/17 | | 25 Vickers barrels + mounting cups drawn from Corps reserve. Collected 288 18-pdr and 120 – 4.5" How ammunition carriers from Fifth Army Gun Park, also 576 – 18pdr and 240 – 4.5" How ammunition carriers for O.O. XVIII Corps Troops. | |
| " | 28/7/17 | | Trucks 7459 + 35899 – 8 tons – general stores. Truck 66967 – 79 Wheels. Received 1 Vickers gun for 232 Machine Gun Co. Received 2 pivot mountings anti-aircraft. Received new Electric torches signalling for intercommunication in trenches – 6 per Battalion. Conference with A.D.O.S. XVIII Corps. | |

A5834 Wt. W4973 M687 750,000 8/16 D. D. & L. Ltd. Forms/C.2118/13.

Army Form C. 2118.

Instructions regarding War Diaries and Intelligence Summaries are contained in F. S. Regs., Part II. and the Staff Manual respectively. Title pages will be prepared in manuscript.

# WAR DIARY
~~or~~
~~INTELLIGENCE SUMMARY.~~

(Erase heading not required.)

| Place | Date | Hour | Summary of Events and Information | Remarks and references to Appendices |
|---|---|---|---|---|
| Sheet 27. F27 B 8.8 | 29/7/17 | | QF 18pdr without B.M. issued to C/255 Bde. R.F.A. | |
| " | 30/7/17 | | Truck 4206 - 5 tons - general stores. D.A.D.O.S to Saint Omer to purchase watercans for burial spraying purposes. Carriage Field 18pdr with sights issued to A/256 Brigade, R.F.A. | |
| " | 31/7/17 | | Truck 47635 - 5 tons - general stores. Pistols Webley + lamps siege began to arrive. | |
| | | | GENERAL. | |
| | | | About 105 tons of stores were received from Base, excluding vehicles. The Division was refitted during the month. It came to light however that despite frequent questions, personal visits and letters, several units had neglected to complete their battle equipment. A notable case, which came to the notice of the Army Commander, was that of magnetic compasses. 114 were found to be deficient whereas only 16 were on indent. This, and the necessity for economy in bulk stores, such as clothing, were the main points discussed at conferences attended during the month by all Quartermasters QMS's (in the case of units without Quartermasters) and Staff Captains of Brigades. The new graphs, showing in contrast the expenditure, month by month, of each unit, in each of the main items, proved useful. All bulk issues were normal or less than normal except:- | |
| | | | GROUND SHEETS. 90% above. — SOAP YELLOW. 50% above | |
| | | | OIL LUBRICATING. 50% " — " SOFT. 12% " | |
| | | | MINERAL JELLY 100% " — FLANNELETTE. 70% " | |
| | | | SHOES HORSE & MULE. 35% above. | |
| | | | The amount spent in local purchases was 366 francs, the lowest on record: and this | |

A5834 Wt. W4973 M687 750,000 8/16 D. D. & L. Ltd. Forms/C.2118/13.

Instructions regarding War Diaries and Intelligence Summaries are contained in F. S. Regs., Part II. and the Staff Manual respectively. Title pages will be prepared in manuscript.

# WAR DIARY
*or*
# INTELLIGENCE SUMMARY.
*(Erase heading not required.)*

Army Form C. 2118.

| Place | Date | Hour | Summary of Events and Information | Remarks and references to Appendices |
|---|---|---|---|---|
| | | | 276 francs for cutch, bought under instructions from A.D.O.S. XVIII Corps, the greater part of which was handed to OO XVIII Corps Troops. | |
| | | | LORRIES. | |
| | | | The 4 lorries covered journeys aggregating to about 1040 miles empty and 1800 miles full carrying about 550 tons gross. | |
| | | | SALVAGE. | |
| | | | About 69 tons of unserviceable stores were returned by units through Refilling Points, sorted and sent to Base. There were still, however, large discrepancies between amounts of new stores issued to units and amounts returned which were brought to notice of Headquarters 'Q' 51st (H) Division. | |
| | | | WORK OF THE SHOPS. | |
| | | | 528 Rifles, 12 machine guns & 23 cycles were among the articles repaired. 2030 burial discs were made. In spare time manufacture was begun of a number of curry combs. These are not allowed but most units have bought them. They are always in demand. 113 pairs of boots were repaired. 12 red flags, 26 pairs puttees 17 armbands 127 medal ribbons for presentation were made up. | |
| | | | 2/9/17. | |
| | | | R Morrison<br>Capt.<br>D.A.D.O.S.<br>51st (H) Division | |

A5834 Wt. W4973 M687 750,000 8/16 D. D. & L. Ltd. Forms/C.2118/13.

Army Form C. 2118.

# WAR DIARY
*or*
# INTELLIGENCE SUMMARY.
*(Erase heading not required.)*

Instructions regarding War Diaries and Intelligence Summaries are contained in F. S. Regs., Part II. and the Staff Manual respectively. Title pages will be prepared in manuscript.

Vol 28

| Place | Date | Hour | Summary of Events and Information | Remarks and references to Appendices |
|---|---|---|---|---|
| | | | 51st (HIGHLAND) DIVISION.<br>D. A. D. O. S.<br>WAR DIARY<br>AUGUST 1917.<br>SECRET.<br>R. Holmson [signature]<br>Capt<br>D.A.D.O.S.<br>51 (H) DIVISION | |

A5834 Wt. W4973 M687 750,000 8/16 D. D. & L. Ltd. Forms/C.2118/13.

Instructions regarding War Diaries and Intelligence Summaries are contained in F. S. Regs., Part II. and the Staff Manual respectively. Title pages will be prepared in manuscript.

# WAR DIARY
*or*
# INTELLIGENCE SUMMARY.
*(Erase heading not required.)*

Army Form C. 2118.

| Place | Date | Hour | Summary of Events and Information | Remarks and references to Appendices |
|---|---|---|---|---|
| F 27 B.8.8. SHEET 27 | 1/8/17. | | Truck No 76618 with 1 limbered wagon 18-pdr for C/255 Bde R.F.A. | |
| " | 2/8/17. | | 2 Vickers guns received for 152 M.G.C. | |
| " | 3/8/17. | | Truck No 56179 - 6 tons - general stores. Lorry to Calais to collect socks and braziers urgently required owing to weather conditions. 40 Pistols received also wagon parts off old indents. Representatives visited Battalion Quartermasters to ascertain losses in recent operations. Bulk demand drawn up for Division. Carriage Field QF 18-pdr issued to C/256 Bde R.F.A. | |
| " | 4/8/17 | | Trucks 207 and 149286 - 7 tons - general stores. D.A.D.O.S. to Calais with two lorries to collect special clothing. 1 lorry borrowed at Calais and 3 lorry loads of stores sent to depot. 2 extra lorries borrowed from 51st Divisional Supply Column to help in getting stores to dumps and clearing 2 trucks from railhead. 3 Lewis guns received for 1/7 Gordon Highlanders. 6 Lewis guns received for 1/5 Gordon Highlanders. 8 Lewis guns received for 1/6 Black Watch. O.Q.F. 4.5" How. issued to D/256, R.F.A. Conference with A.D.O.S. XVIII Corps. | |
| " | 5/8/17 | | Truck No 80544 - 38 wheels. Truck No 27435, 1 wagon ammunition 18 pdr for B/256 Bde R.F.A. 3 Lewis guns issued to 51st Divl Advanced Training Camp for training purposes. | |
| " | 6/8/17 | | Received one 9.45 trench howitzer long range pattern. Truck No 6491, - 4 tons - general stores. Truck No 56158, 2 G.S. poles and 3 limbs for 1/9 The Royal Scots. | |

A5834 Wt. W4973 M687 750,000 8/16 D. D. & L. Ltd. Forms/C.2118/13.

Instructions regarding War Diaries and Intelligence Summaries are contained in F. S. Regs., Part II. and the Staff Manual respectively. Title pages will be prepared in manuscript.

# WAR DIARY
*or*
# INTELLIGENCE SUMMARY.
*(Erase heading not required.)*

Army Form C. 2118.

| Place | Date | Hour | Summary of Events and Information | Remarks and references to Appendices |
|---|---|---|---|---|
| F27 B.8.8. SHEET 27 | 7/8/17. | | 2 Lorries to Calais to collect urgent stores. Truck 55526 - 4 tons - general stores. 1 Lewis gun received for 1/9 The Royal Scots. | |
| " | 8/8/17. | | Carriage Field QF 18 pdr issued to B/255 Bde. R.F.A. | |
| " | 9/8/17 | | Truck No 64467 - 6 tons - general stores. Truck No 32598 - 1 K.T. body for 1/5 Seaforth Highlanders. Carriage Field 4.5 How issued to D/255 Bde R.F.A. | |
| " | 10/8/17 | | Lorry with stores to Back area for 154 Infantry Brigade and on to Calais to collect latrine buckets required by 152 Infantry Brigade. S/Condr Ellis A.O.C. left to administer 154 Infantry Brigade in Back area. | |
| " | 11/8/17 | | Trucks 164029 and 57149 - 11 tons. general stores. 8025 Cart Officer's mess for 1/5 Gordon Highlanders and cart water tank for 1/4 Gordon Highlanders. Lorry left for Back area with stores for 154 Infantry Brigade. Conference with A.D.O.S. XVIII Corps | |
| " | 12/8/17 | | Truck 39590 - 1 wagon limbered G.S. for 154 M.G.C. | |
| " | 13/8/17. | | Truck 15461 - 1 wagon G.S. for No 1 Section, D.A.C. Lorry to Calais to collect urgent stores. 1 Q.F. 18-pdr without B.M. issued to B/256 Bde R.F.A. | |
| " | 14/8/17 | | Truck 56795 - 1 bow piece pontoon for 404 Field Co. R.E. Truck 61142 - 6 tons - general stores. Lorry left for back area with stores for 154 Infantry Bde. | |

A5834 Wt. W4973 M687 750,000 8/16 D. D. & L. Ltd. Forms/C.2118/13.

Instructions regarding War Diaries and Intelligence Summaries are contained in F. S. Regs., Part II. and the Staff Manual respectively. Title pages will be prepared in manuscript.

# WAR DIARY
*or*
# INTELLIGENCE SUMMARY.
*(Erase heading not required.)*

Army Form C. 2118.

| Place | Date | Hour | Summary of Events and Information | Remarks and references to Appendices |
|---|---|---|---|---|
| F27 B8.S. Sheet 27 | 15/8/17 | | Truck 6169 - 74 bales clothing. OQF 18 pdr without B.M issued to B/256 Bde RFA. | |
| " | 16/8/17 | | Conference at 153rd Infantry Bde's Headquarters. Truck 41374 - 7 tons - general stores. Truck 63950 1 ton clothing. Truck 57734 - 1 cart Officers Mess each for 400 + 401 Field Companies RE. | |
| " | 17/8/17 | | D.A.D.O.S. to Calais and collected 1 lorry load urgent stores. | |
| " | 18/8/17 | | Truck No 11201 - Pontoon bipartite bow piece for 404 Field Co. RE, Trucks 59344 and 145820 - 11 tons general stores. Truck 472374 Cart Officers Mess for 404 Field Co RE. Conference with A.D.O.S. XVIII Corps. | |
| " | 19/8/17 | | D.A.D.O.S. to back area, visited 1/9 the Royal Scots, 1/7 A & S. Hdrs and H.Q. 154 Inf. Bde. Received truck No 43030 - 1 cart water tank for 1/7 A & S. Hdrs. Received truck 5210 - 114 boxes blank ammunition. | |
| " | 20/8/17 | | Truck 55148 - one cart water tank for A/255 Bde RFA. Lorry to back area with stores and returned with salvage. | |
| " | 21/8/17 | | Truck No 42775 - 6 tons - general stores, 4 Peerless lorries exchanged for 4 Albion lorries. | |
| " | 22/8/17 | | Lorry to back area with stores for 154 Infantry Bde. | |
| " | 23/8/17 | | Truck 165377 - 5 tons - general stores. Truck 51669 with 33 bicycles, 21 of which are to replace horses. Lorry to back area for salvage. | |

A5834 Wt. W4973 M687 750,000 08/16 D. D. & L. Ltd. Forms/C.2118/13.

Army Form C. 2118.

# WAR DIARY
*or*
# INTELLIGENCE SUMMARY.
*(Erase heading not required.)*

Instructions regarding War Diaries and Intelligence Summaries are contained in F. S. Regs., Part II. and the Staff Manual respectively. Title pages will be prepared in manuscript.

| Place | Date | Hour | Summary of Events and Information | Remarks and references to Appendices |
|---|---|---|---|---|
| F27 B.8.8, SHEET 27. | 24/8/17 | | Nothing to report. | |
| " | 25/8/17 | | Truck 147582 - 8 tons. general stores. Lorry to back area with stores for Divl Baths. Conference with A.D.O.S. XVIII Corps. | |
| " | 26/8/17 | | Truck 5561 - 1 KT body for 1/4 Gordon Highlanders, and 1 cart Maltese for 1/8 A.&S. Hdrs. Carriage Field 18 pdr No 35524 issued to A/256 Bde. R.F.A. | |
| " | 27/8/17 | | Truck 17062 - 4 tons. general stores and truck 1194 one wagon ammunition for A/256 Bde R.F.A. | |
| " | 28/8/17 | | Truck 163301 - 6 tons - general stores. Truck 132 with 936 trays ammunition. QF 18/pdr without B.M issued to A/255 Brigade R.F.A. | |
| " | 29/8/17 | | Truck 43375 1 K.T. body received for 1/4 Gordon Highlanders, 1 Lewis Gun issued to 1/8 The Royal Scots. | |
| " | 30/8/17 | | O.Q.F 18pdr No 6598 issued to A/255 Bde R.F.A. | |
| " | 31/8/17 | | Truck 90750 - 5 tons - general Stores, Railhead - PESELHOEK. | |

Instructions regarding War Diaries and Intelligence Summaries are contained in F. S. Regs., Part II. and the Staff Manual respectively. Title pages will be prepared in manuscript.

# WAR DIARY
*or*
# INTELLIGENCE SUMMARY.
*(Erase heading not required.)*

Army Form C. 2118.

| Place | Date | Hour | Summary of Events and Information | Remarks and references to Appendices |
|---|---|---|---|---|
| | | 39<br>17 | | |

GENERAL.

About 143 tons of stores were received from Base, excluding vehicles. Bulk issues of several items were abnormally heavy eg. jackets 20% above the average: trousers 200% above: pantaloons 20% above: Caps 10%: puttees 50% above: drawers 13% above: socks 56% above: bags nose 13% above, nets hay 20% above: grounds sheets 50% above and yellow Soap 75% above. The amount spent on local purchase was 51 francs, the lowest on record for the Division

Lorries.

The 4 lorries covered journeys aggregating to about 1541 miles empty & 2120 miles full, carrying about 511 tons gross.

Salvage

About 144 tons of unserviceable and other stores were returned by units through Refilling Points and sent to Base.

Work of the Shops.

670 rifles, 250 bayonets (cleaned), 18 machine guns ~~and~~ 26 bicycles and 170 Lewis

A5834 Wt. W4973/M687 750,000 8/16 D. D. & L. Ltd. Forms/C.2118/13.

Instructions regarding War Diaries and Intelligence Summaries are contained in F. S. Regs., Part II. and the Staff Manual respectively. Title pages will be prepared in manuscript.

# WAR DIARY
*or*
# INTELLIGENCE SUMMARY.
*(Erase heading not required.)*

Army Form C. 2118.

| Place | Date | Hour | Summary of Events and Information | Remarks and references to Appendices |
|---|---|---|---|---|
| | | | gun magazines were among the articles repaired. 103 pairs of boots were repaired, 354 pairs puttees made up and 66 military medal ribbons prepared for presentation during the month. | |
| | | | R.H. Johnson Capt. D.A.D.O.S. 51 (H) Division. | |
| | | | 3/9/17 | |

A5834 Wt. W4973 M687 750,000 8/16 D. D. & L. Ltd. Forms/C.2118/13.

Instructions regarding War Diaries and Intelligence Summaries are contained in F. S. Regs., Part II. and the Staff Manual respectively. Title pages will be prepared in manuscript.

# WAR DIARY
*or*
# INTELLIGENCE SUMMARY.
*(Erase heading not required.)*

Army Form C. 2118.

Vol 29

| Place | Date | Hour | Summary of Events and Information | Remarks and references to Appendices |
|---|---|---|---|---|
| | | | 51st (HIGHLAND) DIVISION.<br>D. A. D. O. S.<br>— WAR DIARY —<br>SEPTEMBER 1917.<br>SECRET.<br>[signature]<br>Capt.<br>D.A.D.O.S.<br>51st (H) Division | |

A5834 Wt. W4973 M687 750,000 8/16 D. D. & L. Ltd. Forms/C.2118/13.

Instructions regarding War Diaries and Intelligence Summaries are contained in F. S. Regs., Part II. and the Staff Manual respectively. Title pages will be prepared in manuscript.

# WAR DIARY
*or*
# INTELLIGENCE SUMMARY.
*(Erase heading not required.)*

Army Form C. 2118.

| Place | Date | Hour | Summary of Events and Information | Remarks and references to Appendices |
|---|---|---|---|---|
| SHEET 27 F27 B 8.5. | 1/9/17. | | Received truck No 56689 – 7 tons – general stores and truck 37770 – 70 bales clothing | |
| " | 2/9/17. | | Nothing to report. | |
| " | 3/9/17. | | Received truck No 7442 – 5 tons – general stores. Carriage Field QF 18 pdr No 14911 issued to B/256 Bde RFA through Fifth Army Gun Park. DADOS. to Calais, Base. | |
| " | 4/9/17. | | Received 53262 – 1 cart water tank for 154 Machine Gun Co. D.A.D.O.S. to Calais for urgent stores. 1 Lorry load stores received from Calais. Truck 72029 – 4 tons – general stores. Received 5 water Carts for reserve from 11th Division, through 51st Divl Train. | |
| " | 5/9/17. | | Truck 91979 – 1 wagon G.S. for Divl Signal Co also 12 wheels. O.QF 18-pdr No 2259 and Carriage Field QF-18 pdr No 6413 issued through Gun Park to A/255 Bde, RFA. O.QF 18 pdr No 4726 and carriage Field 18 pdr No 33357 issued through Gun Park to C/255 Bde, RFA. | |
| " | 6/9/17 | | Manufacture begun of carriers, rifle grenades (51 (H) D pattern) wood parts in depot, canvas parts in Divisional laundry | |
| " | 7/9/17 | | Truck No 23959 – 6 tons – general stores. | |
| " | 8/9/17. | | Drew A.D.O.S. attention to return of stretchers with handles sawn off, presumably to fit in lorries. | |
| " | 9/9/17. | | Truck No 21731 – 5 tons. general stores. Lorry load of stores to WATTEN for 51st Divl Baths. D.A.D.O.S. to WATTEN re Grenade Carriers | |

A5834 Wt. W4973 M687 750,000 8/16 D. D. & L. Ltd. Forms/C.2118/13.

Instructions regarding War Diaries and Intelligence Summaries are contained in F. S. Regs., Part II. and the Staff Manual respectively. Title pages will be prepared in manuscript.

# WAR DIARY
*or*
# INTELLIGENCE SUMMARY.
*(Erase heading not required.)*

Army Form C. 2118.

| Place | Date | Hour | Summary of Events and Information | Remarks and references to Appendices |
|---|---|---|---|---|
| SHEET 27 F27 B 8. 8. | 10/9/17 | | Issued paint to all units, with pattern helmets, for 51 (H) D pattern, roughened Khaki colouring. | |
| " | 11/9/17. | | DADOS. to Watten re Grenade Carriers. | |
| " | 12/9/17 | | Truck No 86965 - 6 tons - general stores. | |
| " | 13/9/17 | | Nothing to report. | |
| " | 14/9/17 | | Truck No 57911 - 5 tons - general stores, 48391 - 1 Kitchen travelling complete for 1/6 Gordon Highlanders and 5098 - 1 cart officer's mess for A/256 Brigade R.F.A. Carriage field QF 4.5" howitzer No 2121 issued to D/255 Bde R.F.A. | |
| " | 15/9/17 | | Painted 64 T.S. lamps with slit, in lieu of siege lamps, owing to shortage of the latter. | |
| " | 16/9/17 | | Truck 47596 - 5 tons - general stores. Lorry to WATTEN to collect skeleton grenade carriers for making up in shops. | |
| " | 17/9/17 | | 2 short and 1 long range pattern 9.45 trench howitzers received from 51/V Trench Mortar Battery for transmission to Calais. | |
| " | 18/9/17 | | 1 new long range pattern 9.45 trench howitzer received for 51/V Trench Mortar Batty. O.QF 18-pdr No 4102 issued through Gun Park to C/255 Bde R.F.A. and O.QF 18pdr No 6615 to C/255 Bde R.F.A | |
| " | 19/9/17 | | Truck No 144706 - 6 tons - general stores. Units circularized re indents for winter clothing. Notification received of arrival of first draft minus ground sheets. | |

A5834 Wt. W4973 M687 750,000 8/16 D. D. & L. Ltd. Forms/C.2118/13.

Instructions regarding War Diaries and Intelligence Summaries are contained in F. S. Regs., Part II. and the Staff Manual respectively. Title pages will be prepared in manuscript.

# WAR DIARY
*or*
# INTELLIGENCE SUMMARY.
*(Erase heading not required.)*

Army Form C. 2118.

| Place | Date | Hour | Summary of Events and Information | Remarks and references to Appendices |
|---|---|---|---|---|
| Sheet 27. F27 B 8 9 | 20/9/17 | | Received 2 Vickers guns for 153 Machine Gun Company from Gun Park. O.Q.F 18 pdr No 6390 issued to C/256 Bde through Gun Park. | |
| " | 21/9/17 | | 3" Stokes trench mortar issued to 153 Trench Mortar Battery. Truck No 64972 - 6 tons - general stores. First indent received for American officer (attached 1/2 (H) Field Ambulance). | |
| " | 22/9/17 | | Truck 60627 - 27 bales blankets. 47574 - 1 wagon limbered for 1/6 Seaforth Highlanders and 1 wagon pontoon for 401 Field Co R.E. Carriage field QF 18-pdr issued through Gun Park to B/255 Bde. R.F.A. + Carriage field QF 18 pdr to C/256 Bde R.F.A. | |
| " | 23/9/17 | | Truck 6248 - 7 tons - general stores and 20215 20 bales blankets. Received 2 - 3" Stokes Mortars for 154 Trench Mortar Battery, 5 Lewis guns 1/4 Seaforth Hdrs 4 Lewis guns for 1/7 A & S Hdrs and 4 Vickers guns for 154 Machine Gun Co. Sent patterns of units distinguishing marks to A.D.O.S. XVIII Corps for ~~British~~ National War Museum. | |
| " | 24/9/17 | | Received 1 Vickers gun for 154 Machine Gun Co, 4 Lewis guns for 1/4 Gordon Hdrs and 3 Lewis guns for 1/9 the Royal Scots. O.Q.F. 18-pdr No 6757 issued through Gun Park to C/255 Bde R.F.A. Also OQF 18 pdr No 4957 to B/256 Bde R.F.A. and No 6574 to A/255 Bde R.F.A. Moved 51st Divisional Artillery to 11th Division and despatched personnel (2 clerks, 1 storeman). Suspended issues leaving Calais 26-29th. Notified Havre and Rouen could accept stores leaving 29th. Cancelled indents from Fifth Army Gun Park. | |

Instructions regarding War Diaries and Intelligence Summaries are contained in F. S. Regs., Part II. and the Staff Manual respectively. Title pages will be prepared in manuscript.

# WAR DIARY
*or*
# INTELLIGENCE SUMMARY.
*(Erase heading not required.)*

Army Form C. 2118.

| Place | Date | Hour | Summary of Events and Information | Remarks and references to Appendices |
|---|---|---|---|---|
| SHEET 27 F27 B 8.8 | 25/9/17 | | Nothing to report. | |
| " | 26/9/17 | | Truck No 40853 - 6 tons - general stores Armourers Shop and personnel and anti-gas reserve left by train to new area. | |
| " | 27/9/17 | | Nothing to report. | |
| " | 28/9/17 | | Dump and office moved to Achiet le Petit by road. Bases now Havre & Rouen & Calais. Transferred tridents to Third Army Gun Park. | |
| ACHIET LE PETIT. | 29/9/17 | | Visited A.D.O.S. VI Corps and inspected new dump. Recalled personnel with 51st Divl Artillery. | |
| " | 30/9/17 | | Received two Vickers guns for 152 Machine Gun Company, 1 Lewis gun for 1/5 Seaforth Highlanders and 2 Lewis guns for 1/8 A & S. Hdrs. | |
| | | | GENERAL. | |
| | | | About 79 tons of stores were received from Base during the month, excluding Vehicles. A shortage of compasses prismatic was experienced. | |
| | | | WORK OF THE SHOPS. | |
| | | | Armourers. | |
| | | | 285 rifles, 8 Lewis guns, 6 Vickers guns, 115 Lewis gun magazines, 1 Pistol and 31 Bicycles were overhauled during the month. 150 ammunition carriers and 780 rifle grenade carriers were made | |

Instructions regarding War Diaries and Intelligence Summaries are contained in F. S. Regs., Part II. and the Staff Manual respectively. Title pages will be prepared in manuscript.

# WAR DIARY
*or*
# INTELLIGENCE SUMMARY.
*(Erase heading not required.)*

Army Form C. 2118.

| Place | Date | Hour | Summary of Events and Information | Remarks and references to Appendices |
|---|---|---|---|---|
| | | | Shoemakers. | |
| | | | 79 pairs of boots were repaired | |
| | | | Tailors. | |
| | | | 34 nosebags were repaired, 86 pairs of puttees were cleaned and repaired. 31 red flags were made and 35 military medal ribbons made up for distribution. | |
| | | | LORRIES. | |
| | | | The 4 lorries covered journeys aggregating 1230 miles empty and 1664 miles full carrying 394 tons gross. | |
| | | | SALVAGE. | |
| | | | 102 tons of unserviceable stores were returned to Base during the month. | |
| | | | 3/10/17. | |
| | | | R. H. Murray [signature] Capt. D.A.D.O.S. 51 (H) Division | |

A5834 Wt. W4973 M687 750,000 8/16 D. D. & L. Ltd. Forms/C.2118/13.

Instructions regarding War Diaries and Intelligence Summaries are contained in F. S. Regs., Part II. and the Staff Manual respectively. Title pages will be prepared in manuscript.

# WAR DIARY
*or*
# INTELLIGENCE SUMMARY.
*(Erase heading not required.)*



Army Form C. 2118.

Vol 30

| Place | Date | Hour | Summary of Events and Information | Remarks and references to Appendices |
|---|---|---|---|---|

51st (HIGHLAND) DIVISION.

D. A. D. O. S.

WAR DIARY.

— OCTOBER 1917. —

SECRET.

[signature]
Capt
D.A.D.O.S.
51(H) DIVISION.

A5834 Wt. W4973 M687 750,000 8/16 D. D. & L. Ltd. Forms/C.2118/13.

Army Form C. 2118.

Instructions regarding War Diaries and Intelligence Summaries are contained in F. S. Regs., Part II. and the Staff Manual respectively. Title pages will be prepared in manuscript.

# WAR DIARY
*or*
# INTELLIGENCE SUMMARY.

*(Erase heading not required.)*

| Place | Date | Hour | Summary of Events and Information | Remarks and references to Appendices |
|---|---|---|---|---|
| Achiet le Petit. | 1/10/17 | | DADOS visited new Railhead (Achiet le Grand). | |
| " | 2/10/17 | | Nothing to report. | |
| " | 3/10/17 | | Received Vickers' gun for 153 Machine Gun Company through Third Army Gun Park. Received truck No 42040 – 9 tons – clothing. Infantry Battalions, Trench Mortar Batteries and Machine Gun Companies circularized as to equipment in possession. | |
| " | 4/10/17 | | Nothing to report. | |
| " | 5/10/17 | | Moved Office and dump to BOISLEUX-AU-MONT. Truck 130328 – 6 tons – 20 wheels, 6 cycles, dubbin &c. Found no accommodation. Engaged in erecting Billets and Offices. | |
| SHEET 51 B. 52 D. 8.4. | 6/10/17 | | Received truck 150104 – 6 tons – clothing. Building billets and offices. Moved VII Corps troops units from 50th Division to 51st Division. | |
| " | 7/10/17. | | Received truck No 51676 – mess cart for 1/4 Gordons and wagon limbered G.S. fore for 1/4 Gordon Highlanders. Moved HQ. Jo M Sections, No 3 Special Coy R.E. 181 Tunnelling Coy. R.E. HQ. 23 A.F.A. Bde, 108 Batty, A. Batty 23rd A.F.A Bde and 23rd A.F.A Brigade ammn Column from 50th Divn to 51st Divn. Moved 107 Batty 23rd A.F.A Bde from 62nd Divn to 51st Divn. | |

A5834 Wt. W4973 M687 750,000 8/16 D. D. & L. Ltd. Forms/C.2118/13.

Instructions regarding War Diaries and Intelligence Summaries are contained in F. S. Regs., Part II. and the Staff Manual respectively. Title pages will be prepared in manuscript.

Army Form C. 2118.

# WAR DIARY
*or*
# INTELLIGENCE SUMMARY.
*(Erase heading not required.)*

| Place | Date | Hour | Summary of Events and Information | Remarks and references to Appendices |
|---|---|---|---|---|
| SHEET 51B S2 D8.4. | 8/10/17 | | Received cart water tank for 232nd A.F.A Bde Ammn Col. D.A.D.O.S. to AMIENS for local purchases. | |
| " | 9/10/17 | | Truck 132294 - 1211 horserugs & 24044 - 1200 horserugs. Truck No 43404 - 7 tons - clothing. Lieut H.R. Webb. A.O.D arrived for training. | |
| " | 10/10/17 | | Received trucks 85943 & 137792 - 14 tons - clothing and 1303 pairs gum boots. Truck 8011 - 669 pairs gum boots. | |
| " | 11/10/17 | | Received truck of 1769 blankets. | |
| " | 12/10/17 | | Truck 969 - 5 tons timber, horseshoes and respirators. | |
| " | 13/10/17 | | Truck 8756 - 7 tons - clothing & 20222 - 7 tons - clothing. | |
| " | 14/10/17 | | Nothing to report. | |
| " | 15/10/17 | | Truck No 131647 - 8 tons - 11 bicycles, helmets tube, general stores and blankets. Truck 1452 - 400 braziers. D.A.D.O.S. to A.D.O.S. conference. Confirmed move of 293 A.F.A Bde from 24th Division to this Division. | |
| " | 17/10/17 | | Received 1250 blankets. | |
| " | 18/10/17 | | Lieut W.B. Bannerman A.O.D arrived in relief of Capt R.F. Johnson A.O.D. | |
| " | 19/10/17 | | Truck 27341. 9 tons - Soap & horseshoes. | |

A5834 Wt. W4973 M687 750,000 8/16 D. D. & L. Ltd. Forms/C.2118/13.

Instructions regarding War Diaries and Intelligence Summaries are contained in F. S. Regs., Part II. and the Staff Manual respectively. Title pages will be prepared in manuscript.

# WAR DIARY
*or*
# INTELLIGENCE SUMMARY.
*(Erase heading not required.)*

Army Form C. 2118.

| Place | Date | Hour | Summary of Events and Information | Remarks and references to Appendices |
|---|---|---|---|---|
| SHEET 51B 52 D.8.4. | 20/10/17 | | Capt R.J. Johnson A.O.D left for H.Q. Third Army. Received Trucks 51991, 206175 and 42565 - 22 tons - clothing. Trucks 23384, - 2500 blankets, 41310, - 2900 blankets, 24044 - 2500 blankets, 35967 2050 blankets 139149 - 2500 blankets, 57561 - 3350 blankets, 58781 - 2400 blankets, 26900 - 2400 blankets 2590 - 2330 blankets. | |
| " | 21/10/17 | | 1348 blankets received. 139863 - 14 tons - clothing. Received 2 OQF 18pdrs Nos 7124 and 6759 for 293 A.F.A Brigade. 4 OQF 18pdrs for 23 A.F.A Bde Nos 6778, 6753, 6656 and 8048. Confirmed move of 51st Divisional Artillery from 18th Division to 51st Division. | |
| " | 22/10/17 | | DADOS to AMIENS for local purchases. Received truck 32033 with 1 Kitchen body for 1/7 A&S Hdrs Truck 168 - 8 tons horseshoes and general stores. Moved 23 A.F.A Bde to XVIII Corps Troops. | |
| " | 23/10/17 | | Received trucks 7792 and 23762 - 17 tons - clothing, 22820, 6829 + 59184 - 25 tons clothing and 39272 - 8 tons - pillow cases latrine buckets &c. 2" T.M. issued to Z/51 Trench Mortar Batty. | |
| " | 24/10/17 | | Truck 228648 - 9 tons - clothing. | |
| " | 25/10/17 | | Confirmed move of 77 A.F.A Bde from XVIII Corps Troops to 51st Division. | |
| " | 26/10/17 | | Truck 4855 - 7 tons - 11 wheels, horseshoes and soap. 59214 with 433 cases N.C. containers. 36425 - 3 tons - general stores. Collected 4 - 6in T.M's from IV Corps Troops. Stopped issues to this Division by code wire to bases. | |

A5834 Wt. W4973 M687 750,000 8/16 D. D. & L. Ltd. Forms/C.2118/13.

Instructions regarding War Diaries and Intelligence Summaries are contained in F. S. Regs., Part II. and the Staff Manual respectively. Title pages will be prepared in manuscript.

# WAR DIARY
*or*
# INTELLIGENCE SUMMARY.
*(Erase heading not required.)*

Army Form C. 2118.

| Place | Date | Hour | Summary of Events and Information | Remarks and references to Appendices |
|---|---|---|---|---|
| SHEET 51B 52 D8.4 | 27/10/17 | | Truck 7497 - 7 tons - Clothing. Confirmed move of 62nd Divl Artillery to 51st Divn, QQF 18pdr Carriage No 2/33121 issued to B/255 Bde RFA. Vicker's gun issued to 153 Machine Gun Coy | |
| " | 28/10/17 | | 4 - 6 in trench mortars received from XVII Corps Troops. | |
| " | 29/10/17 | | Issued 8 - 6 in trench mortars to 62nd D.A.C. Railhead changed to AGNEZ. LES DUISANS. | |
| " | 30/10/17 | | Moved 293 A.F.A. Brigade to XIX Corps Troops. Received Vicker's gun for 232nd Machine Gun Coy. Moved HQ 51st Divl RE's 400 and 401 Field Coys to 36th Divn. | |
| " | 31/10/17 | | 51st Divl Arty moved to 34th Divn. Moved VII Corps Troops units to 34th Divn. | |
| | | | GENERAL. | |
| | | | About 243 tons of stores were received from Base during the month, excluding vehicles. | |
| | | | Work of the Shops. | |
| | | | Armourers. | |
| | | | 469 Rifles, 175 Bayonets and Scabbards, 3 Vicker's guns, 5 Lewis guns, 24 bicycles 6 Pistols and 1012 Lewis gun magazines were overhauled in the shops during the month. | |

A5834 Wt. W4973 M687 750,000 8/16 D. D. & L. Ltd. Forms/C.2118/13.

Instructions regarding War Diaries and Intelligence Summaries are contained in F. S. Regs., Part II. and the Staff Manual respectively. Title pages will be prepared in manuscript.

# WAR DIARY
*or*
# INTELLIGENCE SUMMARY.
*(Erase heading not required.)*

Army Form C. 2118.

| Place | Date | Hour | Summary of Events and Information | Remarks and references to Appendices |
|---|---|---|---|---|
| | | | Shoemakers. 56 pairs of boots were repaired during the month. | |
| | | | Lorries. The 4 lorries covered journeys aggregating 1371 miles empty and 1723 miles full carrying 635 tons gross. | |
| | | | Salvage. 80 tons of unserviceable clothing were returned to the Base during the month. | |
| | | | Winter clothing. During the month the issue of second blanket per man, Boots F.S. Waistcoats cardigan, Drawers, Vests, Cap covers, Gloves worsted, Overalls for night patrols, and Soles [illegible] for ankle boots was completed. The issue of leather jerkins or undercoats fur to Infantry Battalions and Pioneers was completed. | |
| | | | 5/11/17. [illegible] Capt DADOS 51(H) Division | |

A5834 Wt. W4973 M687 750,000 8/16 D. D. & L. Ltd. Forms/C.2118/13.

51

Vol 31

Confidential

War Diary

of

D. A. D. O. S.

51st (Highland) Division

From 1st to 30th November, 1917.

Secret

57th Highland Division

Instructions regarding War Diaries and Intelligence Summaries are contained in F. S. Regs., Part II. and the Staff Manual respectively. Title Pages will be prepared in manuscript.

# WAR DIARY
*or*
# INTELLIGENCE SUMMARY
*(Erase heading not required.)*

D.A.D.O.S.

November 1917

Army Form C. 2118.

(1)

| Place | Date | Hour | Summary of Events and Information | Remarks and references to Appendices |
|---|---|---|---|---|
| Boisleux | 1 | | Arrangements made for move to Hermaville. | |
| Hermaville | 2 | | Dump and office opened at Hermaville. The following moves of units were made 77 A.F.A. Brigade to 16 Div: 62nd Div Arty to 34 Div to which were also transferred; - 60 Aux Steam Coy, 27 Reserve Park, 3 Special Coy R.E., 20 & 43 C.C.S. 38 & 71 San. Section, 45 & 62 Labour Groups, 11, 125, 183 & 190 Labour Coys 37 & 38 Naval Labour Corps, 181 Tunnelling Coy R.E., 3rd M.A.C., 255 & 256 Bde R.F.A. 57 D.A.C. & No 1 Coy Train, 57 X, Y, Z, T.M. Btys. | |
| " | 3 | | Dump & office squared up – Routine work | |
| " | 4 | | 293 A.F.A. Brigade moved to XIX Corps Trucks. Truck 22865, 6 tons Horseshoes & General Stores – R'head Agny Le Duizans. | |
| " | 5 | | Truck 26296, 5 tons equipment, dubbin. Received 1000 Cutters wire S.A. No 1 and issued 500 each to 152 & 153 Infty Brigades. | |
| " | 6 | | Truck 55150 – 9 tons clothing | |
| " | 7 | | " 40761 – 5 tons Box Resp – dubbin, horseshoes | |
| " | 8 | | Routine work – visited Corps | |
| " | 9 | | Truck 91729 ~~[illegible]~~ – 7 tons clothing, 255 & 256 Bdes, 57 DAC 57/X Y V Z T.M's & 1 Coy train moved from 34 Div to 57 Div. | |
| " | 10 | | 57338 5 Tons Clothing | |
| " | 12 | | 16757 6 tons Resp. horse, Tube Helmets & Gas Stores 7224 - 19.S Waggon for 153 HQ | |
| " | 13 | | 26234 1 Cart water tank for 1/3 Field Amb | |
| " | 14 | | 64003 5 Tons Clothing | |
| " | 15 | | 86775 400 Braziers | |
| " | 16 | | 1536 4 tons Soap, Nosebags etc. 33307 1 Cart Resv B/255 - 19263 1 Q.F. 4.5 How | |

2449 Wt. W14957/M90 750,000 1/16 J.B.C. & A. Forms/C.2118/12.

Instructions regarding War Diaries and Intelligence Summaries are contained in F. S. Regs., Part II. and the Staff Manual respectively. Title Pages will be prepared in manuscript.

# WAR DIARY
*or*
# INTELLIGENCE SUMMARY
*(Erase heading not required.)*

Army Form C. 2118.

| Place | Date | Hour | Summary of Events and Information | Remarks and references to Appendices |
|---|---|---|---|---|
| LECHELLE | 17 | | Moved office & dump to Lechelle. T.M. Battery Camp | |
| " | 18 | | 210816 – 7 tons – wheels, horseshoes, 91598 – 7 tons clothing 71 6 tons H'shoes etc | |
| " | 19 | | Office & dump moved to 6 Can. Ry Troops Lechelle | |
| " | 20 | | 216420, 407452 :– 14 tons clothing – 1600 tins water – Moved 1/8 Royal Scots 400 secs Field Coys from 36 to 57 Div. | |
| " | 22 | | 48915 – 5 – 18 pr pieces 8450 – 4 tons [illegible] bags & dubbin | |
| " | 24 | | Move office & dump from Lechelle to Baisieux. | |
| BAISIEUX | 26 | | 63320 – 5 tons clothing | |
| | 27<br>28<br>29 | | Routine work: visited units | |
| | 30 | | 63804 83259 – 16 tons clothing – 44290 1 Limber Cart for D/255 | |
| | | | General<br>126 tons of stores received and issued 123 tons Salvage returned. | |
| | | | Shops 88 pairs boots repaired – Tailor – 20 pairs puttees, 370 flags made, 100 Armlets, 7 Medal ribbons, 4 Jackets repaired, 2 pairs pantaloons<br>Armourers:– Rifles 237, M. Guns, 23, Lewis Magazine 520, Bicycles 36, 300 Wire rods for Burial Discs, Bayonets 160<br>During the month the Armourer Staff Sergts inspected & overhauled all M'Guns & rifles etc of their Battalions 152, 153, 154 & 232 M.G. Coy. | |
| | | | [illegible] Capt. [illegible] | |

2449 Wt. W14957/M90 750,000 1/16 J.B.C. & A. Forms/C.2118/12.

Confidential
No. 21/A.
Highland Division.

The Officer i/c.
A.G.'s Office
at the Base.

---

In continuation of this office No. as above, dated 15th instant, the War Diary of D.A.D.O.S., 51st (Highland) Division, for December, 1917, is forwarded herewith.

[signature] Lt
for Brigadier-General,
Commanding
51st (Highland) Division.

18th January, 1918.

Army Form C. 2118. 51

Instructions regarding War Diaries and Intelligence Summaries are contained in F. S. Regs., Part II. and the Staff Manual respectively. Title Pages will be prepared in manuscript.

# WAR DIARY
*or*
# INTELLIGENCE SUMMARY

*(Erase heading not required.)*

Vol 32

| Place | Date | Hour | Summary of Events and Information | Remarks and references to Appendices |
|---|---|---|---|---|
| | | | SECRET | |
| | | | War Diary | |
| | | | D. A. D. O. S. | |
| | | | 57th H.D. | |
| | | | December 1917. | |

2449 Wt. W14957/M90 750,000 1/16 J.B.C. & A. Forms/C.2118/12.

Instructions regarding War Diaries and Intelligence Summaries are contained in F. S. Regs., Part II. and the Staff Manual respectively. Title Pages will be prepared in manuscript.

# WAR DIARY
*or*
# INTELLIGENCE SUMMARY
*(Erase heading not required.)*

Army Form C. 2118.

| Place | Date | Hour | Summary of Events and Information | Remarks and references to Appendices |
|---|---|---|---|---|
| Baizieux | 1 | – | Moved Office and Dump to Bapaume | |
| Bapaume | 2 | – | Visited Fremicourt, to take over from 58th; dump & office. | |
| Fremicourt | 3 | – | Moved Office and Dump to Fremicourt. | |
| ″ | 4 | – | Routine work. | |
| ″ | 5 | – | 100 Tents received from Corps | |
| ″ | 6 | – | Routine work. Visited Casualty Clearing Stations for Revolvers, Binoculars etc. | |
| ″ | 7 | – | 16 Tons clothing received Trucks 57254, 6894 | |
| ″ | 8 | – | 57121 – 8 tons nosebags & general stores, 159 lbs. 6 tons Horseshoes etc, 265227 6 tons Chaff-cutting machines & general stores. | |
| ″ | 9 | – | Routine work – Visited Railhead. | |
| ″ | 10 | – | 25210 5 tons – Wheels, limbers & general stores, 41011 – G.S. wagons, Limbers – 33422 G.S. wagon, Water Cart, & Mess Cart, 53761 Limber wagons, 90241 – Kitchen Mess Cart, RE Limber wagon. | |
| ″ | 11 | – | 5789 – 6 tons Clothing – Visited Salvage Dumps. | |
| ″ | 12 | – | 91602 – 6 tons clothing – | |
| ″ | 13 | – | Visited 5th A.F.A. Brigade to inspect & report on guns & stores. 256 – 8 tons wheels, horse-shoes – 279 – 208 wagons, nosebags – 18525 G.S. wagon. | |
| ″ | 14 | – | 4063 – 8 tons Clothing 19444, watercart & Mess Cart – Moved 56th Div Artillery | |
| ″ | 15 | – | Routine work | |
| ″ | 16 | – | | |
| ″ | 17 | – | 76 4 tons – Cycles, Tube Helmets, Blankets, 17081 – Ponton wagon | |
| ″ | 18 | – | 23144 – 4 tons Clothing. | |

2449 Wt. W14957/M90 750,000 1/16 J.B.C. & A. Forms/C.2118/12.

Instructions regarding War Diaries and Intelligence Summaries are contained in F. S. Regs., Part II. and the Staff Manual respectively. Title Pages will be prepared in manuscript.

# WAR DIARY
or
# INTELLIGENCE SUMMARY
*(Erase heading not required.)*

Army Form C. 2118.

| Place | Date | Hour | Summary of Events and Information | Remarks and references to Appendices |
|---|---|---|---|---|
| Fremicourt | 19 | – | 147433 – 8 tons Nosebags – Steel Helmets & General Stores. | |
| " | 20 | – | 60343 – 5 tons – Dubbin, Detail Stores. | |
| | | | 11478 – Mess Carts & Limber G.S. | |
| " | 21 | – | 92995 – 7 tons clothing. Visited Refilling point & C.C.S. | |
| " | 22 | – | 62756 – 10 tons Horseshoes. | |
| " | 23 | – | 10 sets Tent Boards received from Corps. | |
| " | 24 | – | Routine work. | |
| " | 25 | – | 68375. 2 Limbers & Wagons – 50832, 8 tons clothing. | |
| " | 26 | – | Routine work. | |
| | 27 | | | |
| " | 28 | – | 165216 – 5 tons Clothing. | |
| | 29 | – | Routine work. | |
| " | 30 | | 3267 – 6 tons Clothing. | |
| " | 31 | | Routine work. | |
| | | | General. The issue of Jerkins leather for the whole division was completed. Demands were very well met by the Base during a period of stress of active operations. Armourers Shop repaired 197 Rifles, 12 Lewis Guns, 3 Vickers, 35 Cycles, 27 Bayonets & Scabbards, 498 Magazines Lewis Gun. Bootmaker repaired 165 pair boots. Lorry Mileage 1288 Loaded, 1262, Empty. 60 Revolvers collected from C.C.S. | |
| | | | [illegible] Capt. DADOS | |

2449 Wt. W14957/M90 750,000 1/16 J.B.C. & A. Forms/C.2118/12.

Instructions regarding War Diaries and Intelligence Summaries are contained in F. S. Regs., Part II. and the Staff Manual respectively. Title Pages will be prepared in manuscript.

# WAR DIARY
*or*
# INTELLIGENCE SUMMARY
*(Erase heading not required.)*

Army Form C. 2118.

Vol 323

| Place | Date | Hour | Summary of Events and Information | Remarks and references to Appendices |
|---|---|---|---|---|
| | | | Secret. | |
| | | | D.A.D.O.S. | |
| | | | 51 (H) Division | |
| | | | January 1918. | |

2449 Wt. W14957/M90 750,000 1/16 J.B.C. & A. Forms/C.2118/12.

Instructions regarding War Diaries and Intelligence Summaries are contained in F. S. Regs., Part II. and the Staff Manual respectively. Title Pages will be prepared in manuscript.

# WAR DIARY
~~or~~
# ~~INTELLIGENCE~~ SUMMARY

*(Erase heading not required.)*

Army Form C. 2118.

| Place | Date | Hour | Summary of Events and Information | Remarks and references to Appendices |
|---|---|---|---|---|
| FREMICOURT | 1 | – | Truck No. 210584 – 8 tons clothing and blankets – | |
| | 2 | – | " " 12280 – 7 tons, timber, nose bags, postings. | |
| | 3 | – | " " 41182 – 9 tons, wheels, dubbin, rifle covers etc. 64916 – 5 tons clothing | |
| | 4 | – | Routine work. | |
| | 5 | – | Truck 81261 – 10 tons horseshoes, postings, wheels. | |
| | 6 | – | Routine work. – 6 tons timber, harness, nosebags & general stores. | |
| | 7 | – | 41281 – Wagon Ammunition G/2055 – 2 L.H.A. limbers – 2 Sect. DAC | |
| | 8 | – | 61409 – 6 tons clothing | |
| | 9 | – | 90289 – 5 tons Dubbin, Fire buckets, 22624 – 2 Forepart limbers & 1 G.S. wagon – 28902 limber G.S. and water cart. | |
| | 10 | – | 183489 – 9 tons – wheels, steel, horseshoes etc. – 23811 wagon Amm. | |
| | 11 | – | Routine work. | |
| | 12 | – | 60524 – limber wagon. Visited New HQ at Achiet-le-petit – Saw Town Major re new dump. | |
| | ~~12~~ | | 48798 – 1 wagon Amb. | |
| | 13 | – | 77737 – 2 water carts – 3 Ress Carts – 32052 – 1 Forepart limber – 1 G.S. wagon, 1 limbered G.S. wagon & 2 wheels | |
| | 14 | – | 58968 – 7 tons clothing. | |
| | 15 | – | Routine work. | |
| | 16 | – | 76053 – 2 watercarts, 1 limbered G.S. – 1 R.E. wagon limber & limbered G.S. wagon. Visited Achiet-le-petit re new dump – CARLTON HOUSE | |
| | 17 | – | Visited 3 Army HQ. 300 Tents returned wet by 5th Brigade – tents pitched to dry | |
| | 18 | – | DADOS 6th Div called to arrange taking over. | |
| | 19 | – | 157 – New Braziers. | |
| | 20 | – | Stores arranged for taking over & Camp cleared. | |
| ACHIET-LE-PETIT | 21 | – | Handed over to 6th Div – Moved to New Dump Sheet 57c G 14 a central – Accommodation not yet ready – huts unfinished & repairs to CARLTON HOUSE incomplete. | |
| | 22 | – | Detailed 1 AOC to OO 3rd Army Clearing Depot for temporary duty ACHIET-LE-GRAND | |
| | 23 | – | Routine work. | |

2449 Wt. W14957/M90 750,000 1/16 J.B.C. & A. Forms/C.2118/12.

Army Form C. 2118.

# WAR DIARY
*or*
# INTELLIGENCE SUMMARY
*(Erase heading not required.)*

Instructions regarding War Diaries and Intelligence Summaries are contained in F. S. Regs., Part II. and the Staff Manual respectively. Title Pages will be prepared in manuscript.

| Place | Date | Hour | Summary of Events and Information | Remarks and references to Appendices |
|---|---|---|---|---|
| ACHIET-LE-PETIT | 24 | | 46263 - 12 tons - Cycles, postcops & detail Stores. Visited Railhead - 49 CCS - 3rd Army Clearing Depot | |
| | | | 25597 - 12 tons clothing | |
| | 25 | | Visited Corps & Army - 19574 - 8 tons wheels, dubbin, respirators & equipment. | |
| | 26 | | 26001 - 9 tons wheels, timber, horseshoes, nosebags, etc. Visited Railhead - 152 & 153 Refilling Points - 49 CCS. | |
| | 27 | | 26524 - 8 tons timber, general stores. Visited Railhead & Refilling Points. | |
| | 28 | | 30690 - 3 tons clothing. Visited 3rd Army Clearing Depot & DDOS IV Corps Troops. | |
| | 29 | | Visited IV Corps Troops & Railhead. | |
| | 30 | | Routine work. | |
| | 31 | | 56162 - 6 tons horseshoes, dubbin. | |
| | | | General: 142 tons of stores received and issued: 150 tons Salvage returned. | |
| | | | Shops: Armourers: Rifles - 79 Lewis guns 12 - Pistol revolvers 4 - Cycles 47 - 64 Lewis gun butt cabinets fitted to tripods | |
| | | | Tailors: 11 Jackets, 3 Coats, 5 prs pantaloons, 2 flags made, 1 Armband made, 8 prs puttees repd | |
| | | | Bootmakers: 114 pairs of boots repaired | |
| | | | The lorries covered 1,822 miles with 402 Tonnage. | |
| | | | Demands were met by Bases very satisfactorily except certain articles unobtainable except very slowly - eg electric torch bulbs. | |
| | | | "1914 Star" Ribbon was also unobtainable - only 6 inches being received, off large demands still outstanding. | |
| | | | [signature] Capt. DADOS 37 (H) Div | |

2449 Wt. W14957/M90 750,000 1/16 J.B.C. & A. Forms/C.2118/12.

Vol 34

- Confidential -

War Diary

for

D.A.D.O.S. 51st. (H) Division.

From 1st to 28th. February, 1918.

Instructions regarding War Diaries and Intelligence Summaries are contained in F. S. Regs., Part II. and the Staff Manual respectively. Title Pages will be prepared in manuscript.

# WAR DIARY
*or*
# INTELLIGENCE SUMMARY

*(Erase heading not required.)*

Army Form C. 2118.

| Place | Date | Hour | Summary of Events and Information | Remarks and references to Appendices |
|---|---|---|---|---|
| ACHIET-LE-P. | 1 | | Truck No 58162 – 10 tons General Stores; 34072 – 10 tons Shirts, Drawers, Boots, Waistcoats. | |
| | 2 | | Routine work: visited railhead. | |
| | 3. | | Truck No 24415 – Nets Hay, Stoves Soyer, Bags Nose etc. – 4770, 3 Carts W. Tank, 2 Wagons G.S. Limber – 52679 – 429075, 4 wagons G.S. – 132322, Gloves hedging, Blankets etc. General stores. | |
| | 4. | | Visited by ADOS IV Corps. – Capt Rickby, AOD. | |
| | 5 | | Routine work. | |
| | 6 | | Truck 474839 – 10 tons clothing & accessories: visited 15 Bde Brigade: | |
| | 7 | | Notification from "Q" of move of 1 Brigade on 10th, another on 11th and Div HQ on 13th back to FREMICOURT – take over from 6th Div and hand over to 25th Div. | |
| | 8 | | 55952 – 3 tons clothing. | |
| | 9 | | 59373 – 8 tons – 5 Wheels, equipments, horseshoes, dubbin, general stores. | |
| | 10 | | To FREMICOURT – D.A.D.O.S. 6th Division. 45088 – 1 G.S. wagon, 2 Carts W.T. – Kitchen body. – 14761 – 1 G.S. wagon & 1 Cart. | |
| | 11 / 12 | | } Routine work: Armourers and some stores to FREMICOURT. | |
| FREMICOURT. | 13 | | D.D.O.S III Army called: Moved Dump and Office to FREMICOURT | |
| | 14 | | 42385 – 8 tons: – 50 pieces timber, horseshoes. 56379 – 6 tons, 27 wheels tube helmets, dubbin, 650231 – 1 limber kitchen & 1 G.S. wagon | |
| | 15 | | D.A.D.O.S. to ZENINGHEM No 14 O.D. for 14 days Ammunition Course. A/D.A.D.O.S. Lieut W.M. LEDINGHAM, R.E. | |

Instructions regarding War Diaries and Intelligence Summaries are contained in F. S. Regs., Part II. and the Staff Manual respectively. Title Pages will be prepared in manuscript.

# WAR DIARY
*or*
# INTELLIGENCE SUMMARY

*(Erase heading not required.)*

Army Form C. 2118.

| Place | Date | Hour | Summary of Events and Information | Remarks and references to Appendices |
|---|---|---|---|---|
| FREMICOURT | 16 | | 55396 – 5 tons – clothing. | |
| | 17 | | 64908 – 8 tons – Respirators, equipment & general stores | |
| | 18 | | 26799 – 1 G.S. wagon for Corps. Condr Fishwick & Sub Condr Ellis to H.Q. III Army for interview with D.D.O.S. | |
| | 19 | | 40084 – ten tons – clothing 3 wheels. | |
| | 20 | | Routine Work. | |
| | 21 | | 5 Tables & 16 Forms received from O.O. IV Corps troops, | |
| | 22 | | 132983 – 8 tons – 22 wheels, dubbing & horseshoes. Lt. Macpherson Intell. Corps arrived on 2 days course. | |
| | 23 | | 63968 – 7 tons – clothing. | |
| | 24 | | 8279 – 71 packages – clothing | |
| | 25 | | Visited Railhead. | |
| | 26 | | Routine Work. | |

2449 Wt. W14957/M90 750,000 1/16 J.B.C. & A. Forms/C.2118/12.

Army Form C. 2118.

Instructions regarding War Diaries and Intelligence Summaries are contained in F. S. Regs., Part II. and the Staff Manual respectively. Title Pages will be prepared in manuscript.

# WAR DIARY
*or*
# INTELLIGENCE SUMMARY

*(Erase heading not required.)*

| Place | Date | Hour | Summary of Events and Information | Remarks and references to Appendices |
|---|---|---|---|---|
| FREMICOURT | 27 | | 5"4 352 – 2 pontoons for 400 Field Coy R.E. | |
| | 28 | | 20 Manure Forks received from O.O. Corps Troops | |
| | ~~1st March~~ | | | |
| | | | General. 95 tons of stores received. 80. Tons Salvage returned. | |
| | | | Shops | |
| | | | Armourers Rifles 85; Vickers 3; Lewis 4; Cycles 41; | |
| | | | Alterations in Lewis gun grips 100; | |
| | | | Webley Pistols 16; Colt 3; Very Pistols 2; | |
| | | | Food Containers (Repair) 12; Discs (Red & Green) Marking 170 | |
| | | | Tailor: Articles Repaired. Trousers 6; Jackets 15; Pantaloons 1; | |
| | | | Caps 3; Raincoat 1; Mats 3; | |
| | | | Lorries Mileage Loaded 821 Empty 725 Tonnage 634 | |

W.M. Lechingham Lieut
for Capt DADOS 51st (H) Divn

2449 Wt. W14957/M90 750,000 1/16 J.B.C. & A. Forms/C.2118/12.

Army Form C. 2118.

Instructions regarding War Diaries and Intelligence Summaries are contained in F. S. Regs., Part II. and the Staff Manual respectively. Title Pages will be prepared in manuscript.

SECRET

# WAR DIARY
*or*
# INTELLIGENCE SUMMARY

*(Erase heading not required.)*

VII 35

| Place | Date | Hour | Summary of Events and Information | Remarks and references to Appendices |
|---|---|---|---|---|
| | | | WAR DIARY<br>–<br>MARCH 1918<br>–<br>D. A. D. O. S<br>57 D. | |

2449 Wt. W14957/M90 750,000 1/16 J.B.C. & A. Forms/C.2118/12.

Army Form C. 2118.

# WAR DIARY
*or*
# INTELLIGENCE SUMMARY
*(Erase heading not required.)*

Instructions regarding War Diaries and Intelligence Summaries are contained in F. S. Regs., Part II. and the Staff Manual respectively. Title Pages will be prepared in manuscript.

SECRET

MARCH 1918

| Place | Date | Hour | Summary of Events and Information | Remarks and references to Appendices |
|---|---|---|---|---|
| FREMICOURT | 1 | – | Routine work | |
| | 2 | – | 72 Trench covers drawn from O.O. 3rd Army Tps No 1 (Destalling 60. S.M.T.O. 12). Truck 36860 – 6 tons Horseshoes etc., 28245 – 1 Light Van Body + 1 G.S. wagon | |
| | 3 | – | D.A.D.O.S. returned from Ammunition Course at ZENEGHEM. | |
| | 4 | – | Routine work – 25694 – 1 Wheels, 3 Tubs Washing – 2150, 6 Tons General Stores. | |
| | 5 | – | Calls at Salvage – Fire orders revised at depot + appliances rearranged – New fire orders + drill | |
| | 6 | | 11761 – G.S. wagon | |
| | 7 | | 30180 – 6 tons clothing. | |
| | 8 | | 142391 – 6 tons dubbing soap. soda etc | |
| | 9 10 11 | | Routine work | |
| | 12 | | Lorry to MIDDLESEX CAMP to move Signalling School to ACHIET LE PETIT. 145431 2 tons detail stores – 24963 2 Watercarts, Fire limber G.S. wagon. Collected 25 tents from O.O. 4 Corps. Issued 3000 rounds Ammn S.A. blank to NAIL, NICE, NORMAL | |
| | 13 | | 74197, 41905 – 4 limb. G.S. wagons, 8 covers – 1 G.S. wagon, 1 R.E. limb. wag. body | |
| | 14 | | 90440 – 1 limb wag 4.5 – 62449 – 5 tons clothing. | |
| | 15 | | 36813, 15141, 13 tons stores | |
| | 16 | | Railhead changed to BAPAUME | |
| | 17 | | No 9 ENTRENCHING Battn joins division. | |
| | 18 | | 56292 – 5 tons clothing – 43009 – 1 limb G.S. wagon to G.S. wagon | |
| | 19 | | 130830 – 5 tons stores – Corps wire – "prepare for thaw precautions" | |
| | 20 | | 210665 – 3 tons dubbin, soap, soda. Visited Brigade H.Q. 152 – 153 – 154. | |
| | 21 | | Storehouses cleared and stores dumped by roadside ready for moving. 4 Ordnance lorries sent to H.Q. to stand by. 4 in relief arrived 6 p.m. when "Q" orders moved to GRÉVILLERS Stores abandoned 1 Marquee Scottish Churches – about 40 Brazziers, 12 Shot [illegible] Containers, 8 repairable bicycles, Days supply of soap, soda + dubbin, + five tents. | |

2449 Wt. W14957/M90 750,000 1/16 J.B.C. & A. Forms/C.2118/12.

Instructions regarding War Diaries and Intelligence Summaries are contained in F. S. Regs., Part II. and the Staff Manual respectively. Title Pages will be prepared in manuscript.

SECRET.

# WAR DIARY
*or*
# INTELLIGENCE SUMMARY

*(Erase heading not required.)* II MARCH 1918

Army Form C. 2118.

| Place | Date | Hour | Summary of Events and Information | Remarks and references to Appendices |
|---|---|---|---|---|
| GREVILLERS | 21 | | Ordered by CORPS to move to DIV WING at ACHIET LE PETIT. Div advised that lorries would not go back to Fremicourt to pick up any stores left | |
| ACHIET-LE PETIT | 22 | | Visited DIV. HQ also Q.M.s at wagon lines – Visited Gun Park & 2nd Army | |
| | 23 | | Visited Div HQ. & Corps. Stores collecting at MIRAUMONT – lorries delayed by shell fire hearing bridge | |
| | | | Office & dump to PUSIEUX thence to BERTRANCOURT. Visited Army & Gun Park also Div HQ. | |
| BERTRANCOURT | 24 | | Moved to MARIEUX – Saw Corps. – Obtained from Corps probable destination of Div & arranged accordingly | |
| MARIEUX | 25 | | Moved to OCCOCHES – Collected stores from Div Wing – Clothing, Canteen etc, also Div Rest Camp Salvage. | |
| OCCOCHES. | 26 | | Moved to NEUVILLETTE – Saw Q.M.s Wired estimated requirements of Div to Base [illegible] to consign to LILLERS | |
| NEUVILLETTE | 27 | | Obtained from units all deficiencies in battle stores & forwarded list to Base for urgent refit. Consign to LILLERS. | |
| | 28 | | | |
| FOUQUIERES | 29 | | Moved to FOUQUIERES. – Saw ADOS Corps. I.O.M. No 1 at GOSNAY. Took over large number of stores from dump 42nd DIV at LABEUVRIERE by orders Corps & issued to the division. | |
| | 30. | | Issuing all available stores for refit and collecting from G. Park | |
| | 31 | | Division on Priority for all stores from Base – Refit completed in five days. | |

Generally.

– Stores lost at FREMICOURT owing to lorries being detailed by HQ to stand by & no relief lorries until night. Otherwise everything could have been got away.

About 70 tons stores received by rail. Lorry Mileage Loaded 1303 Empty 1085.

Tonnage 398 tons

Salvage returned:–

| Jackets | Pantaloons | Trousers | Puttees | Bottles water | W. Sacks | Tins [illegible] | Bottles Camp | Boots Pr | Sheets Ground | Coats Great | Belts Ankle | Helmets Pth |
|---|---|---|---|---|---|---|---|---|---|---|---|---|
| 1618 | 750 | 501 | 180 | 88 | 146 | 253 | 57 | 328 | 147 | 320 | 1028 | 1297 |

[illegible] Capt.
D.A.A.D.
[illegible] HD
31/3/18.

2449 Wt. W14957/M90 750,000 1/16 J.B.C. & A. Forms/C.2118/12.

Instructions regarding War Diaries and Intelligence Summaries are contained in F. S. Regs., Part II. and the Staff Manual respectively. Title Pages will be prepared in manuscript.

SECRET

# WAR DIARY
*or*
# INTELLIGENCE SUMMARY
*(Erase heading not required.)*

APRIL 1918

Army Form C. 2118.

DADOS 51 D

WA 36

| Place | Date | Hour | Summary of Events and Information | Remarks and references to Appendices |
|---|---|---|---|---|
| | | | WAR DIARY<br>April 1918.<br>D.A.D.O.S<br>HD<br>— | |

2449 Wt. W14957/M90 750,000 1/16 J.B.C. & A. Forms/C.2118/12.

Army Form C. 2118.

Instructions regarding War Diaries and Intelligence Summaries are contained in F. S. Regs., Part II. and the Staff Manual respectively. Title Pages will be prepared in manuscript.

# WAR DIARY
*or*
# INTELLIGENCE SUMMARY

*(Erase heading not required.)*

APRIL 1918 — II — SECRET

| Place | Date | Hour | Summary of Events and Information | Remarks and references to Appendices |
|---|---|---|---|---|
| FOUQUIERES | 1 | | Truck 16167 – 5 tons General Stores – 32221, 32487 – 2 C. Water Tanks, 1 Wagon Limb G.S., 100 Cases Respirators 59 Bales Clothing. | |
| | 2 | | 32650, 32646, 33793, 136631, 4 Carts Tool R.E., 4 tons General stores, 1 C. Water Tank. 2372, 143822 of Clothing. | |
| | 3 | | 135308 – 3 limb Car the 18 pr. – 41294, 1 limb Way G.S. + 1 Cart Maltese 265632 – 4 Tons General Stores | |
| | 4 | | 35120, 95076, 95072, 285215, 29478, 6003, 26109, 32998, 4005, 1706, 7070. – 17 tons General Stores + Vehicles for distribution. | |
| LABOUVRIERE | 5 | | Took over from 3rd Div. Issued Sports Gear to 4th Seaforths 35075, 27077, 185257, 8364, 68775, 9352, 71740 13 tons General Stores, Vehicles + 141 Bicycles | |
| | 6. | | 2060, 5211, Pontoon Parts for R.E. 58341, 11757, 92064, 41776, 18769, 2453, 12 tons General Stores + Vehicles. 5755, 473584, 50950, 7761, 16546, 52756 Vehicles for Artillery. | |
| | 7 | | All copies of I Corps Standing Orders etc. returned to A.D.O.S. 6141 – 5 tons General Stores | |
| ROBECQ. | 8. | | Move office + dump to ROBECQ. 24514, 31421, 57010, 16859, 11 tons General stores, 6 tons boots + chaff cutters, 33 wheels + vehicles. | |

2449 Wt. W14957/M90 750,000 1/16 J.B.C. & A. Forms/C.2118/12.

Instructions regarding War Diaries and Intelligence Summaries are contained in F. S. Regs., Part II. and the Staff Manual respectively. Title Pages will be prepared in manuscript.

Army Form C. 2118.

# WAR DIARY
*or*
# ~~INTELLIGENCE SUMMARY~~
*(Erase heading not required.)*

SECRET III April 1918

| Place | Date | Hour | Summary of Events and Information | Remarks and references to Appendices |
|---|---|---|---|---|
| ROBECQ | 9 | | 62930, 47216, 20 [illegible] & 2 tons Saddlery | |
| | | | 60523, 11989, Pontoon gear. | |
| | | | 12475, 91308, 2 tons general stores & vehicles. | |
| | 10 | | Moves stores & dump to HAM EN ARTOIS – Office at ROBECQ | |
| | 11 | | Routine work: Stores distributed from HAM. | |
| BUSNES | 12 | | Office moved to BUSNES | |
| | 13 | | Large Number of Vickers & Lewis Guns obtained from 9 Parks – [illegible], Magazines etc. Rifles collected and issued. Box Respirators & Cutters Wire. Very Pistols etc. | |
| | 14 | | 6, 18pr & 2. 4.5 How drawn by Arty. 30 Lewis Guns issued to 153 & 154 Brigades – also Steel Helmets etc | |
| | 15 | | 33149, 32193 – Vehicles | |
| | | | 57889, 44767, 54009, 24060, – Vehicles, 100 Boxes Horseshoes, 36 cases respirators & field dressings. | |
| | | | 9365, 17773, 57474, 23877, 4405, Vehicles for 16 Div Arty. | |
| LAMBRES | 16 | | Moved office to LAMBRES. | |
| | | | 7538, 29583 – Vehicles | |
| | 17 | | Horse & Mules shoes for 16 Div Arty collected from 16th Div. | |
| | | | 41643 – 9 tons general stores | |
| | | | 60982. – 8 tons general stores | |
| LAMBRES | 18 | | ~~[illegible]~~ | |
| | | | 41797, 53323, 41459, 58694, 251 cases equipment, 10 Wheels, 4 tons clothing, & Vehicles. | |
| | | | Store & dump moved to LAMBRES. | |
| | 19 | | 16656 – 6 tons general stores | |
| | | | 59333 – 4 tons general stores | |
| NORRENT FONTES | 20 | | Move office & dump. | |

SECRET WAR DIARY IV April 1918.

| Place | Date | Summary of Events & Information | Ref |
|---|---|---|---|
| NORRENT FONTES | 20 | 144688 - 35 Cases Respirators - 159 boxes Horseshoes. | |
| | 21 | 35035, 3259, 48006 - 97751<br>15 tons General stores & vehicles, & stores for 39 M.G. Battn | |
| | 22 | 18888 - 19 wheels, 1 vehicles - 41316, 9 tons clothing | |
| | 23 | | |
| | 24 | 217, 32408, 74000, 98678, 59248,<br>7 tons general stores, 26 wheels, 6 tons vehicle parts, 4 bicycles 5 tons harness, 22 wheels & 147 boxes horseshoes | |
| | 25 | 5708 - Vehicles. 1118 - Vehicle | |
| | 26 | 5365 - Vehicle - 56660, 129079, 11 tons general stores<br>24744. Vehicles. | |
| | 27. | 15616 - 47 sacks accoutrements. 16521 - 1 W. Limb G.S.<br>40 trench shelters & 67 pairs hedging gloves collected from 00 C.T.s. | |
| | 28 | 62006 - 6 tons general stores ; 97751 - 6 tons stores for 39 M.G. Battn | |
| | 29 | 91436 - 59991 - 11 tons clothing. | |
| | 30 | Collection 3 Revolvers, 5 Very Pistols, 40 Compasses Magnetic from C.C.S.s & Railhead. | |

SECRET. WAR DIARY. April 1918.

| Place | Date | Summary of Events & Information | Ref |
|---|---|---|---|

General. 240 tons of Stores received on rail – not including vehicles.
Total number of trucks received was 95.

A great number of stores have been collected from Gun Park No 1 by lorry, consisting of Vickers & Lewis Guns, Trench Mortars, and their various parts, also 18 pdr & 4.5 spare parts.

39th M. G. Battalion & 16 Divisional Artillery attached to this Div for Stores.

Lorry Mileage – miles full, – miles empty – tonnage.

Artificers
Tailors
Shoemakers

Armourers :– 7 Lewis Guns, 1 Vickers, 1 Hotchkiss, 1026 Rifles, 582 Bayonets, 35 Cycles

Tailors :–

Shoemakers :– Repairs 103 Boots Ankle, 26 Boots F.S.

Salvage:

| | S.D. Jackets | S.D. Pantaloons | S.D. Trousers | Puttees | Kilts | Coats Great | Boots Ankle pr | Caps S. Dress | Shirts Flannel | Drawers woollen | " Cotton | Socks woollen | Vests woollen | Haversacks | Bottles water | Tins Mess | Flannel Belts | Shoes Horse | " Mule | Sheets Ground |
|---|---|---|---|---|---|---|---|---|---|---|---|---|---|---|---|---|---|---|---|---|
| Totals returned to Salvage:– | 1325 | 683 | 435 | 527 | 366 | 543 | 798 | | | | | | | | | | | | | |
| Totals Issued from Store during Month | 2254 | 1519 | 1019 | 3770 | 1275 | 4007 | 2427 | 1063 | 3000 | 5 | – | 3000 | – | 1766 | 1761 | 5527 | 15070 | 6311 | 1530 | 4944 |

[signature] Capt
D.A.D.O.S.
30th April 1918 57 Div

Army Form C. 2118

Instructions regarding War Diaries and Intelligence Summaries are contained in F. S. Regs., Part II. and the Staff Manual respectively. Title Pages will be prepared in manuscript.

# WAR DIARY
*or*
# INTELLIGENCE SUMMARY
*(Erase heading not required.)*

Vol. 37

| Place | Date | Hour | Summary of Events and Information | Remarks and references to Appendices |
|---|---|---|---|---|
| | | | War Diary. for May. 1916. | |



1875 Wt. W593/826 1,000,000 4/15 J.B.C. & A. A.D.S.S./Forms/C. 2118.

SECRET War Diary (1) May 1916

| Place | Date | Summary of Events | Remarks |
|---|---|---|---|
| NORRENT FONTES | 1 | 18517 . 1 Cart water tank 21994 - 50 Crates Anti-gas Stores - 59376 - 2 tons clothing visited railhead | |
| | 2 | 23967 - 8 tons general stores - 93743 . 66 crates anti gas stores , 46960, 150 boxes horseshoes, 22 wheels. | |
| | 3 | 90277, 37681, 12 tons general stores, 36235 . 22 wheels, 84077 1 C.W.T to R.E. body | |
| | 4 | } Routine work | |
| | 5 | 6114 2 G.S. limbered wagons . Moved 16 D.A. 39 M.G. Batty for Div. Arty. C 61 Div. | |
| | 6 | Routine work - Move from NORRENT FONTES to MAROEIL | |
| MAROEIL | 7 | Called on ADOS XVII Corps. A.O.C. C Troops. | |
| | 8 | 40347 . 2 wagons G.S. Called at Railhead | |
| | 9 | A.D.O.S. called. Trucks 99138, 3021 - oil, grease reconsigned to 61 Div for 16 Div Arty & 39 M.G. Batty . Lorry to AIRE with oil for D.A. Lorry to BEURIE to pick up Anti gas appliances. 15 Hot Food Containers drawn from 17 Corps Salvage & issued to 1/6 Seaforths. | |
| | 10 | 183574 - 6 tons general stores, 52283 1 Cwt Lorry to Gun Park. Lorries Exchanged. | |
| | 11 | Called on 56 Div & collected 600 Cups Firing Grenade for 61 Gordons. Visited 152 & 153 Brigades. Also ADOS XVII Corps & XVII Corps | |
| | 12. | 90107 - 2 tons general stores. Lorry to Gun Park. Lorry to 61 Div. Stores for 51 D.A. | |
| | 13 | 3 loads Salvage to Railhead . - 30655 - 2 tons clothing. | |
| | 14 | Returned attached men to units. Lorry to SAVY for bayonets. | |
| | 15 | 59269 - 5 tons general stores, 57338 - vehicles. 2 lorries to 1.O.M. No 33 . load of Salvage to R'head. | |

Instructions regarding War Diaries and Intelligence Summaries are contained in F. S. Regs., Part II. and the Staff Manual respectively. Title Pages will be prepared in manuscript.

SECRET

# WAR DIARY
or
# ~~INTELLIGENCE SUMMARY~~ (2)

(Erase heading not required.)

May 1918

Army Form C. 2118

| Place | Date | Hour | Summary of Events and Information | Remarks and references to Appendices |
|---|---|---|---|---|
| MAROEIL | 16 | | 1 Positioning Machine received from Base for trial M.G. Battn. 72 Lewis Guns from Park to complete to Scale to = 24 per Battn. | |
| | 17 | | 67486 – 5 tons general stores – 47204 Vehicles – Visited three railheads & received 5 revolvers – 1 Telescope, 2 prs Binoculars N.P. 22 No 33 periscopes received from Base – 10 Forward Area Sights & 1 Muzzle Pizzle [?] drawn from 17 C.T. | |
| | 18. | | Lorry to G. Park to draw 4.5" How. Barrels [?] for I.O.M. No 4 H Shops. | |
| | 19 | | Visited Corps Salvage at Wanquetin – Lorries changed. | |
| | 20 | | 56382 – 3 tons clothing. Lorry to Aire, Gun Park & Savy for I.O.M. | |
| | 21. | | Visited Officers' Clothing Depot No 1 – 91438 – Vehicle. | |
| | 22 | | 1730 – 6 tons general stores. A.D.O.S. called. Visited 56 Div. & 18 C.T.[?] 3323 – [illegible] tons clothing & boots. | |
| | 23. | | 66 Rifles sent from Shops to Corps for A.D.O.S. | |
| | 24. | | 15565 – 6 tons general stores. | |
| | 25 | | 79, 32683, Vehicles. 59738 – 3 tons clothing. 40 Cups grenade repaired to 56 Div. S/Cond. Wilson left for duty HQ. 5th Army. | |
| | 26 | | 93658 – 5 tons general stores. 905 pairs socks repaired 56 Div. Salvage to railhead. | |
| | 27 | | Visited Corps Salvage – Court of Enquiry M.V. Park [?]. Prices of lost stores submitted – 139607 – 8 tons clothing. | |
| | 28 | | 54014 – Vehicles – 70 Syringes given A.D.M.S. for San. Sect. 50 Hot Food containers available. 4.5" How & Carr from G. Park for 58 Bty 5th Canadian R.G.A. | |

1875 Wt. W593/826 1,000,000 4/15 J.B.C. & A. A.D.S.S./Forms/C. 2118.

Instructions regarding War Diaries and Intelligence Summaries are contained in F. S. Regs., Part II. and the Staff Manual respectively. Title Pages will be prepared in manuscript.

SECRET.

# WAR DIARY or INTELLIGENCE SUMMARY

(Erase heading not required.)

(3) May 1918

Army Form C. 2118

| Place | Date | Hour | Summary of Events and Information | Remarks and references to Appendices |
|---|---|---|---|---|
| MAROEUIL | 29 | | 5000 Summer Drawers arrive. 44440 – 10 tons general stores – 7811 Vehicles. 4 Rubber Puzzle Mountings A.A. received. | |
| | 30. | | 25399 – Vehicles. 2 Radium Spotters No 7 Dial Sights received – Shoemakers to Army | |
| | 31 | | 37380, 47014 – 9 tons general stores, 25230 – 1 ton clothing. ·2· 4.5 Hows for 57 Battery – replace worn. | |

Issues & Returns of Stores for Month

← Per 1000 Men → ← Per 1000 Animals →

| | | Coats Great | | Waterproof? | | Jackets SD | | Trousers SD | | Pantaloons | | Puttees | | Caps SD | Shirts | Drawers | Socks | Vests | H'sacks | W'bottles | Mess tins | G-Sheets | Flannelette | Shoes Horse | " Mule |
|---|---|---|---|---|---|---|---|---|---|---|---|---|---|---|---|---|---|---|---|---|---|---|---|---|---|
| | | Issued | Retd | Issued | Retd | Issued | Retd | Issued | Retd | Issued | Retd | Issued | Retd | ← | | | | Issued | | | | | → | | |
| Total | Issued. | 1180 | 600 | 1777 | 850 | 2709 | 1120 | 1000 | 500 | 2524 | 507 | 2228 | 798 | 1037 | 430 | 1024 | 852 | 20 | 457 | 878 | 296 | 345 | [illegible] | 1163 | 416 |
| Per | 1000 | 62 | 32 | 93 | 45 | 142 | 60 | 71 | 100 | 250 | 100 | 117 | 40 | | | | | | | | | | | | |

Strength Div Services. 14000
" Mounted 4800
18800
Animals 6000

Includes Issues to 57 Div Artillery
& 15 Cav Div Artillery

[signature] Capt.

D.A.D.O.S. 51st (HIGHLAND) DIVISION.

1875 Wt. W593/826 1,000,000 4/15 J.B.C. & A. A.D.S.S./Forms/C. 2118.

Army Form C. 2118

Instructions regarding War Diaries and Intelligence Summaries are contained in F. S. Regs., Part II. and the Staff Manual respectively. Title Pages will be prepared in manuscript.

Secret

# WAR DIARY
*or*
# INTELLIGENCE SUMMARY
*(Erase heading not required.)*

June 1918

Vol 38

| Place | Date | Hour | Summary of Events and Information | Remarks and references to Appendices |
|---|---|---|---|---|
| | | | WAR DIARY<br>JUNE 1918<br>D. A D O S<br>HD | |

1875 Wt. W593/826 1,000,000 4/15 J.B.C. & A. A.D.S.S./Forms/C. 2118.

Instructions regarding War Diaries and Intelligence Summaries are contained in F. S. Regs., Part II. and the Staff Manual respectively. Title Pages will be prepared in manuscript.

SECRET

# WAR DIARY
*or*
# ~~INTELLIGENCE SUMMARY~~
*(Erase heading not required.)*

June 1918

Army Form C. 2118

(1)

| Place | Date | Hour | Summary of Events and Information | Remarks and references to Appendices |
|---|---|---|---|---|
| MAROEUIL | 1st | | Lorries exchanged. 3 Armourers to Div. Wing to inspect Arms. Recd 1 Hotchkiss Gun from Gun Park for 1 Co. 5 Bn Div Train. 1st supply | |
| | 2. | | Routine work | |
| | 3. | | Truck 28230 40 bales S.D. Jackets (Reserve for change) | |
| | | | " 76503 1 Wagon G.S. for 2/1 Field Ambce. | |
| | | | " 1384 1 Kitchen limber body for 1/4 Sea Hrs + 1/7 Gordon Hrs | |
| | | | " 28599 1 Cart Water for 1/6 Black Watch 1 Wagon limb G.S. limb for 1/6 Sea Hrs | |
| | | | " 37380 1 Truck general stores principally Vehicle parts. | |
| | | | " 47014 Dubbin Oil. Paint Soap. Accoutrements Picketing Gear etc | |
| | 4 | | 51 Div Arty joined from 4th Div. D.D.O.S. First Army visited Ord Dump | |
| | 5 | | Truck 2845 5 tons General Stores inc. 105 Yds Muslin for distribution | |
| | | | " 4809 Fringes browband 4000 Yds Flannelette for Reserve | |
| | 6 | | Demanded 8000 prs Drawers cotton to complete to two pairs per man | |
| | | | Truck 16022 4 tons Clothing including Hosiery, Boots, Accessories. Kilts Titles. 6000 Towels for Baths | |

1875 Wt. W593/826 1,000,000 4/15 J.B.C. & A. A.D.S.S./Forms/C. 2118.

Instructions regarding War Diaries and Intelligence Summaries are contained in F. S. Regs., Part II. and the Staff Manual respectively. Title Pages will be prepared in manuscript.

[illegible]

# WAR DIARY
*or*
# INTELLIGENCE SUMMARY
*(Erase heading not required.)*

(2)

June 1918

Army Form C. 2118

| Place | Date | Hour | Summary of Events and Information | Remarks and references to Appendices |
|---|---|---|---|---|
| MAROEUIL | 6 | | Issued 1/7 A&S Hrs with 23 prs Trousers for raiding party | |
| | | | Received 19 Camouflage Suits from 17 Corps Camouflage Depot and issued to 152 Bde 6 153 Bde 6 154 Bde 6 Q.1 | |
| | 7 | | Routine Work. Awaiting Kilt Aprons from Base. Demanded 1 Wagon Ambulance for 1/3 Field Amb to replace condemned by I.O.M. | |
| | 8 | | Demanded 1. 6 inch Trench Mortar for 51st Div TMB to replace one destroyed by fire | |
| | | | Received 13 Pistols Webley from Base. Truck 7980 7 tons General Stores including 83 boxes horseshoes. 9 [illegible] Box Respirators. Stable necessaries. Truck 364 1 Wagon [illegible] GS for 1/7 Black Watch. Truck 683 1 Cart [illegible] for 58 Bty. [illegible] FA. | |
| | 9 | | Received 228 Half bag [illegible] Lewis Gun [illegible] from [illegible] Park and issued to 152 Bde 72. 153 Bde 72 154 Bde 72 = 24 per Battalion. Pio. Bn. 12 | |
| | | | Truck 75829 1 Pontoon wagon for 400 Field Co RE | |
| | 10 | | " 152453 Accoutrements. [illegible] Soap. Picketing Gear. Truck 584 1 GS wagon for 160 [illegible] 17 wheels – Truck 70 – 21 wheels | |

1875 Wt. W593/826 1,000,000 4/15 J.B.C. & A. A.D.S.S./Forms/C. 2118.

Instructions regarding War Diaries and Intelligence Summaries are contained in F. S. Regs., Part II. and the Staff Manual respectively. Title Pages will be prepared in manuscript.

Secret

# WAR DIARY
*or*
# INTELLIGENCE SUMMARY
*(Erase heading not required.)*

(3)

June 1918.

Army Form C. 2118

| Place | Date | Hour | Summary of Events and Information | Remarks and references to Appendices |
|---|---|---|---|---|
| MAROEUIL | 11 | | Truck 76666 1 Wagon Lim G.S for 1/4 Gordon Hrs. Visited Corps Salvage. | |
| | 12 | | " 30838 1 Wagon Lim G.S for 1/6 Black Watch. 1 Wagon G.S for B. 255 Bde | |
| | | | Received 81 Trie [illegible] A.A. sights from 17 Corps Troops and issued 12 to each Infy Bde and 600 1 each Pio. Bn. 6 51 D.A. 17 [illegible] Bde 19 – Received 1 18 pdr Carriage for A/255 Bde – Recd [illegible] stores from 4 [illegible] for 51 D.A. – Recd 12 [illegible] from [illegible] 15 [illegible] – Issued following medal ribbon to 154 Bde for presentation. 5. D.S.O. 20 M.C. 15 D.C.M. 150 M.M. 4 Croix de Guerre. | |
| | 13 | | Truck 168630 3 ton Clothing inc Boots and Laundry | |
| | 14 | | " 29838 2 ton General Stores principally Iron + timber – Truck 14757-98 boxes horseshoes 72 pouches Rifle Grenade Discharger G.R.O 441 – 8 to each I. Bn. – Purchased 17 Flatirons and issued to 154 Bde. | |
| | 15 | | Truck 136434 – 1 Wagon G.S for 2 Sect. 5. [illegible] – Truck 135821 – 1 [illegible] for 51 Div. Co 1 [illegible] for 53 Bty R.F.A. – Truck 3234 8000 prs cotton drawers Received 24 [illegible] from [illegible] 15 [illegible] – Demanded 1. 18 pdr for 60 Bty R.F.A. | |
| | 16 | | Demanded 1 Wagon G.S for 3 Sect 5. [illegible] 1 Wag. Lim G.S for 1/7 A+S Hrs Issued following medal ribbons to 153 Bde for presentation. 2 D.S.O 14 M.C. 10 D.C.M. 100 M.M. 3 Croix de G. | |

1875 Wt. W593/826 1,000,000 4/15 J.B.C. & A. A.D.S.S./Forms/C. 2118.

Instructions regarding War Diaries and Intelligence Summaries are contained in F. S. Regs., Part II. and the Staff Manual respectively. Title Pages will be prepared in manuscript.

Secret

# WAR DIARY
*or*
# INTELLIGENCE SUMMARY
*(Erase heading not required.)*

(4)

June 1918

Army Form C. 2118

| Place | Date | Hour | Summary of Events and Information | Remarks and references to Appendices |
|---|---|---|---|---|
| MAROEUIL | 17 | | Routine work | |
| | 18. | | Truck 39473 1 G.S body each for 1/7 BW + 1/4 Gor. Hrs – Truck 30538 1 Wag L.G for B/255 1 Wag Lim G.S for 1/6 B.W. – Truck 714 11 tons General Stores inc 216 pouches rifle grenade dischargers – 36 M.V. connectors ARO 4497 – Truck 4053 Accoutrements Oil Dubbin Soap &c | |
| | 19 | | Truck 470921 – 6 tons General Stores chiefly vehicle parts – Recd 1 Horse clipper with protection for teeth from O.O. 17 C. Y and issued to Mob. Vet. Sect – Retd 100 [illegible] to O.O. No 1 Main Park. | |
| | 20 | | Routine work. Truck 21980 4 tons clothing. | |
| | 21 | | Truck 28380 1 G.S Wagon for 3 Sect 5 Bn DAC, 1 Wag Lim G.S for 1/7 A+S Hrs Truck 403 1 G.S wagon for AAA Sect 51 DAC. – Truck 4303 10 tons General Stores | |
| | 22 | | Routine work. Visited Corps Salvage | |
| | 23 | | Truck 577 General Stores inc 1 German MG for instructional purposes – Truck 4225 11 tons General Stores – Truck 42888 1 Wag Lim G.S each for MG Bn + 1/7 A+S Hrs 1 Merchant for 1/4 Sea Hrs | |
| | 24 | | Routine work. Visited Railhead + Corps Salvage | |
| | 25 | | Truck 92051, 3 tons general Stores. 216 Rifle Grenade Dischargers – Recd 23 new wood hut bottoms from Corps Troops for 1/2 Field Amb. 73 Trench shelters from 17 Corps Troops | |

Army Form C. 2118

(5)

# WAR DIARY
*or*
# INTELLIGENCE SUMMARY
*(Erase heading not required.)*

June 1918

Instructions regarding War Diaries and Intelligence Summaries are contained in F. S. Regs., Part II. and the Staff Manual respectively. Title Pages will be prepared in manuscript.

| Place | Date | Hour | Summary of Events and Information | Remarks and references to Appendices |
|---|---|---|---|---|
| MAROEUIL | 26 | | Recd 4 Spotted No 7 dial sights from 17 C.S.[?] for 5 Sea Bn. Recd 1 Rifle converted for discharger and issued to 154 Bde. | |
| | 27 | | Routine work. Recd 2 German machine Guns. | |
| | 28 | | Truck 3797 146 Boxes horseshoes. Truck 23135 6 lorry General stores. | |
| | 29 | | Obtained 20 torches for 153 Bde for special purpose. Recd 4 Tarpaulins from OO 17 C.S.[?] for 6 RA | |
| | 30 | | Routine work. Visited Corps Salvage & Railhead. Demanded 1 Trav[elling] Kitchen body for 5 Sea Hrs. | |

Issues & Returns of Stores for month

| | Coats Great | | Boots Ankle | | Jackets SD | | Trousers SD | | Pantaloons | | Puttees | | Caps SD | Shirts | Socks | Drawers | Cloaks | Blankets | Water bottles | Mess tins | Haversacks | Horseshoes | Shoes horse | Nails |
|---|---|---|---|---|---|---|---|---|---|---|---|---|---|---|---|---|---|---|---|---|---|---|---|---|
| | Issd | Recd | Issd | Recd | Issd | Recd | Issd | Recd | Issd | Recd | Issd | Recd | | | | | | | | | | | | |
| Total Issd | 503 | 405 | 2488 | 1639 | 3534 | 2436 | 1315 | 684 | 2258 | 1414 | 4587 | 2975 | 1400 | - | 1000 | 13000 x | - | 378 | 936 | 1420 | 539 | 11740 | 9444 | 2558 |
| Per 1000 | 24 | 19 | 118 | 78 | 168 | 118 | 87 | 45 | 364 | 236 | 218 | 141 | 738 | - | 1 | - | - | 17 | 44 | 68 | 26 | 535 | 1574 | 431 |

← Per 1000 men → | Per 1000 animals

Strength Div Services 15000
Attd " 5800
Total 20800
Animals 6000

Includes issues to 5 Sea Bn
x 1st issue GRO 3934
Summer scale

Lt for Major
D.A.D.O.S.
51st (HIGHLAND) DIVISION

1875 Wt. W593/826 1,000,000 4/15 J.B.C. & A. A.D.S.S./Forms/C. 2118.

Instructions regarding War Diaries and Intelligence Summaries are contained in F. S. Regs., Part II. and the Staff Manual respectively. Title Pages will be prepared in manuscript.

SECRET

Army Form C. 2118

# WAR DIARY
*or*
# INTELLIGENCE SUMMARY
*(Erase heading not required.)*

JULY 1918

Vol 39

| Place | Date | Hour | Summary of Events and Information | Remarks and references to Appendices |
|---|---|---|---|---|
| | | | WAR DIARY<br>JULY 1918<br>D.A.D.O.S<br>(HD) | |

1875 Wt. W593/826 1,000,000 4/15 J.B.C. & A. A.D.S.S./Forms/C. 2118.

Instructions regarding War Diaries and Intelligence Summaries are contained in F. S. Regs., Part II. and the Staff Manual respectively. Title Pages will be prepared in manuscript.

Secret

# WAR DIARY
*or*
# INTELLIGENCE SUMMARY
*(Erase heading not required.)*

July 1918

(1)

Army Form C. 2118

| Place | Date | Hour | Summary of Events and Information | Remarks and references to Appendices |
|---|---|---|---|---|
| MAROEUIL | 1/7/18 | | Truck 50 1. Cart water for D/255. 1 Wheel M.G. for 1 bo 51. Train. - Truck 30749 4 Vermorel Sprayers for Gas Officer. - Truck 30749 5 tons general stores including Oil. Soap &c | |
| | 2/7/18 | | Demanded 1 M.G. wagon for 4 bo. Train. - Recd 16 Yukon Packs from Gun Park No1 for 1/4 Gordon Hrs. - Demanding 1 Off mess cart for H.Q. 255 Bde R.F.A. | |
| | 3/7/18 | | Recd from Vendroux 14 T.M. Sub-beds for 51. T.M.B. Attended conference at ADOS. 17.6 re indents - G.O.6. [illegible] visited Dump. Truck 3844. 1 K.T. body for 1/5. Sea Hrs | |
| | 4/7/18 | | Truck 91266 5 tons General Stores inc Boots &c - 56 prs limber for 1/7 Black Watch. Demanded 1. 18 pdr. carriage for 55 Bty to F.A. replace condemned for wear | |
| | 5/7/18 | | Truck 218 contg. 28 wheels - Truck 21651 - 57 prs limber. 17 bales. 42 sacks shirts + socks for Baths - Truck 100152 - 43 wheels - Demanded 1. 18 pdr and carriage for A Bty 256 Bde | |
| | 6/7/18 | | Truck 41193 - 6 tons general stores inc 3 Vermorel Sprayers 54 Strombos horn cylinders 73 boxes horseshoes. 1000 prs S.D. Trousers, caps, [illegible] &c Truck 89156. 37 bicycles - Truck 82415 1 K.T. body for 6. Sea Hrs. | |

1875 Wt. W593/826 1,000,000 4/15 J.B.C. & A. A.D.S.S./Forms/C. 2118.

Instructions regarding War Diaries and Intelligence Summaries are contained in F. S. Regs., Part II. and the Staff Manual respectively. Title Pages will be prepared in manuscript.

# WAR DIARY
*or*
# INTELLIGENCE SUMMARY
*(Erase heading not required.)*

Army Form C. 2118

Dent. July. 1918 (2)

| Place | Date | Hour | Summary of Events and Information | Remarks and references to Appendices |
|---|---|---|---|---|
| MAROEUIL | 6/7/18 | | Truck 536. 1 G.S. wagon for 4 Coy Train. 1 Sect. Om for HQ 255 Bde | |
| | 7/7/18 | | Routine work. Visited Railhead and Corps Salvage. Recd 1 blackboard & easel from 17 C. Sps for Div Class. 2 Spotted Bail sights for Ord. Ba - Recd 2 Kempressors Lewi type with metallic tubing and issued 1 each to HQ 255 Bde + 256 | |
| | 8/7/18 | | Truck 3046. 5 tons General Stores, inc Picketing Gear. Oil, paint & soap. 600 blankets for 154 Bde to complete to 25% Dischargers Rifle Grenade 1 M.Gun, German demanded 12 Lewis Guns 4 each for Field Coy R.E. 1 Vickers Gun for M.G.Bn. Wired suspension of stores to Base. | |
| | 9/7/18 | | Visited Railhead + D.A.D. - Sent 4 Lorry loads Salvage to Railhead - Reconsigned Truck 132540 contg 3 tons General Stores from Mont-St-Eloy to Tinques. | |
| | 10/7/18 | | Visited Salvage Dump - Routine work - Sent 3 Lorry loads Salvage to Railhead. | |
| | 11/7/18 | | Moved from MAROEUIL TO ROULLECOURT - Moved 5 ton Div Arty from 51 Div to 4 Can Div. | |
| ROULLECOURT | 12/7/18 | | Recd 12 Lewis Guns 4 each for Field Coys. R.E. - 1 Vickers for M.G.Bn. - Truck 132540 General Stores, inc, Harness Boots, Clothing. Box Recpt. - Wired ACCEPT to Base. Recd 2 Marquees for 152 Bde from 17 C.Y. | |

Instructions regarding War Diaries and Intelligence Summaries are contained in F. S. Regs., Part II. and the Staff Manual respectively. Title Pages will be prepared in manuscript.

Secret

# WAR DIARY
*or*
# INTELLIGENCE SUMMARY July. 1918

(3)

*(Erase heading not required.)*

Army Form C. 2118

| Place | Date | Hour | Summary of Events and Information | Remarks and references to Appendices |
|---|---|---|---|---|
| ROUELLECOURT | 13/7/18 | | Moved from Rouellecourt to Tinquette. | |
| TINQUETTE | | | | |
| -"- | 14/7/18 | | Routine work | |
| -"- | 15/7/18 | | 17 Corps moved 51 Div from Calais to Havre Base - Moved from Tinquette to Aubigny Railhead | |
| AUBIGNY | " | | Entrained | |
| " | 16/7/18 | | Left Aubigny | |
| | 17/7/18 | | Train journey | |
| OGNES | 18/7/18 | | Arrived MERY STATION thence to OGNES. | |
| PIERRY-MOUSSY | 19/7/18 | | Left Ognes and arrived Pierry-Moussy - Demanded two complete Wag. Lim. G.S. for 152 Bde | |
| -"- | 20/7/18 | | Routine work. Visited Railhead, JALONS | |
| " | 21/7/18 | | Demanded 1 Trav Kitchen Limber for 1/4 Gor. Hrs. - Demanded 320 box Resp to complete Reserve. Demanded 2 Vickers Guns for M.G. Bn | |
| -"- | 22/7/18 | | Demanded 5000 each of the following for Div Baths. Socks, shirts, towels. Also 1000 prs cotton drawers. - Demanded 27 Lewis Guns - 10 Sets Pack saddlery - 72 Pistols Sig. 1" | |
| | 23/7/18 | | Demanded 1 Wagon G.S. for 360 Train - 12 suspension bars for Thomas' splints for 1/2 Field Ambce - Demanded 4. No 200 wheels for 1/8 Royal Scots. | |

1875 Wt. W593/826 1,000,000 4/15 J.B.C. & A. A.D.S.S./Forms/C. 2118.

Army Form C. 2118.

# WAR DIARY
*or*
# INTELLIGENCE SUMMARY.
(*Erase heading not required.*)

Instructions regarding War Diaries and Intelligence Summaries are contained in F. S. Regs., Part II. and the Staff Manual respectively. Title pages will be prepared in manuscript.

Secret

July 1918 (4)

| Place | Date | Hour | Summary of Events and Information | Remarks and references to Appendices |
|---|---|---|---|---|
| PIERRY-MOUSSY | 25/7/18 | | Truck 116225. 25 wheels - 42 bicycles - 24 breeches wire ML 3" Stokes. T.M. | |
| | | | Routine work. Visited Railhead | |
| " | 26/7/18 | | Truck 40659 2 Vic Guns for M.G.B. 1 Aux Tripod - 16 brass box Reels - demanded 1 G.S. wagon for S.A.A. Sect. DAC. | |
| | 27/7/18 | | Drew 400 Petrol tins from R.S.O. [illegible] and sent next day to S.A.A. Sect. DAC. at AY. | |
| | | | Routine work. Visited Railhead | |
| | 28/7/18 | | Railhead from 20th OIRY. Demanded 1 18 pr. carriage for D/256 Bde Demanded 1/18 pr and carriage for C/256 Bde | |
| | | | Routine work | |
| | 29/7/18 | | Demanded 1 Vic Gun for M.G. Bn. Also 8 Vickers for M.G. Bn demanded from 22nd Corps | |
| | 30/7/18 | | Received 8 Vickers Guns from Corps | |
| " | 31/7/18 | | Routine Work. Received Orders for move. | |

[illegible signature]
MAJOR



A5834 Wt. W4973/M687 750,000 8/16 D. D. & L. Ltd. Forms/C.2118/13.

Army Form C. 2118.

Instructions regarding War Diaries and Intelligence Summaries are contained in F. S. Regs., Part II. and the Staff Manual respectively. Title pages will be prepared in manuscript.

# WAR DIARY
*or*
# INTELLIGENCE SUMMARY.
*(Erase heading not required.)*

August 1918

9/82 40

| Place | Date | Hour | Summary of Events and Information | Remarks and references to Appendices |
|---|---|---|---|---|
| | | | WAR DIARY FOR AUG 1918 | |

D.A.D.O.S.,
51ST
(HIGHLAND) DIVISION.
No.........................
Date.........................

A5834 Wt. W4973/M687 750,000 8/16 D. D. & L. Ltd. Forms/C.2118/13.

Army Form C. 2118.

Instructions regarding War Diaries and Intelligence Summaries are contained in F. S. Regs., Part II. and the Staff Manual respectively. Title pages will be prepared in manuscript.

# WAR DIARY
*or*
# INTELLIGENCE SUMMARY.
*(Erase heading not required.)*

Secret — August 1918.

| Place | Date | Hour | Summary of Events and Information | Remarks and references to Appendices |
|---|---|---|---|---|
| MOUSSY | 1/8/18 | | Packed up for move | |
| | 2/8/18 | | Entrained at EPERNAY (MARNE) | |
| | 3/8/18 | | Train journey | |
| | 4/8/18 | | Detrained at TINQUES. Arrived MINGOVAL. | |
| MINGOVAL | 5/8/18 | | Truck 210553 1 bale 9 bales boots. 10200 prs socks. 10000 Shirts. 10000 Towels. 21000 Drawers for Div Baths. Trucks 43983 1 6.0 in for A/256. 1 18 pdr limber for B/256. K.Y. limber for 4 Gor. Hrs. 1 G.W.Y. for 6 Seaforth Hrs. | |
| | | | Truck 61815 - Vehicle components. 60 Tubs washing. 6 Bales Camp Kettles. Hay nets. Picketing Gear. 25 boxes box Reap. Demanded 1 Lewis Gun for A/255 Bde | |
| | | | Demanded 1 18 pdr and carr for B/256 Bde replace condemned. | |
| -"- | 6/8/18 | | " 17 Lewis Guns to complete Infy Bns - Demanded 1. 18 pdr + carr for C/256 Bde | |
| | | | ADOS. VIII Corps called. - Passed refit indents for 6 Sea + 6 Gor ~~Hrs~~ 5 Sea Armourer left for duty with Bn. - Lorries exchanged | |
| -"- | 7/8/18 | | Equip Officer 51 DA called. Demanded 37 Lewis Guns. - Passed refit Indents for 6 BW. 7 BW. 7 Gor. 4 Sea. 4 Gor. 7 A&S Hrs. | |

A5834 Wt. W4973 M687 750,000 8/16 D. D. & L. Ltd. Forms/C.2118/13.

WAR DIARY
*or*
# INTELLIGENCE SUMMARY.
*(Erase heading not required.)*

Army Form C. 2118.

(2)

Aug. 18

Instructions regarding War Diaries and Intelligence Summaries are contained in F. S. Regs., Part II. and the Staff Manual respectively. Title pages will be prepared in manuscript.

| Place | Date | Hour | Summary of Events and Information | Remarks and references to Appendices |
|---|---|---|---|---|
| MINGOVAL | 8/8/18 | | Truck 45013 from Rouen. 5 tons Clothing includ. 1800 Kilt Aprons | |
| | | | Recd 1. 18 pdr + Carr each for B & C Bty 256 Bde from Mun Park No 1. | |
| | | | Truck 4656 - 37 wheels 44 pieces timber. 12 Lewis Guns. Oil and Grease. 117 boxes horseshoes. | |
| | | | Truck 5297 from TROYES. 2 Vic Guns for M.G. Bn. - Truck 137782 - 7 Vic Guns for M.G. Bn. 72 Pistols Sig. 1" 2700 yds Flannelette. 912 Rods cleaning 1st supply under ACRO 4392 - 11 Guns Lewis complete. | |
| | | | Demanded 2 Lewis Guns each for Btys RFA to complete to 4 per Bty | |
| | | | Routine work. Visited Railhead. | |
| -"- | 9/8/18 | | Visited Mun Park No 1 6 Seaforths Armourers joined for duty. Cr S.S. Strollon joined for duty from Mun Park No 1. - Passed Refit indent for 5 Seaforth Hrs. | |
| | | | Truck 75811 - 1 Wag Lim G.S. complete for 1/7 Gordon Hrs. | |
| | | | The following have been demanded from Base for Refitment of Division - | |
| | | | Hooks Hedging prs 185 Guns Lewis complete 84 Vickers 9. 18 pdrs 2 18 pdr Carr 2 Periscopes 386 Cups firing Rifle Grenade 222. Cutters wire 455 Binoculars 115 Cartridges Grenade 577. Dischargers RG 64 Pistols 178. Compasses 94. Watches 38 Stretchers 32. Pistols Signals 80. Telescopes Sig 3. Kilts 1132 Aprons Kilt 2832 Bonnets T.O.S 916 | |

A5834 Wt. W4973/M687 750,000 8/16 D. D. & L. Ltd. Forms/C.2118/13.

Instructions regarding War Diaries and Intelligence Summaries are contained in F. S. Regs., Part II. and the Staff Manual respectively. Title pages will be prepared in manuscript.

Secret

# WAR DIARY
*or*
# INTELLIGENCE SUMMARY.
*(Erase heading not required.)*

Army Form C. 2118.

| Place | Date | Hour | Summary of Events and Information | Remarks and references to Appendices |
|---|---|---|---|---|
| MINGOVAL | 10/8/18 | | Truck 2279 from Gun Park with 55 Lewis Guns + 18 pdr parts | |
| | 11/8/18 | | " 4233 Soap Accoutrements Picketing Gear. Flannelette 5 tons - Truck 4365 with 24 wheels - Truck 92376 2 complete Wagons Lim G.S for HQ 152 Infy Bde Lorries exchanged | |
| | 12/8/18 | | Routine Work. Visited ADOS Corps and Railhead - Trucks 92286. 21424. 1 G.S Wagon for SAA Sect. DAC 1. Wag Lim G.S for 1/7 Gordon Hrs | |
| | 13/8/18 | | Routine work. ~~[illegible]~~ | |
| | 14/8/18 | | Visited Railhead + Dados 52 Div. Trucks 39315. 67189 6583 8994 57316 67751. 33644 + 4381 inc Bicycles vehicles &c | |
| | 15/8 | | Visited New Area. Truck 200404 with Refit Stores | |
| MAROEUIL | 16/8/18 | | Dump moved from Mingoval to Maroeuil. Took over from 52 Div - Trucks 160353 + 68639. Horseshoes and Refit Stores | |
| | 17/8/18 | | Visited Railhead Routine Work | |

A5834 Wt. W4973/M687 750,000 8/16 D. D. & L. Ltd. Forms/C.2118/13.

Army Form C. 2118.

Instructions regarding War Diaries and Intelligence Summaries are contained in F. S. Regs., Part II. and the Staff Manual respectively. Title pages will be prepared in manuscript.

# WAR DIARY
*or*
# INTELLIGENCE SUMMARY.
*(Erase heading not required.)*

| Place | Date | Hour | Summary of Events and Information | Remarks and references to Appendices |
|---|---|---|---|---|
| MAREUIL AGNEZ-LES-DUISANS | 18/8 | | Moved from Mareuil to Agnez-Duisans. Trucks 95080 + 51681 with 13 Tons General Stores received. Visited Corps Salvage Dump and Railhead, ADOS visited. | |
| -"- | 19/8 | | Visited Railhead. Trucks 28807 and 33072 with necessaries and vehicles received. Took over arms and ammunition of 312 Infy Bn US Forces. | |
| -"- | 20/8 | | Routine work, ADOS visited Depot. | |
| -"- | 21/8 | | Trucks 63310 and 130428. Clothing and Refit Stores received. Routine work. | |
| -"- | 22/8 | | Routine work, visited Railhead, DDOS 1st Army visited Dump | |
| -"- MAREUIL | 23/8 | | Moved from Agnez-les-Duisans to Mareuil. | |
| -"- | 24/8 | | Routine Work | |
| " | 25/8 | | Trucks 467818, 95406, 11995, 53331, General Stores and Vehicles | |
| " | 26/8 | | Routine work, Magazines handed over to Gun Park Completing transaction with 312 Infy Bn USA, 100 Sets packsaddlery and 1000 Petrol tins received. | |
| VICTORY CAMP ECURIE | 27/8 | | Main Office moved to Victory Camp and Routine work | |
| " | 28/8 | | Routine work, Boots and Clothing received | |
| " | 29/8 | | — " — Visited Gun Park, Transferred from Can: Corps to XXII Corps | |
| " | 30/8 | | Trucks 145627, 1450 and 1431 General Stores + Vehicles. Recd 1 3" Stokes Mortar for TMB. | |

Instructions regarding War Diaries and Intelligence Summaries are contained in F. S. Regs., Part II. and the Staff Manual respectively. Title pages will be prepared in manuscript.

Secret

(5)

Army Form C. 2118.

# WAR DIARY
*or*
# INTELLIGENCE SUMMARY.
*(Erase heading not required.)*

| Place | Date | Hour | Summary of Events and Information | Remarks and references to Appendices |
|---|---|---|---|---|
| VICTORY CAMP ECURIE | 31/8/18 | | Routine Work Visited Railhead and Salvage Dump. Obtained from ROO DIEVAL. 12 Pistols 2 Pistols Signal 1". 3 prs Binoculars 5 Pistol Holsters | |
| | | | Issues and Returns of Stores for Month | |

| | Coats Great | | Boots Ankle | | Jackets SD | | Trousers SD | | Pantaloons | | Puttees | | Caps SD | Shirts | Socks | Drawers | Haversacks | Water bottles | Mess tins | Ground sheets | Flannelette | Horse shoes | " Mule | |
|---|---|---|---|---|---|---|---|---|---|---|---|---|---|---|---|---|---|---|---|---|---|---|---|---|
| | ISSD | RETD | I | R | I | R | I | R | I | R | I | R | | | | | | | | | | | | |
| | 479 | 471 | 2768 | 2428 | 3372 | 3875 | 1295 | 1227 | 1985 | 1728 | 3936 | 3511 | 867 | x 1500 | x 1500 | 50 | 200 | 532 | 1604 | 420 | 12920 | 6758 | 2357 | TOTAL ISSD |
| | 23 | 22 | 132 | 115 | 161 | 137 | 93 | 82 | 330 | 288 | 187 | 167 | 144 | - | - | - | 40 | 25 | 76 | 20 | 615 | 1159 | 393 | PER 1000. |

| Strength Division | 15000 |
|---|---|
| Att'd | 5800 |
| Total | 20800 |
| Animals | 6000 |

Includes issues to 16 Div Arty

X for Div Baths, for which a like No of U/S were retd to Base

Following to replace lost
- Caps SD 77
- Bottles water 231
- Tins mess 879
- Sheets Ground 138
- Haversacks 28

Major

Instructions regarding War Diaries and Intelligence Summaries are contained in F. S. Regs., Part II. and the Staff Manual respectively. Title pages will be prepared in manuscript.

1

SECRET

# WAR DIARY
*or*
# INTELLIGENCE SUMMARY.
*(Erase heading not required.)*

SEPTEMBER 1918

Army Form C. 2118.

WO 95/ 41

| Place | Date | Hour | Summary of Events and Information | Remarks and references to Appendices |
|---|---|---|---|---|
| | | | WAR DIARY<br>SEPTR. 1918<br>D.A.D.O.S.<br>51ST (H) DIV<br>D.A.D.O.S., 51ST (HIGHLAND) DIVISION<br>No. ..........<br>Date .......... | |

A5834 Wt. W4973 M687 750,000 8/16 D. D. & L. Ltd. Forms/C.2118/13.

Instructions regarding War Diaries and Intelligence Summaries are contained in F. S. Regs., Part II. and the Staff Manual respectively. Title pages will be prepared in manuscript.

Army Form C. 2118.

# WAR DIARY
*or*
# INTELLIGENCE SUMMARY.
*(Erase heading not required.)*

SECRET

SEPTEMBER 1918

| Place | Date | Hour | Summary of Events and Information | Remarks and references to Appendices |
|---|---|---|---|---|
| VICTORY CAMP ECURIE | 1/9/18 | | Lorries exchanged. Moved Dump from MAROEUIL to VIC. CAMP ECURIE | |
| | | | Truck 16 from Gun Park with 1 Limber, carr. 4.5 Hows for D/256 Bde. | |
| | | | " 35 " " " 1. 4.5 How + carr for D/256 | |
| | | | " 8259 " " " 1 18 pdr. for B 177 Bde | |
| | | | " 8950 " " " 1. 18 " for A/255 Bde Truck 54 1·18 pdr + carr for 177 Bde | |
| | | | " 31 " " " 1 18 " carr for A/180 Bde " 1958 1·18 pdr for C.180 Bde | |
| | | | " 1958 " " " 1 " " C/177 " | |
| " | 2nd | | Truck 14076 1. Wagon G.S for No1 Co. Train - Truck 8737 6 tons General stores | |
| | | | Routine Work. Visited Railhead. | |
| " | 3rd. | | Recd 1·18 pdr for A/180 Bde - Cr. S.Sgt Stratton AOC Armr 1/4 Gor. H[illegible] left for duty with 6 Ockal. | |
| | | | Moved 16th Div Artillery to O.O XXII Corps Troops - Routine work. Visited Railhead | |
| " | 4TH | | Truck 10644 from G.P with Gun stores - Routine work visited Railhead | |
| " | 5TH | | " 46767 5 tons General stores inc. Clothing Boots Artillery &c | |
| " | 6TH. | | " 48126 with 3500 Shirts, 3600 Socks, 3600 Towels for Div. Baths | |
| | | | " 1731 " Gun stores from Gun Park - Truck 47217 1. Cart water for 5 Seaforth Hrs | |
| | | | Routine work. Visited Railhead. 1 " Mess for B/256 Bde. | |
| " | 7th. | | Truck 50 from G.P. with 1 Wagon Ammn Limber 18 pdr for B/256 Bde | |
| | | | Demanded 4 Lewis Guns each for 4 Gor. Hrs + 7 A[illegible] Hrs. 1 Lorry to advance Gun Park for stores | |

A5834 Wt. W4973 M687 750,000 8/16 D. D. & L. Ltd. Forms/C.2118/13.

Instructions regarding War Diaries and Intelligence Summaries are contained in F. S. Regs., Part II. and the Staff Manual respectively. Title pages will be prepared in manuscript.

SECRET

# WAR DIARY
*or*
# INTELLIGENCE SUMMARY.
*(Erase heading not required.)*

SEPT 1918

(2)

Army Form C. 2118.

| Place | Date | Hour | Summary of Events and Information | Remarks and references to Appendices |
|---|---|---|---|---|
| VIC. CAMP ECURIE | 8TH | | Trucks 797 5929 Gun Stores from G.P. Truck 3598 7 tons general stores. Demanded 2 boilers water tank for I.O.M. No 2 + 55 Shops. - Routine Work. Visited Railhead. | |
| " | 9TH | | Truck 4827 - 6 tons General inc Equip. Oil Grease etc. Recd 1-18 pdr for B.255 Bde | |
| " | 10TH | | Routine Work. Visited Railhead | |
| " | 11 " | | Warning Order received. Recd 28 watches from Base. 8 Lewis Guns from G.P. 4 tank for 4 Gor. Hrs and 7 A.S. Hrs - Routine work. | |
| " | 12TH | | Truck 1197 = 5 tons general stores inc Boots clothing + Saddlery also 140 Spectacles [illegible] under GRO 4914. Routine work. Visited Railhead | |
| " | 13TH | | Routine work. Recd 25 condenser tubes from O.C. XXII. C Sps and issued to 51 M.G.B for mac | |
| MAROEUIL | 14TH | | Moved Office + Dump from VIC. CAMP TO MAROEUIL - Truck 163868 9 tons general stores = Horseshoes accessories etc - Routine Work Trucks 38968 39417 4 boilers water 2 each for I.O.M. No 2 and 55 Shop. - Lorries exchanged | |
| " | 15TH | | Routine work. Visited Railhead. Demanded 1-18 pdr for B 255 and for [illegible] | |
| " | 16 | | Truck 40380 6 tons General Stores. Demanded Do " Do Do. Visited Ord. Depot Calais Inspector of Boot shops visited Depot | |

A5834 Wt. W4973/M687 750,000 8/16 D. D. & L. Ltd. Forms/C.2118/13.

Instructions regarding War Diaries and Intelligence Summaries are contained in F. S. Regs., Part II. and the Staff Manual respectively. Title pages will be prepared in manuscript.

SECRET

# WAR DIARY
*or*
# INTELLIGENCE SUMMARY.
*(Erase heading not required.)*

SEPTEMBER 1918

(3)

Army Form C. 2118.

| Place | Date | Hour | Summary of Events and Information | Remarks and references to Appendices |
|---|---|---|---|---|
| MAROEUIL | 17TH | | Recd 1 · 18 pdr Wagon Amm and 1 · 18 pdr limber wagon for NO 2 Sect 51 DAC. Routine Work. Visited Railhead. Collected 30 Tents 6. 5 L from Main Park and delivered to Town Major FREVIN CAPELLE | |
| " | 18 | | Main Stores from Main Park. Recd 18 pdr NC 7008 for B 256 to replace 2422 condemned. 1 Lewis Gun recd for 6 Bde Hrs. 2 · 18 pdrs for B. 255 Btte | |
| " | 19. | | Truck 6413 Main Stores from MP. - Routine work. | |
| " | 20 | | " 447 7 tons general stores inc Clothing Boots Saddlery &c Truck 5042 1 limber for 7 BW. Routine Work. Visited Railhead | |
| " | 21. | | Truck 5254 with Main Stores from MP. Truck 23113 3 tons General Stores inc Horseshoes. Lorries exchanged. | |
| " | 22 | | Trucks 165313. 7377. 145 bales Blankets. 147197 5 tons General Stores. Picketing Gear &c. Visited Victory Camp. Ecurie | |
| | 23 | | Moved part of Dump to Victory Camp. Visited B 2500 49. Bde and Railhead. Recd 10 German Machine Guns ~~for~~ on Loan from OO. XXII Corps | |
| " | 24 | | Recd. 30 Long Jackets & Trousers Anti-Gas from 50. Distributed 10 to each Infy Btte. Routine Work. Visited Railhead | |
| VIC. CAMP ECURIE. | 25 | | Moved from MAROEUIL TO VIC. CAMP, ECURIE Truck 29540 7 Tons Gen. Stores inc Boots Saddlery &c. Trucks 22972. 22352 Contg. Blankets. | |

A5834 Wt. W4973 M687 750,000 8/16 D. D. & L. Ltd. Forms/C.2118/13.

Instructions regarding War Diaries and Intelligence Summaries are contained in F. S. Regs., Part II. and the Staff Manual respectively. Title pages will be prepared in manuscript.

SECRET

# WAR DIARY
*or*
# INTELLIGENCE SUMMARY.
*(Erase heading not required.)*

(4)

Army Form C. 2118.

SEPTR. 1918

| Place | Date | Hour | Summary of Events and Information | Remarks and references to Appendices |
|---|---|---|---|---|
| VIC. CAMP ECURIE. | 26. | | Truck 10676 Gun stores from Gun Park. Routine Work. Visited Railhead. | |
| -"- | 27. | | Truck 16604. 8 tons General stores = Kilts, accessories, Horseshoes | |
| -"- | 28. | | Routine Work. Visited Railhead and Officers Clothing Depot. | |
| -"- | 29. | | Lorries exchanged. 2 Armourers exchanged from Div. Arms Shop. Trucks 19760 36050 9 tons General Stores. Equip Oil & Grease. Routine Work Visited Railhead. | |
| -"- | 30. | | Recd 8 sets Pack saddlery from O.O. 22.6 Yps & issued 1 set each to 8 Bdys RFA for carrying telephone wire. Routine Work - Visited Railhead and Officers Clothing Depot | |

STATEMENT OF ISSUES & RETURNS OF CERTAIN ARTICLES FOR MONTH

| COATS GREAT | | BOOTS ANKLE | | JACKETS SD | | TROUSERS SD | | PANTALOONS | | PUTTEES | | CAPS SD | SHIRTS | SOCKS | H'SACKS | WATER BOTTLES | TINS MESS | GD SHEETS | FLANNELETTE | SHOES HORSE | MULE | |
|---|---|---|---|---|---|---|---|---|---|---|---|---|---|---|---|---|---|---|---|---|---|---|
| H | R | H | R | H | R | H | R | H | R | H | R | | | | | | | | | | | |
| 360 | 809 | 1343 | 1238 | 1069 | 1202 | 803 | 680 | 747 | 641 | 1728 | 1238 | 660 | 3600 x | 3600 x | 55 | 288 | 710 | 146 | 14280 | 3544 | 1627 | TOTAL |
| 19 | 43 | 71 | 65 | 108 | 116 | 51 | 48 | 149 | 108 | 91 | 117 | 132 | | | 3 | 15 | 48 | 8 | 756 | 886 | 407 | PER 1000 |

STRENGTH. DISMTD 14000
MTD 4800
TOTAL 18,800
ANIMALS 4000

X ISSD TO DIV. BATHS -

A5834 Wt. W4973 M687 750,000 8/16 D. D. & L. Ltd. Forms/C.2118/13.

Instructions regarding War Diaries and Intelligence Summaries are contained in F. S. Regs., Part II. and the Staff Manual respectively. Title pages will be prepared in manuscript.

(5)

Army Form C. 2118.

# WAR DIARY
*or*
# ~~INTELLIGENCE SUMMARY.~~

*(Erase heading not required.)*

September 1918

| Place | Date | Hour | Summary of Events and Information | Remarks and references to Appendices |
|---|---|---|---|---|
| | | | Work performed in Div Armrs Shop for month: Inspecting Cleaning & Overhauling Rifles 192. Bicycles 36 Machine Guns 10. Binoculars 21. Pistols 11 - 4 Armrs working. | |
| | | | 30/9/18 | |

[signature]
MAJOR

D.A.D.O.S.,
51ST
(HIGHLAND) DIVISION
No.

A5834 Wt. W4973 M687 750,000 8/16 D. D. & L. Ltd. Forms/C.2118/13.

Instructions regarding War Diaries and Intelligence Summaries are contained in F. S. Regs., Part II. and the Staff Manual respectively. Title pages will be prepared in manuscript.

SECRET

# WAR DIARY
*or*
# INTELLIGENCE SUMMARY.
*(Erase heading not required.)*

Army Form C. 2118.

Vol 42

| Place | Date | Hour | Summary of Events and Information | Remarks and references to Appendices |
|---|---|---|---|---|
| | | | WAR DIARY<br>OCTOBER 1918<br>D.A.D.OS 51ST(H) DIV<br>D.A.D.O.S., 51ST (HIGHLAND) DIVISION<br>No.........<br>Date......... | |

A5834 Wt. W4973/M687 750,000 8/16 D. D. & L. Ltd. Forms/C.2118/13.

Instructions regarding War Diaries and Intelligence Summaries are contained in F. S. Regs., Part II. and the Staff Manual respectively. Title pages will be prepared in manuscript.

Army Form C. 2118.

# WAR DIARY
*or*
# INTELLIGENCE SUMMARY.
*(Erase heading not required.)*

[illegible] October 1918

| Place | Date | Hour | Summary of Events and Information | Remarks and references to Appendices |
|---|---|---|---|---|
| VICTORY CAMP ECURIE | 1ST | | Demanded 5000 pairs Socks for Div. Baths - Demanded 1 [illegible] for 1/7 Gor. Hrs | |
| | | | Truck 7888 from Gun Park with Gun Stores. - Handed 15 sets Packsaddlery to 8th Div | |
| | | | Routine Work. Visited Railhead. | |
| " | 2nd | | Railhead moved to Mont-St-Eloi   Dump moved to Mont-St-Eloi | |
| | | | Trucks 6216 2490 with Blankets   Trucks 57180 16698 - 9 tons General Stores | |
| | | | " 39996 1 Wagon Limb. G.S. for S.A.A. Sect. [illegible] | |
| CHATEAU D'ACQ | 3rd | | Moved Office from Ecurie to Chateau D'acq. Routine Work. Visited Railhead. | |
| " | 4TH | | Truck 2572 1. K.T. body for 6 Gor. Hrs. Truck 35188 5 tons General. 44614 1. K.T body for 1/6. Black Watch. | |
| " | 5TH | | Truck 6539 General Stores - Routine Work. Visited Railhead. | |
| | 6TH | | Recd. 15 each Type A & B Safety Trigger Guards from O.C. 6.T. for fmg. Authy Q.M.G. 4059/15 (Q.B.1) of 21.9.18. Drew 360 No 32 Grenades from XVII Dump for Div. HQ | |
| | | | Truck 27485 5 tons General Stores. Consigned 14 Surplus Guns Lewis to Reception Camp. from Surplus with 7. Gor. Hrs. Received instructions re Amalgamation of 6 and 7 Gordon Hrs, and Reorganization of 1/6 A&S. Hrs from Pio. Bn to Infy. Bn. | |

A5834 Wt. W4973/M687 750,000 8/16 D. D. & L. Ltd. Forms/C.2118/13.

Instructions regarding War Diaries and Intelligence Summaries are contained in F. S. Regs., Part II. and the Staff Manual respectively. Title pages will be prepared in manuscript.

# WAR DIARY
*or*
# INTELLIGENCE SUMMARY.
*(Erase heading not required.)*

Army Form C. 2118.

Deml — October 1918

(2)

| Place | Date | Hour | Summary of Events and Information | Remarks and references to Appendices |
|---|---|---|---|---|
| QUEANT | 7th | | Moved Office and Camp to QUEANT. Collected 1 Tent + 50 Trench Shelters from O.C. 6T and returned to Camp Commandant. Routine Work | |
| " | 8th | | Railhead moved to ARRAS. Collected 50 Trench covers from Ord Dep INCHY-EN-ARTOIS | |
| " | 9th | | Routine Work. | |
| " | 10th | | Moved Office and Camp to Bourlon - Demanded 36 Lewis Guns to complete Bde to | |
| CHATEAU BOURLON | " | | Scale "G" | |
| " | 11 | | Railhead changed to CROISELLES | |
| ESCADOEUVRES | " | | Moved Office to ESCADOEUVRES Routine Work. Visited Railhead. | |
| " | 12th | | Moved Camp from Bourlon to ESCADOEUVRES - Demanded 1 Wagon G.S. for 1 Co. Train. Routine Work. Visited Railhead | |
| NAVES. | 13 | | Moved Office to NAVES. - Truck 92945 to Ord General Stores inc. Horseshoes. Received 100 Trench Shelters from O.C. Corps Troops - Railhead changed to CANTIMPRE | |
| " | 14 | | Demanded 1 Wag. Lim G.S. for [illegible]. Recd 7100 prs Socks 2040 Shirts 2000 Towels. Recd. 288 Dischargers Rifle Grenade under GRO 5147. Recd. notification that indents for picking must state whether for Infantry or Other troops | |

A5834 Wt. W4973/M687 750,000 8/16 D. D. & L. Ltd. Forms/C.2118/13.

Instructions regarding War Diaries and Intelligence Summaries are contained in F. S. Regs., Part II. and the Staff Manual respectively. Title pages will be prepared in manuscript.

(3)

# WAR DIARY
*or*
# INTELLIGENCE SUMMARY.
*(Erase heading not required.)*

Army Form C. 2118.

~~Diary~~ October 1918

| Place | Date | Hour | Summary of Events and Information | Remarks and references to Appendices |
|---|---|---|---|---|
| NAVES | 15 | | Recd 36 Lewis Guns to complete SW to Scale G. Demanded 1 - 18 pdr. Wagon Amm for 2nd. D.A.C. - Truck 41092 5 tons General Truck 45641 Clothing Truck 24950 with clothing inc 4000 drawers 9000 Vests. - Railhead Fontaine - NOTRE DAME | |
| " | 16 | | Demanded 3 Stokes T.M's for 152 I.M.B. Demanded 5 Mk IV M.G. Mountings for M.G. Bn Truck 57155 50 bales Vests Truck 93556 Boots [illegible] Truck 12445 with 4380 waistcoats Cardigan | |
| " | 17 | | Routine Work. Visited Railhead | |
| " | 18 | | " " " Demanded 2 Vickers Guns for M.G. Bn. | |
| " | 19 | | Trucks 62219. 5754 3250 Rugs horse. Recd 50 covers with sling L.G. from O.O. 22 Corps Tps. Received notification that No 1B Adv Gun Park ready to function | |
| " | 20 | | Routine Work | |
| AVESNES LE SEC. | 21 | | Moved Office from NAVES to AVESNES-LE-SEC. Truck 56137 7 tons General. | |
| LIEU-ST-AMAND. | 22 | | Moved Office ~~[illegible]~~ from AVESNES-LE-SEC TO LIEU-ST-AMAND Dump from Escaudoeuvres Recd 37 Lewis Guns + 3 Stokes T.M's from Gun Park | |
| - " - | 23 | | Truck 59521 7 tons General. Trucks 43178. 2260 23648 with leather jerkins and coats sheepskin lined. | |

A5834 Wt. W4973/M687 750,000 8/16 D. D. & L. Ltd. Forms/C.2118/13.

Instructions regarding War Diaries and Intelligence Summaries are contained in F. S. Regs., Part II. and the Staff Manual respectively. Title pages will be prepared in manuscript.

# WAR DIARY
*or*
# INTELLIGENCE SUMMARY.
*(Erase heading not required.)*

Secret

(4)

Army Form C. 2118.

October 1918

| Place | Date | Hour | Summary of Events and Information | Remarks and references to Appendices |
|---|---|---|---|---|
| LIEU-ST AMAND | 24 | | Truck 60236 1 Wagon G.S for No1 Co. Train. Truck 56306 8 tons General | |
| | | | Received 250 Expendable belts via Train from Gun Park & issued to 51 Bn M.G.C | |
| | | | Received 2000 pairs socks from Ord. 49 Div | |
| " | 25 | | Routine Work. | |
| " | 26 | | Truck 55473 6 tons General. Truck 112 1 Lim wagon for SAA Sect D.A.C | |
| " | 27 | | Routine Work. Recd 1. 18 pdr. Ammn Wagon for 2 Sect. 51 D.A.C | |
| " | 28 | | Recd 1. 18 pdr. carr for C 255 Bde. Truck 82171 Boots. Clothing &c | |
| " | 29 | | Routine work Demanded 1. 4.5 How Ammn wagon for D. 256 Bde | |
| | | | 1 Fore limber available at No1 A Gun Park for 1/8 Royal Scots. | |
| | | | Truck 2808 6 tons General. | |
| " | 30 | | Routine Work. | |
| IWUY | 31 | | Moved Office & Dump from LIEU-ST-AMAND TO IWUY | |

A5834 Wt. W4973/M687 750,000 8/16 D. D. & L. Ltd. Forms/C.2118/13.

Instructions regarding War Diaries and Intelligence Summaries are contained in F. S. Regs., Part II. and the Staff Manual respectively. Title pages will be prepared in manuscript.

# WAR DIARY
*or*
# INTELLIGENCE SUMMARY.
*(Erase heading not required.)*

Secret

October 1918

(5)

Army Form C. 2118.

| Place | Date | Hour | Summary of Events and Information | Remarks and references to Appendices |
|---|---|---|---|---|

STATEMENT OF ISSUES AND RETURNS OF CERTAIN ARTICLES FOR MONTH.

| COATS GREAT | | BOOTS ANKLE | | JACKETS SD | | TROUSERS SD | | PANTALOONS | | PUTTEES SD PRS | | CAPS SD | SHIRTS | SOCKS | DRAWERS | VESTS | H'SACKS | BOTTLES WATER | TINS MESS | SHEETS GD | FLANNELETTE | SHOES HORSE | SHOES MULE | | |
|---|---|---|---|---|---|---|---|---|---|---|---|---|---|---|---|---|---|---|---|---|---|---|---|---|---|
| ISSD | RETD | I | R | I | R | I | R | I | R | I | R | | | | | | | | | | | | | | |
| 237 | 290 | 1252 | 1211 | 1482 | 1332 | 514 | 504 | 789 | 737 | 1521 | 1422 | 281 | | φ 3100 | x 13780 | x 13000 | 86 | 235 | ⊗ 773 | 339 | 13200 | 4095 | 1973 | | TOTAL |
| 16 | 17 | 75 | 71 | 84 | 78 | 32 | 31 | 197 | 184 | 90 | 84 | 16 | | | | | 5 | 14 | 45 | 20 | 77 | 1019 | 493 | | PER 1000 |

STRENGTH

| | |
|---|---|
| DISMTD | 13000 |
| MTD | 4000 |
| TOTAL | 17000 |
| ANIMALS | 4000 |

x. FIRST SUPPLY UNDER GRO 5103 (WINTER CLO)

φ FOR DIV BATHS

⊗ 50 ISSD TO REPLACE LOST

[signature] MAJOR

D.A.D.O.S., 51ST (HIGHLAND) DIVISION

A5834 Wt. W4973/M687 750,000 8/16 D. D. & L. Ltd. Forms/C.2118/13.

Instructions regarding War Diaries and Intelligence Summaries are contained in F. S. Regs., Part II. and the Staff Manual respectively. Title pages will be prepared in manuscript.

SECRET

# WAR DIARY
*or*
# INTELLIGENCE SUMMARY.
*(Erase heading not required.)*

Army Form C. 2118.

98 43

| Place | Date | Hour | Summary of Events and Information | Remarks and references to Appendices |
|---|---|---|---|---|
| | | | WAR DIARY FOR NOV. 1918 | |
| | | | D.A.D.O.S., 51ST (HIGHLAND) DIVISION<br>No.........<br>Date......... | |

A5834 Wt. W4973/M687 750,000 8/16 D. D. & L. Ltd. Forms/C.2118/13.

Army Form C. 2118.

Instructions regarding War Diaries and Intelligence Summaries are contained in F. S. Regs., Part II. and the Staff Manual respectively. Title pages will be prepared in manuscript.

# WAR DIARY
*or*
# INTELLIGENCE SUMMARY.

*(Erase heading not required.)*

Secret    Nov 1918

| Place | Date | Hour | Summary of Events and Information | Remarks and references to Appendices |
|---|---|---|---|---|
| IWUY | 1st. | | Truck 2252 1 Wagon Lim G.S. for 17 A.S. Hqs. Truck 10859 Gun Stores. Advanced No1 Gun Park moved to 51A B13.D.8.2. Routine work visited Railhead | |
| | 2 | | Truck 36786 5000 Drawers for Baths Truck 35559 1 Wagon Lim G.S. for 4 Gordon Hrs. Routine work. Visited Railhead. | |
| | 3rd. | | Routine work. Visited Railhead | |
| | 4 | | Truck 55291 6000 Vests. Truck 36808 8 tons General. Railhead changed to MALAKOFF. Visited Infy Bdes and Railhead. | |
| | 5 | | Truck 467163 5 tons General = Oil. Equip. &c. Delivered Stores to Div. Coy at MAING | |
| | 6 | | Routine work. Visited Railhead + Bdes. | |
| | 7 | | Railhead changed to CANTIMPRE Routine work. | |
| | 8 | | Routine work. Issued 2000 rounds Blank Amm to 4 Gor. Hrs Truck 2016 Boots &c | |
| | 9 | | Routine work. Visited Railhead. | |
| | 10 | | Truck 63188 - 168 Bales F.S. Boots | |
| | 11 | | Truck 55261 1. K.T. body for MG. Bn Truck 28573 1 Cart Oil for D.255 Bde Truck 63642 6 tons General. Recd Gun Stores from GP. | |

A5834 Wt. W4973 M687 750,000 8/16 D. D. & L. Ltd. Forms/C.2118/13.

Instructions regarding War Diaries and Intelligence Summaries are contained in F. S. Regs., Part II. and the Staff Manual respectively. Title pages will be prepared in manuscript.

# WAR DIARY
*or*
# INTELLIGENCE SUMMARY.
*(Erase heading not required.)*

Army Form C. 2118.

Nov 1918

(2)

| Place | Date | Hour | Summary of Events and Information | Remarks and references to Appendices |
|---|---|---|---|---|
| IWUY | 12 | | Routine work | |
| | 13 | | Do visited Bdes and Railhead | |
| | 14 | | Do do | |
| | 15 | | Do. Truck 51149 6 tons General. Issued 1 each B.S. [illegible] to 5+6 [illegible] Hrs for use of Special Railway Guard. Routine work. | |
| | 16 | | Routine Work. Under Army Authy 1 Blanket may be issued to each British Pris of War coming into our lines. | |
| | 17 | | Truck 23537. Kits, [illegible] etc. Routine work | |
| | 18 | | Truck 11592 1 K.T. body for M.G. Bn. also 1 Wagon [illegible] G.S. [illegible] Routine work | |
| | 19 | | Truck 58904 11 tons General Stores. Demanded 1 Wagon G.S. for 2/60 [illegible] 1 6 W T for 7 A&S Hrs | |
| | 20 | | Routine work. Visited Bdes + Railhead | |
| | 21 | | Do Do | |
| | 22 | | Truck 30054 6 tons General Stores. Oil Grease etc Truck 61326 4 tons Gen. Stores Boots Equip etc | |

A5834 Wt. W4973/M687 750,000 8/16 D. D. & L. Ltd. Forms/C.2118/13.

Instructions regarding War Diaries and Intelligence Summaries are contained in F. S. Regs., Part II. and the Staff Manual respectively. Title pages will be prepared in manuscript.

Secret.

# WAR DIARY
*or*
# INTELLIGENCE SUMMARY.
*(Erase heading not required.)*

NOV. 1918

(3)

Army Form C. 2118.

| Place | Date | Hour | Summary of Events and Information | Remarks and references to Appendices |
|---|---|---|---|---|
| Ivuy | 23 | | Truck 32210 18 Wheels. Truck 132518 8 tons General stores | |
| | | | Truck 35016 / 467053 } 3850 Blankets. Truck 150250 / 77905 } 4150 Blankets. | |
| | 24 | | Truck 48201 / 57227 / 21798 } 14010 Drawers / 14000 Vests } for Baths | |
| | 25 | | Routine work. Visited Railhead | |
| | 26 | | Trucks 97004 85 Boxes horseshoes Truck 95196 Equip. Oil & Grease Truck 82677 9 tons General stores | |
| | 27. | | Routine Work | |
| | 28 | | Do | |
| | 29 | | Do | |
| | 30 | | Do. Trucks 17271. 6 tons General stores. 1607 1 Cart Maltese for 1/3 Fd Amb / " 1 Wagon G.S. for 260 Men | |
| | | | Truck 43524 1. Cart Water for 7 A&S Hrs. 1 Wagon Lim G.S. fore for 8 Royal Scots 1 Wagon Lim G.S. hind for MG Bn. 1 Wagon Lim G.S. fore 1 hind 1 for 404 Field Co. | |

A5834 Wt. W4973/M687 750,000 8/16 D. D. & L. Ltd. Forms/C.2118/13.

Army Form C. 2118.

# WAR DIARY
*or*
# INTELLIGENCE SUMMARY.
*(Erase heading not required.)*

Instructions regarding War Diaries and Intelligence Summaries are contained in F. S. Regs., Part II. and the Staff Manual respectively. Title pages will be prepared in manuscript.

NOV 1918

(4)

| Place | Date | Hour | Summary of Events and Information | Remarks and references to Appendices |
|---|---|---|---|---|

STATEMENT OF ISSUES + RETURNS OF CERTAIN EQUIP FOR MONTH

| Boots Mud | | Boots Ankle | | Jackets lb | | Trousers lb | | Pantaloons | | Puttees lb | | CAPS SD | SHIRTS | SOCKS | DRAWERS | VESTS | HAVERSACKS | BOTTLES W | TINS MESS | SHEETS GD | FLANNELETTE | SHOES HORSE | MULE |
|---|---|---|---|---|---|---|---|---|---|---|---|---|---|---|---|---|---|---|---|---|---|---|---|
| I | R | I | R | I | R | I | R | I | R | I | R | | | | & | & | | × | ⊗ | ·x· | | | |
| 151 | 342 | 1640 | 1622 | 845 | 1665 | 444 | 516 | 600 | 523 | 1560 | 1722 | 197 | – | – | 14010 | 20000 | 70 | 289 | 759 | 166 | 6340 | 5 F 9 8 | 3 F 8 7 |
| 11 | 25 | 117 | 116 | ~~119~~ 94 | 119 | 38 | 47 | 206 | 174 | 111 | 123 | | | | | | 5 | 20 | 54 | 8 | 453 | 1 3 T F | 371 |

| STRENGTH | DIS | 11000 |
|---|---|---|
| | MTD | 3000 |
| | TOTAL | 14000 |
| | ANIMALS | 4000 |

× 54 lost
⊗ 236 "
·x· 5 "
& Issues to Div Baths

D. Christie Capt Hor

D.A.D.O.S.,
51ST
(HIGHLAND) DIVISION

A5834 Wt. W4973/M687 750,000 8/16 D. D. & L. Ltd. Forms/C.2118/13.

Army Form C. 2118.

Instructions regarding War Diaries and Intelligence Summaries are contained in F. S. Regs., Part II. and the Staff Manual respectively. Title pages will be prepared in manuscript.

SECRET

# WAR DIARY
or
# INTELLIGENCE SUMMARY.

(*Erase heading not required.*)

DECEMBER 1918

V8 44

| Place | Date | Hour | Summary of Events and Information | Remarks and references to Appendices |
|---|---|---|---|---|
| | | | D.A.D.O.S | |
| | | | 51st (H) DIV | |

D. D. & L., London, E.C.
(A8004) Wt. W1771/M2 31 750,000 5/17 Sch. 52 Forms/C2118/14

Army Form C. 2118.

Instructions regarding War Diaries and Intelligence Summaries are contained in F. S. Regs., Part II. and the Staff Manual respectively. Title pages will be prepared in manuscript.

# WAR DIARY
*or*
# INTELLIGENCE SUMMARY.

(*Erase heading not required.*)

SECRET

DECR 1918

| Place | Date | Hour | Summary of Events and Information | Remarks and references to Appendices |
|---|---|---|---|---|
| IWUY | 1st | | Truck 61136 - 2100 Blankets 21742 - 6 tons Gen Stores 33091 66 Boxes Shoes | |
| | 2nd | | Truck 64438 - 6 tons Gen Stores - Kits, Grindery &c | |
| | 3 | | Truck 61293 5 tons Clothing - Kits &c Truck 12565 6 tons - Oil Grease &c | |
| | 4 | | 1 · 18 pdr truck for B 255 + 6 256 [illegible] by S O M No 55 Shop [illegible] | |
| | 5 | | Routine Work | |
| | 6 | | Demanded 1 Wagon [illegible] for 8 Royal Scots - Truck 48724 - 6 tons - Bags [illegible] Boots &c | |
| | | | 5100 Socks for Baths | |
| | 7 | | Truck 92270 - 5 tons - Boots &c | |
| | 8 | | Truck 2933 - 6 tons - Kits, Necessaries &c | |
| | 9 | | Trucks 24509 - 14100 Socks<br>181667 14000 Shirts for Baths<br>151981 14000 Towels | |

D. D. & L., London, E.C.
(A8004) Wt. W1771/M2 31 750,000 5/17 Sch. 52 Forms/C2118/14

Instructions regarding War Diaries and Intelligence Summaries are contained in F. S. Regs., Part II. and the Staff Manual respectively. Title pages will be prepared in manuscript.

SECRET

# WAR DIARY
*or*
# INTELLIGENCE SUMMARY.
*(Erase heading not required.)*

DECR 1918

Army Form C. 2118.

| Place | Date | Hour | Summary of Events and Information | Remarks and references to Appendices |
|---|---|---|---|---|
| IWUY | 1st | | Truck 61136 - 2100 Blankets. 21742 - 6 tons Gen Stores. 33091 66 Boxes Shoes | |
| | 2nd | | Truck 64438 - 6 tons Gen Stores - Kits, Armoury etc | |
| | 3 | | Truck 61293 5 tons Clothing - Kits etc. Truck 12565 6 tons - Oil, Grease etc | |
| | 4 | | 1. 18 pdr truck for B 255 & 6 256 [illegible] by 1 Om No 55 Shop for cleaning | |
| | 5 | | Routine Work | |
| | 6 | | Demanded 1 Wagon from M.S. for 8 Royal Scots - Truck 48724 - 6 tons - Bags & Boots etc<br>5100 Socks for Baths | |
| | 7 | | Truck 92270 - 5 tons - Boots etc | |
| | 8 | | Truck 2933 - 6 tons - Kits, Accessories etc | |
| | 9 | | Trucks 24509 - 14100 Socks<br>181667 14000 Shirts } for Baths<br>151981 14000 Towels | |

(A8004) Wt. W1771/M2 31 750,000 5/17 Sch. 52 Forms/C2118/14 D. D. & L., London, E.C.

Instructions regarding War Diaries and Intelligence Summaries are contained in F. S. Regs., Part II. and the Staff Manual respectively. Title pages will be prepared in manuscript.

Army Form C. 2118.

(3)

# WAR DIARY
*or*
# INTELLIGENCE SUMMARY.
*(Erase heading not required.)*

SECRET DECR 1918

| Place | Date | Hour | Summary of Events and Information | Remarks and references to Appendices |
|---|---|---|---|---|
| INUY | 21st | | Truck 24580 - 1 Water cart for B.256 - 1 Hand cart for HQ 256 | |
| | | | " 38624 1 Wagon limb & fore for 8 Royal Scots | |
| | 22nd | | Routine Work | |
| | 23 | | Truck 57410 - 6 tons. | |
| | 24 | | Truck 152536 - 6 tons - Oil. Grease &c | |
| | 25 | | Xmas Day - Holiday | |
| | 26 | | Truck 65274 - 5 tons - Boots. Armoury &c | |
| | 27 | | Routine Work | |
| | 28 | | | |
| | 29 | | " | |
| | 30 | | Truck 35287 - 73 Boxes Horseshoes - 28 Bags Armoury. | |
| | 31 | | Truck 12767 - 4 tons - Oil. Grease &c | |

D. D. & L., London, E.C.
(A8004) Wt. W1771/M2'31 750,000 5/17 Sch. 52 Forms/C2118/14

Army Form C. 2118.

(2)

# WAR DIARY
*or*
# INTELLIGENCE SUMMARY.
*(Erase heading not required.)*

Instructions regarding War Diaries and Intelligence Summaries are contained in F. S. Regs., Part II. and the Staff Manual respectively. Title pages will be prepared in manuscript.

SECRET DECR 1918

| Place | Date | Hour | Summary of Events and Information | Remarks and references to Appendices |
|---|---|---|---|---|
| IWUY | 10 | | Routine work. | |
| | 11 | | Truck 48551 - 4 tons. | |
| | 12<br>13 | | } Routine Work. | |
| | 14 | | Truck 1616 - 3 tons - Ordnance, Clothing &c | |
| | 15 | | Truck 60229 - ~~Truck~~ 1 - 18 pdr. Amm Wagon } for A 255 Bde<br>1 " Lim Wagon } | |
| | 16 | | Truck 24812 - 91 Boxes Horseshoes - Truck 210046 - 6 tons - Kits &c | |
| | 17 | | Routine Work | |
| | 18 | | Truck 40343 - 6 tons - Oil, Grease &c | |
| | 19 | | Truck 85045 - 5670 pieces Purchase. | |
| | 20 | | " 164391 - 5 tons - Boots &c - Truck 162829 300 Latrine Buckets<br>600 Tubs washing | |

D. D. & L., London, E.C.
(A8004) Wt. W1771/M2 31 750,000 5/17 Sch. 52 Forms/C2118/14

Instructions regarding War Diaries and Intelligence Summaries are contained in F. S. Regs., Part II. and the Staff Manual respectively. Title pages will be prepared in manuscript.

Army Form C. 2118.

(3)

# WAR DIARY
*or*
# INTELLIGENCE SUMMARY.
*(Erase heading not required.)*

SECRET DECR 1918

| Place | Date | Hour | Summary of Events and Information | Remarks and references to Appendices |
|---|---|---|---|---|
| INUY | 21st | | Truck 24530 - 1 Water cart for B.256 - 1 Hand cart for HQ 256 | |
| | | | " 38624 1 Wagon limber & fore for 8 Royal Scots | |
| | 22nd | | Routine Work | |
| | 23 | | Truck 67410 - 6 tons. | |
| | 24 | | Truck 152536 - 6 tons - Oil. Grease etc | |
| | 25 | | Xmas Day - Holiday | |
| | 26 | | Truck 65274 - 5 tons - Boots. Armoury etc | |
| | 27 | | Routine Work | |
| | 28 | | | |
| | 29 | | " | |
| | 30 | | Truck 35287 - 73 Boxes Horseshoes - 28 Bags Armoury. | |
| | 31 | | Truck 12767 - 4 tons - Oil. Grease etc | |

D. D. & L., London, E.C.
(A8004) Wt. W1771/M2 31 750,000 5/17 Sch. 52 Forms/C2118/14

Army Form C. 2118.

Instructions regarding War Diaries and Intelligence Summaries are contained in F. S. Regs., Part II. and the Staff Manual respectively. Title pages will be prepared in manuscript.

SECRET

# WAR DIARY
*or*
# INTELLIGENCE SUMMARY.
(*Erase heading not required.*)

DECR 1918 (4)

| Place | Date | Hour | Summary of Events and Information | Remarks and references to Appendices |
|---|---|---|---|---|

RETURN OF EXPENDITURE OF CERTAIN ARTICLES OF EQUIP FOR MONTH

| COATS GREAT | | BOOTS ANKLE | | TROUSERS SD | | JACKETS SD | | PANTALOONS | | PUTTEES SD | | CAPS SD | SHIRTS | SOCKS | DRAWERS | VESTS | H' SACKS | B WATER | TINS MESS | SHTS GD | FLANNELETTE | SHOES HORSE | MULE | Remarks |
|---|---|---|---|---|---|---|---|---|---|---|---|---|---|---|---|---|---|---|---|---|---|---|---|---|
| I | R | I | R | I | R | I | R | I | R | I | R | | | | | | | | | | | | | |
| 306 | 302 | 1197 | 894 | 582 | 502 | 2083 | 1921 | 909 | 864 | 1449 | 1430 | 489 | 12000 FOR BATHS | 14100 FOR BATHS | / | / | 45 | 176 | 337 | 124 | 10200 | 479 | 1760 | TOTAL |
| 22 ×ϕ | 21 | 85 × | 64 | 53 × | 45 | 148 × | 137 | 303 × | 288 | 103 × | 102 | 35 × | - | - | | | 3 | 12 | 24 | 9 | 728 | 1045 | 840 | PER 1000 |

× 50% INCREASE AUTH BY GOC FOR DA

ϕ 50 TO REPLACE L.

| | |
|---|---|
| D.M. | 11000 |
| M | 3000 |
| TOTAL | 14000 |
| ANMLS | 4000 |

[signature] Capt for MAJOR

D.A.D.O.S., 51ST (HIGHLAND) DIVISION

2 JAN 1919

D. D. & L., London, E.C. (A8004) Wt. W1771/M2 31 750,000 5/17 Sch. 52 Forms/C2118/14

Army Form C. 2118.

Instructions regarding War Diaries and Intelligence Summaries are contained in F. S. Regs., Part II. and the Staff Manual respectively. Title pages will be prepared in manuscript.

# WAR DIARY
*or*
# SECRET INTELLIGENCE SUMMARY.
*(Erase heading not required.)*

Vol 45

| Place | Date | Hour | Summary of Events and Information | Remarks and references to Appendices |
|---|---|---|---|---|
| | | | D.A.D.O.S. <br> 51ST (H) DIVISION <br> JANUARY 1919 | |

D. D. & L., London, E.C. (A8004) Wt. W1771/M2 31 750,000 5/17 Sch. 52 Forms/C2118/14

Army Form C. 2118.

Instructions regarding War Diaries and Intelligence Summaries are contained in F. S. Regs., Part II. and the Staff Manual respectively. Title pages will be prepared in manuscript.

SECRET

# WAR DIARY
*or*
# INTELLIGENCE SUMMARY. JANUARY 1919

*(Erase heading not required.)*

(1)

| Place | Date | Hour | Summary of Events and Information | Remarks and references to Appendices |
|---|---|---|---|---|
| IWUY | 1st | | Moved Area Stores to Advanced Dump HOUDENG-AIMERIES | |
| | [illegible] | | Truck 19797 6 tons - Boots Grindery &c | |
| | 2nd | | Routine Work | |
| | 3 | | " | |
| | 4 | | " | |
| | 5 | | Moved Office and Stores to LA LOUVIERE | |
| LA-LOUVIERE | 6 | | Routine Work and fixing up new Dump | |
| " | 10 | | " | |
| " | 14 | | Truck 82334 - 500 Lamps F.S. for Educational purposes | |
| " | 15 | | " 12387 - 67 Bales Shirts and Socks | |
| " | 16 | | Routine Work | |
| " | 17 | | Truck 5375 - 5 tons Trucks 61070 156452 142335 - 7500 Blankets | |
| " | 18 | | Routine Work | |
| " | 19 | | Trucks 181882 - 1300 Blankets Truck 4358 - 6 tons - Horseshoes | |

D. D. & L., London, E.C.
(A8004) Wt. W1771/M2731 750,000 5/17 Sch. 52 Forms/C2118/14

Army Form C. 2118.

Instructions regarding War Diaries and Intelligence Summaries are contained in F. S. Regs., Part II. and the Staff Manual respectively. Title pages will be prepared in manuscript.

# WAR DIARY
*or*
# INTELLIGENCE SUMMARY. JANY. 1919

SECRET (2)

*(Erase heading not required.)*

| Place | Date | Hour | Summary of Events and Information | Remarks and references to Appendices |
|---|---|---|---|---|
| LA LOUVIERE | 20 | | Routine Work | |
| " | 21 | | Truck 150471 - 4 tons - Oil &c Truck 35007 - 2100 blankets | |
| " | 22 | | Truck 13006 - 7 tons - Boots &c Truck 46950 - 2500 blankets | |
| " | 23 | | " 10605 - 2 tons - Boots &c | |
| " | 24 | | " 3064 - 5 tons - Horseshoes | |
| | 25 to 31 | | Routine Work | |
| | | | Following work performed in the Armourers Shop for month | |
| | | | Overhauled and Inspected Bicycles 125. Machine Guns 234 | |

D. D. & L., London, E.C.
(A8004) Wt. W1771/M2 31 750,000 5/17 Sch. 52 Forms/C2118/14

Army Form C. 2118.

Instructions regarding War Diaries and Intelligence Summaries are contained in F. S. Regs., Part II. and the Staff Manual respectively. Title pages will be prepared in manuscript.

SECRET

# WAR DIARY
*or*
# INTELLIGENCE SUMMARY.
*(Erase heading not required.)*

JANUARY 1919 (3)

| Place | Date | Hour | Summary of Events and Information | Remarks and references to Appendices |
|---|---|---|---|---|
| | | | Statement of Issues and Receipts of certain items for month | |

| Coats Great I | Coats Great R | Boots Ankle I | Boots Ankle R | Trousers SD I | Trousers SD R | Jackets SD I | Jackets SD R | Pantalns I | Pantalns R | Puttees SD I | Puttees SD R | Caps SD | Shirts | Socks | Drawers | Vests | H/Sacks | Bott W | Tins Mess | Shts Ground | Flannelette | Shoes Horse | Mule | |
|---|---|---|---|---|---|---|---|---|---|---|---|---|---|---|---|---|---|---|---|---|---|---|---|---|
| 173 | 154 | 914 | 802 | 470 | 387 | 1090 | 1093 | 678 | 473 | 944 | 1040 | 314 | | 5000 x | - | 5000 x | 27 | 115 | 418 | 186 | 1560 | 1314 | 601 | TOTAL |
| 13 | 12 | 91 | 80 | 47 | 39 | 84 | 84 | 259 | 157 | 72 | 80 | 21 | | - | - | - | 2 | 9 | 32 | 14 | 120 | 771 | 201 | PER 1000 |

STRENGTH

| | |
|---|---|
| DISMTD | 10000 |
| MTD | 3000 |
| TOTAL | 13000 |
| ANIMALS | 3550 |

x. ISSUES TO DIV BATHS

Scarcity of boots and repair materials became a serious question and to end of month very few boots were received. Boots F.S. were demanded as a temporary measure.

[signature]
MAJOR

D.A.D.O.S.,
51ST
(HIGHLAND) DIVISION.

D. D. & L., London, E.C. (A8004) Wt. W1771/M2 31 750,000 5/17 Sch. 52 Forms/C2118/14

www.ingramcontent.com/pod-product-compliance
Lightning Source LLC
Chambersburg PA
CBHW082011220426
43670CB00014B/2604

*9781474528252*